COOPER'S WOMEN

Also by Jane Ellen Wayne

Crawford's Men
Gable's Women
Kings of Tragedy
The Life of Robert Taylor
Stanwyck

JANE ELLEN WAYNE

COOPER'S WOMEN

PRENTICE HALL PRESS
New York London Toronto Sydney Tokyo

All insert photos courtesy of the Kobal Collection.

Prentice Hall Press
Gulf+Western Building
One Gulf+Western Plaza
New York, New York 10023

Library of Congress Cataloging-in-Publication Data

Wayne, Jane Ellen.
Cooper's women / Jane Ellen Wayne.
p. cm.
Includes index.
ISBN 0-13-172438-X
1. Cooper, Gary, 1901–1961—Relations with women. 2. Motion picture actors and actresses—United States—Biography. I. Title.
PN2287.C59W3 1988
791.43'028'0924—dc 19
[B] 88-19484
CIP

Manufactured in the United States of America

10 9 8 7 6 5 4 3 2 1

First Edition

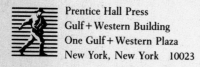

To Aunt Mona
Who Knew Him Well

ACKNOWLEDGMENTS

As the author of star biographies for the past twenty years, I've had the distinct pleasure of interviewing many of the friends and coworkers of Robert Taylor, Barbara Stanwyck, Clark Gable, Joan Crawford, and Gary Cooper. Because Hollywood is in reality a small town, many of the stars' lives crossed socially and professionally. Many of their happy and sad tales were related to me by old-timers, some of whom are no longer alive. My deepest thanks go to them for their goodwill and sense of humor. You can't survive in Hollywood without a measure of both.

CONTENTS

PREFACE

Six feet, three inches tall, blue eyes, dark brown hair, 175 pounds, large hands, lanky and leggy, trim, soft-spoken with a midwestern drawl tinged with a British accent, long-faced and long-necked . . . he had an enormous appetite and could fall asleep anytime. His favorite subjects were horses and hunting. The "yup" and "nope" legend is true. He was a heavy smoker and a moderate drinker. His preference for jeans set a trend, but tuxedos were made for him. His frequent swallowing became the familiar "gulp" in films. He carried Tums and wintergreen to ease his chronic indigestion. He didn't read ten books in his lifetime and couldn't carry a tune.

He was a champion in bed, but fell in love too easily . . .

"It happens that I've made friendships with women who have aided me in my work," Gary Cooper declared.

The year was 1929. The former stuntman had become a star and moviegoers demanded to know more about him. They were curious about his Hollywood love affairs that made him famous even before his recognition as an actor.

Gary Cooper didn't talk much, and he never discussed his intimate relationships. But the girls did. Soon he was a bedroom legend. They paid tribute to his prowess as a cocksman and to his gentle nature. He had an irresistible boyish quality that attracted women.

Ingrid Bergman said, "Every woman who knew Gary fell in love with him." Their affair was no secret despite the fact they were both married. Typically for Cooper, the romance ended by the time the film was finished.

Gary sincerely adored women and strove to make them happy. He made their desires his desires. Though he might be involved with two—maybe three—women at a time, any affair was precious to him. He did very little bragging, if any. Cooper took love and life in his stride. Both caught up with him eventually, but friends remember Gary Cooper as a humble man with few ambitions or pretensions.

Joan Crawford, who was *not* one of Cooper's women, remarked, "Gary made every woman feel as if she were the only woman in the world. I never saw him 'on the make.' I'm told he was very subtle. Women didn't leave him alone and he obliged them, but Gary didn't impress me as an opportunist."

Tallulah Bankhead claimed to have left the stage for a career in Hollywood to "get laid by Gary Cooper." Years later when questioned about the outcome she succinctly responded, "Mission accomplished."

Even demure Helen Hayes, Cooper's costar in *A Farewell to Arms,* confessed, "If Gary had asked me, I would have gone away with him."

Perhaps it was Cooper's devotion to his mother that was responsible for the warmth and respect he had for women. He was a mama's boy as a child and grew up on a Montana ranch to be a rugged cowhand and avid hunter with a love for the outdoors. He was a poor scholar with a mild talent as an artist. Above all else, his mother wanted her son to be a gentleman; and despite a rebellious streak he was a well-mannered fellow with a big heart.

When Gary went to California his parents followed. His mother, Alice, had much to say about his famous girlfriends. Though it's unlikely she found out he proposed to Clara Bow, she did prevent his marriage to Lupe Velez. Overworked and brokenhearted, by 1933 Gary had a nervous breakdown complicated by poor physical health. He wanted to get far away from Hollywood as soon as possible. He secretly planned a European vacation, but just before he boarded the train for New York he heard girlfriend Lupe Velez scream in jealousy, "Garree—you son of a bitch!" As she fired a gun at his head he ducked, jumped on the pullman car, and slammed the door behind him.

Whether Lupe, the Mexican Spitfire, meant to kill or only wound Gary, we'll never know. The incident was kept quiet. Oddly, there was no panic on the station platform. Cooper stayed away for a few months. His mother took this opportunity to tell the press how she never interfered in Gary's life and hoped he would marry a respectable young lady some day.

Gary would surely have married the hot-tempered Velez if his mother had stayed in Montana. It was just as well that he didn't, because he wasn't faithful to any woman and Lupe, who carried a stiletto in one of her garters and had a loaded gun in her night table, eventually might have killed him. A sensitive and misunderstood girl, Lupe was deeply in love with Cooper.

When they were together, however, she often complained about his immunity to anger. If she threatened and punched and kicked, he just ambled out the front door. Alice tended to her son's wounds and the Paramount makeup people worked overtime to conceal the black-and-blue marks on his body, but Gary always went back to Lupe.

Off camera the amusing question was often asked, "Who's duller? Cooper or Gable?" Actress Ava Gardner said, "If you ask Clark, 'How are ya?' he's stuck for an answer." Writer Jim Tully remarked, "Cooper's head is like a gorgeous room with no furniture in it." And Hollywood columnist Hedda Hopper, who adored Gary, admitted he was no genius. "No one remembers anything interesting he said," she commented. "I'd like to scream because I know he has something in that head. You'd think the Hollywood crowd would be totally bored with him, but he's such a nice guy that everyone enjoys just having him around."

Cooper never achieved the same power and status on the screen as his rival, Clark Gable, whose reputation as a great lover was due to the sheer *number* of women he bedded—literally hundreds. However, Carole Lombard, his zany third wife, said publicly, "God knows I love Clark, but he's the worst lay in town." When Gable had the opportunity to spend the night with Lupe, he refused. "Forget it!" he said. "She'll be blabbing it all over town the next day what a lousy lover I am." Maybe this explains Gable's preference for prostitutes. "They go away and keep their mouths shut."

Lupe Velez was very candid. In her Mexican accent she announced, "Garree has the biggest one in town." Clara Bow, the famous "It Girl" of the twenties, agreed: "Coop's hung like a horse and can go all night." He was known to his friends as "Studs." This was the nickname Bow gave to Gary when he was falling off horses as a stuntman in 1926. The nickname stuck.

One can only speculate about what Cooper's destiny might have been without the adorable oversexed flapper. She paved the way for him. Clara got Gary bit parts in her movies, as a newspaper reporter in *It* and a doomed flyer in *Wings*. Ironically, she wasn't trying to make an actor out of him or further his career. Her motives were strictly, and intimately, personal.

Gary lived with Clara Bow and then Lupe Velez and then the wealthy homosexual Anderson Lawler, who introduced him to the upper crust. Bisexuals were common in Hollywood, but Cooper's reputation as a ladies' man made him a most unlikely candidate. After his death, well-known gays hinted they were involved with the cowboy from Montana. No one knows for sure.

Gary ignored the gossip, hopping from Clara's Chinese Den to Lupe's hacienda and back to Anderson's candlelit gourmet dinners. In between, Coop romped with his leading ladies.

It took him twenty-one films and four years to finally become a star in 1929. That year, in *The Virginian,* his name appeared in lights directly below the title. It was in this, Coop's first all-talkie, that he challenged an outlaw with the line he made famous—"If you want to call me that, smile!"

He rarely spoke to fans, but a few drinks might encourage him to say the line again. This was the extent of his communication with the public in the early days. Like Gable, Cooper gave terrible interviews; either he said the wrong thing or put reporters to sleep. Paramount moguls cringed when Gary told the press, "Lupe is primitive and elemental like me."

Hedda Hopper, who always defended Cooper, said, "I think Gary was attracted to both Clara Bow and Lupe Velez because they were the direct opposite of his mother, who was a rather snobbish English Episcopalian. I liked Alice very much, but Gary was her little boy and he acted it around his parents. Sometimes he was almost effeminate. Alice told me she was prepared for a baby girl and dressed her son up like one. He actually wore skirts until he went to school. I asked him about it and Gary told me he played with dolls, but didn't own one. His mother didn't want her little boy to get dirty. So, when he came to Hollywood on his own, he was a sloppy dresser and cared less about clothes. In his own way, he revolted—risking his life as a stuntman, running around with wild girls and trying to manage bootleg booze without getting sick. Of course, when Alice found out, she moved to Los Angeles and tried to take charge."

Gary lived with his parents off and on until he could afford a house of his own. Gossip columnists kept up with him, however, and his escapades were common knowledge. Paramount Studios did not want him to tarnish his "nice boy" image by romancing at the same time a Mexican girl who wore no panties (and proved it at parties), and a flapper who virtually had a waiting room for boyfriends outside her bedroom.

The public chose to believe the simple—almost stupid—interviews he gave, such as the one given by a rookie reporter who asked Gary if he was always so quiet.

"Nope," came Coop's reply.

"Is that all you have to say, Gary?"

"Yep."

Corny, but true.

Gary Cooper didn't care what people thought, but not in a cocky or brazen way. He didn't play the Hollywood game of dating girls chosen by the studio, nor did he pretend to be anybody other than a guy from Montana who lived on a ranch and could ride a horse. Actor Richard Arlen, a close friend, said, "Coop was a mystery and that's one reason women fell for him. He wasn't quoted as saying much so he was a mystery to his fans. Coop let you figure out for yourself who he was."

Gary was a simple fellow when he met Countess Dorothy di Frasso, who introduced him to European society and royalty. She bought him an expensive wardrobe and jewelry, taught him how to select the appropriate wine in several languages, and allowed him to play host at her luxurious villa while her husband, the count, was off dining elsewhere with one of his mistresses.

When Paramount Studios demanded that Gary return from Europe, he stalled until he heard a rumor that an actor by the name of Cary Grant had been chosen to take his place. "My God," he told the countess. "That dude's got my initials—backwards!"

He was greeted on his return with a new contract and a sizable raise. Apparently there was only one Gary Cooper, even in 1933. By the end of the year he would be a married man. Starlets, script girls, and secretaries were crestfallen, but only temporarily.

It was just a matter of time . . .

COOPER'S WOMEN

1

MONTANA COWBOY

Alice Brazier Cooper always detested Montana. She was twenty years old in 1892 when she left Kent, England, to visit her brother Alfred in America's wild West. If she was disappointed by New York, compared with London, Alice was completely disillusioned by her five-day train ride to the gold-rush town of Helena. Looking through the dingy train windows, she was disgusted by the sight of the filthy miners, dirty cowboys, bearded gold prospectors, and drunken Indians. The slaughter of General Custer and the Seventh Cavalry by Sitting Bull and his Sioux braves, which occurred less than two decades earlier, was a favorite topic of conversation. "Last Chance Gulch" was the name of the main thoroughfare, and of the town before it was renamed. The big talk was of Helena becoming the capital of Montana. "It's a barbaric place," she told Alfred. She never changed her mind.

But Alice extended her visit because she adored her brother. She went to the Episcopal church and attended its social get-togethers. Her brother introduced her to eligible bachelors in the hope she would marry and live nearby. One of the bachelors was Charles H. Cooper, the son of a wealthy Bedfordshire, England, family. Charles was a quiet fellow, not much taller than Alice and six years older. During the day he worked for the Northern Pacific Railroad; at night he studied law, which left him very little time for women.

Helena had prospered on its abundant silver mines, but when gold became the chief commodity in the Northwest the price of silver plunged. The banks in Helena were forced to close. A frantic Alice went to Charles for legal advice. How could she get back to England if her assets were frozen? He put his knowledge of banking laws to work and, in the meantime, began to date the prim and proper Miss Brazier. By the time he retrieved her money they were engaged to be married.

Alice was such a happy bride in 1893 it didn't matter that Charles wanted to stay in Montana. She was confident he would change his mind.

In 1895 their first son Arthur was born, and the Coopers settled down in a two-story brick house. Because his small law practice was growing, Charles quit the railroad and became a clerk in the municipal court. A few years later a retiring judge suggested Cooper take his place. Alice was very impressed, but there was a drawback.

"I am still a British subject," Charles reminded her. "That will, I'm sure, stand in my way."

"We'll apply for our U.S. citizenship immediately," she exclaimed.

Alice relished the thought of having her husband become a judge. She had no way of knowing that it wouldn't become a reality for almost fifteen years.

When she became pregnant again Alice was positive the baby would be a girl. Hadn't a fortune-teller told her so? While she fussed over pink curtains and pretty pink bonnets the doctors prepared her gently for a difficult birth, because the likelihood of a second pregnancy had been slim.

On a very hot and humid May 7, 1901, a baby boy was born to the Coopers. They named him Frank James. For the next few years his mother dressed little Frank in dainty frocks. He played with girls because Alice did not want her precious darling getting dirty. When Arthur, Daddy's favorite, was at school, Alice dedicated the days to young Frank.

In 1906, Charles bought the Seven-Bar-Nine ranch fifty miles north of Helena. Years later Gary Cooper remembered, "My father always wanted to raise cattle. He got a spread at a cheap price and figured it would pay for itself. My first recollection as a kid was the day we arrived at the ranch. The cowhands and Indians working the place came to meet us. I looked around and knew the wide open country was for me."

Soon Alice was busy redecorating the ranch house, which she named Sunnyside. Arthur tagged along with his father as usual, leaving Frank on his own for the first time. The brothers attended a little schoolhouse with the Indian children of itinerant workers. It was an exciting new life for the Coopers. That changed when one year sudden floods killed the cattle and almost destroyed the crops. Harsh weather was a constant hardship. Gary remembered as a child watching his mother chop wood in a blizzard and trying to help her in the blinding snow. All the same he was very disappointed when Alice decided to spend only the summer months on the ranch. Frank preferred the little schoolhouse and the unassuming cowboys. He missed old Zeb, the ranch hand who taught him how to ride, shoot, fish, hunt, swim, and curse. Frank was only eight years old, but he knew this was how he wanted to live. As the fall of 1908 approached, he dreaded going back to Helena.

Alice hated the Bar-Nine. When she came down with a serious case of shingles, the doctors attributed her illness to stress. The following summer she and the boys remained in town. Frank was heartbroken, but he cared for his mother as she made a slow recovery. Charles refused to sell the Bar-Nine, but finally allowed Alice and the boys to vacation in England until she regained her strength. There was no doubt in her mind that her husband would follow. But when he was at last appointed judge, Alice returned with mixed emotions, consoling herself with the knowledge that Charles was one of the most influential men in Montana. She would have the social status she had known in England. Still, the education of her sons was a gnawing concern. Arthur was a good student but had no social graces, and Frank cursed like a drunk cowboy.

"We're American citizens now," Charles told Alice. He wanted his sons to grow up in Montana.

"What about tradition?" Alice asked. "You and your father and his father attended Dunstable School. Arthur and Frank should have the same opportunity. Your parents want them to live on the estate in Bedfordshire. This is their message to you."

Charles argued that the elder Coopers were living in the past. "I broke away," he stressed.

"But without your English education as a foundation," Alice spoke up, "you'd never have become a judge. It's only fair that our sons be given the same advantage." Charles eventually gave in.

In 1911 an enthusiastic Arthur and a defiant Frank crossed the Atlantic and enrolled at the Dunstable School. Years later Gary Cooper recalled, "During the three years away from home, my brother and I were close for the first and last time. Arthur was an exceptional student who convinced the headmaster on more than one occasion to let me stay. I was on the defensive, I guess, and got into fistfights if anyone made fun of my speech. I wasn't interested in school very much."

Although he never adjusted to the formality of the British, Frank behaved like a gentleman. He picked up an English accent but would never lose his western drawl. When asked if he was happy in Bedfordshire, Gary Cooper replied, "Nope, but I wasn't unhappy either."

Arthur was being considered for enrollment at Oxford when rumors of war frightened Alice. She ordered the boys returned to Montana in 1915. The Bar-Nine was thriving with five hundred head of cattle. Frank had no real interest in school; if he wasn't yearning to ride his horse he was engrossed in oil painting.

Restless, he hopped a freight train from Helena to the ranch, which made Alice frantic with worry. Frank was not always alone on his ventures, however. He and a chum decided to experiment with some dynamite on the outskirts of the ranch; several head of cattle were lost after a stampede.

Precisely why Frank was "removed" from Helena High School isn't known, but there appears to be some connection between his lack of enthusiasm, his wild pranks, and his running with a gang of mischievous boys. Gary Cooper's explanations in later years vary. He mentions either flunking out or dropping out. The latter is the accepted version, because Arthur enlisted in the army when the United States entered the Great War in 1917. Most of the ranch hands also went into the service, leaving Charles short of help and needing his younger son full-time. Frank disliked hard labor almost as much as school, but he did more than his share. Among his friends in those times was Jay Talbot, a roaming cowboy who occasionally picked up a day's wages on the Bar-Nine. Jim Galen and Jim Calloway, the restless sons of Helena attorneys, liked to go riding with Frank on the range. Their youthful sprees would influence Gary Cooper's start in the movies.

In 1916, Frank Cooper grew fourteen inches in one year. Suddenly he was all legs, skinny and gaunt. "My son had to catch up with himself," Alice said. "He developed a ravenous appetite but until he put on weight, his legs were like stilts. Towering over boys his own age made him awkward and shy."

While Arthur was in the army and Charles presided over his court, Frank and Alice worked fourteen hours a day on the ranch. When he turned seventeen Frank asked for a car, but his parents refused to buy him one. He said he needed one to get to school, but Alice reminded him about Harvey Markham. "He has a Model-T Ford. And he's always offering you a ride."

"I thought you worried 'cause he's crippled."

"The Markhams are very wealthy," Alice said. "That car was custom built and is sturdy. Considering the fact that Harvey can't walk, it's a miracle how he uses hand controls to maneuver the automobile. I think it's wonderful that you take him hunting and fishing. And you can do homework together since Harvey's in the same grade."

"Yeah," Frank mumbled. "We're both two years behind."

"He had polio and you took Arthur's place when he went into the army. We can't prevent illness and war, son." One morning, however, Harvey Markham lost control of his car on a steep curve when the hand brakes failed. Frank was with him on that fateful ride to school. Both boys were thrown clear before the car turned over. Frank was more concerned about Harvey, who was only shaken up, than about himself. It appeared as if they both had escaped injury, but the following morning Frank felt an excruciating pain in his left hip. The Coopers took him to the family physician, who said he seemed okay, but that he had torn some muscles and might have pain for a few days. The best exercise, he advised, was plenty of horseback riding.

For almost a week Frank could barely get out of bed. Charles and Alice agreed he should live at the Bar-Nine for a while. Years later Gary Cooper would find out that his hip had actually been broken. Although it mended, from then on he always favored his left leg. In the saddle he sat at an angle to reduce the pain and allowed his body to move in sync with the horse. A slight limp and casual slouch in the saddle would become one of the distinguishing trademarks of Gary Cooper.

Despite the pain, Frank's dream of becoming "just a cowboy" came true. He slept in the bunkhouse and helped with the branding and bull wrestling. Like a hound dog unleashed, he was free for the next few months. "I did whatever the other ranch hands were expected to do," he said. "They really loved the hard work and I respected them for that. I guess I was kinda lazy because I had no illusions about wanting to be a cowpoke the rest of my life, but I liked their company. Most of 'em couldn't read, but they'd been around. I think we even had a few rustlers workin' on the spread."

Frank's first adventure was in Omaha trading cattle. He went with the other cowboys to market and while there celebrated with a whore. He even got so drunk the others had to carry him back to the train. The Coopers never did find out. Their eighteen-year-old son had finally grown up. When he refused to continue his education so he could pursue a career in art, they had to face up to his independence.

Alice was distraught, whereas Charles was realistic about his son's maturity. He was more concerned about his wife's health, so he used his influence to enroll Frank as a high-school student in the neighboring town of Bozeman. Despite his wife's protests, he gave Frank a motorcycle as an inducement. Years later Gary Cooper recalled, "I wanted to finish school for Mother's sake—to get it over with. It meant doing three years of school in one, but an English teacher helped me make it."

That teacher was Ida Davis, a forty-year-old spinster who took more than a liking to Frank. She told him if he would make an effort the school board might make an exception and graduate him. Miss Davis was a dedicated teacher, but she went beyond the call of duty for Cooper. It's unlikely there was a May–December romance, but she was certainly attracted to him, and Frank knew it. Taking advantage was not difficult for Frank. Ida made it easy for him. "I'm sure you can get into Montana State College right here in Bozeman," she said.

"I dunno," he said with a shrug.

"Have you considered commercial art?"

"What's that?"

Frank graduated in 1920 and wanted to get away from the schoolbooks for a while. To avoid the backbreaking work on the Bar-Nine he got a job as a tour guide at Yellowstone National Park in northwest Wyoming. He enjoyed driving the tour bus, but his usual spiel was short and often incoherent. However, the ladies didn't seem to mind. They often came back for seconds, requesting the tall, easygoing fellow with the dreamy blue eyes. Frank didn't flirt with women. He stared at them. He didn't smile, but gave the impression he might. Because the salary was meager he relied on tips from the tourists. Frank made more money that summer than the other guides, who suspected he was "working after hours." Whatever it was that women liked about him, Frank didn't flaunt it. The bashful cowboy was seen in the company of wealthy ladies who could afford to stay at the nearby hotel. But he never bragged or talked about his conquests. When Frank wasn't charming extra tips from rich women with tall tales about the Old Faithful geyser, he was off hunting alone or sitting with a sketch pad and pencil in a world all his own.

Not knowing what to do with the rest of his life Frank turned to Ida Davis. She urged him again to attend college in Bozeman. He entered, but dropped out before the end of the first semester. His father then helped him apply for admission to several liberal arts colleges. Grinnell, in Iowa, accepted him in 1922. He got a job at a college hangout, the Poweshiek Café, selling hamburgers for ten cents apiece. Classmates called him "Cowboy Cooper," and thought he should participate in campus activities.

"I don't know what gave me the notion I could act," he said. "It was just something that popped into my head. I tried out for the drama society. Not only did I stutter but I spoke my lines so softly that no one could hear me. I was rejected a couple of times." His memories of Grinnell were fond. He managed to keep his marks afloat, got along well with the boys at the dormitory, and . . . he fell in love. Several girls in the town of Grinnell almost captured Frank, but Doris Virden stole his heart. He proposed marriage "for a later date"—his family was having financial problems and he could barely make ends meet with only a part-time job.

It was time to find out if his only talent, that of a commercial artist, would be worth pursuing. Without telling anyone Frank left school and hopped on a bus for Chicago in February 1924 to find a job. For a month he stayed at the unheated YMCA, where he nearly froze to death.

"I hated cold weather," he said. In March Frank returned to Grinnell to pack his belongings. "I'm going home to Helena and getting a job," he told Doris. "Then I'm going to art school so I can work in an advertising agency. When I can afford it, we'll get married." Doris turned down his proposal but wished him "Good luck!"

As soon as Alice Cooper saw her son she burst into tears. "Nothing's gone right since you left," she sobbed. "Your father's no longer a judge. Did he tell you?"

"Nope."

"He had to make a choice, son. His private practice was lucrative but it took up so much of his time. We needed the money."

"Fer me?"

"Oh . . . don't blame yourself, Frank."

"What's Dad gonna do about the ranch?"

"Keep it," she sighed.

Frank was relieved. Still, he dreaded the thought of "ridin' herd" again. Instead he worked in a filling station and sold a few editorial cartoons to the local newspaper. Then Charles took a business trip to California, leaving Alice alone with Frank. Mother and son discussed the future. Frank told her about his proposal to Doris Virden, but before his mother fainted he added, "She never says much in her letters. I get the feelin' she answers mine just to be polite."

"You can't afford a wife." Alice frowned. "Who else have you heard from?"

"Jim Galen and Jim Calloway. They're in Hollywood ridin' horses in moving pictures for ten dollars."

"A day?" she asked.

"Dunno. Still a lotta money for doin' something that comes easy."

"Wicked town, Frank."

"Tom Mix doesn't look like a bad guy to me, Mom," he said.

"Don't be so sure. Fatty Arbuckle makes you laugh, but he killed that young girl. And how about Wallace Reid? That all-American boy . . . looked something like you, son."

"Yeah?"

"He died in a padded cell and do you know why?"

"Nope."

"Wallace Reid was a morphine addict. It started with dope and liquor, but everyone in Hollywood drinks bootleg booze. How they get away with it! Anyway, poor Wallace died a year ago and he was only thirty years old. And who killed William Desmond Taylor?"

"Who's he?"

"He was a famous director at Paramount who got shot to death in '22. The police found filthy love letters from beautiful actresses in his house—among other things."

"Like what?"

"I don't think we should talk about it anymore, but Hollywood is not a place for a respectable young man."

"I was lookin' at a map of California," Frank said thoughtfully, " 'cause I wanted to know where Dad was. Hollywood is really just a little town. It's part of Los Angeles. There's lots of cities nearby."

Alice bowed her head. "You aren't planning to visit your friends, I hope."

"I was thinkin' maybe," he said, taking her hand. "It's nice and warm out there. Lookin' for a job as an artist might be easier. Dad said he'll have to go back and forth to California, so I thought—"

"Are you doing this because that girl in Grinnell turned you down?"

Alice had hit a nerve, but Frank swallowed hard and shook his head. "I'm real glad Arthur got married," he said, smiling. "Gosh, he's got a good job with the Federal Reserve and all, and that's why I couldn't leave you all alone. I won't leave Montana until you and Dad say it's okay. I'd never hurt you."

"I'd worry about you, son."

"And get awful sick."

Frank faced a brick wall until his father returned from California. "I'm trying to settle a complicated estate for a client in San Diego," Charles explained.

"While I was out there I had some pretty good offers. Until I know for sure, I'll have to go back and forth."

"Does it mean we might move to California?" Alice asked.

Charles nodded.

The family sat down and talked. When the discussion was finished, Cowboy Cooper packed his art supplies. He was optimistic and looking forward to seeing the two Jims again, but in the excitement, he forgot their addresses.

2

HOLLYWOOD BOUND

On Thanksgiving Day 1924, twenty-three-year-old Frank Cooper arrived alone by train in Los Angeles. He looked around the depot and innocently asked a porter, "Which way to Hollywood?"

Years later Cooper admitted that the only real reason he went to California was to be a movie star. The odds were so great against it happening that perhaps one has to attribute his success to sheer beginner's luck. Many people in Montana and Iowa told him he should be in the movies, because he had little else going for him. Most likely the ladies handed him this worn-out line and Frank took it seriously.

Dressed in a wrinkled, ill-fitting suit, Frank combed L.A. for Jim Galen's whereabouts, but he couldn't find him. Knowing next to nothing about the film industry, he assumed everybody knew everybody within a few blocks. Wrong. The studios were spread out, he was told. But if his friend was well-known, he reasoned, there was no problem. "Jim falls off horses," he said, expecting a quick response. Instead he got a few snickers and many scowls. Cooper looked and talked like a hick. Hollywood was crawling with hundreds of well-dressed newcomers who at least had some knowledge of where they wanted to go.

When the sun began to set Cooper started looking for a place to sleep. It never occurred to him that he wouldn't be staying with Galen or Calloway. With only $100 in his pocket he was in trouble. "I found a room for a buck a day," Cooper said, "but almost went broke paying for food." Within a few days he located a boardinghouse on Romaine Avenue for $12 a week, which included two meals a day and chicken every Sunday. The other lodgers were bit players in moving pictures, who suggested he sign up with Central Casting. He did, and never heard from them. When asked if he had an agent, he shrugged. "What's that?"

In letters to his mother Frank wrote that people were very nice in Hollywood. He told her they were sober and didn't carry guns. He said he was trying to find a job as a commercial artist and inquired when she and Charles planned to arrive in Los Angeles. "I lied to them," he admitted, "and needed to borrow some money." He did, however, manage once to be at the right place at the right time, landing a job as an extra in a street crowd scene. He was paid $3.00.

Cooper had his problems, but they seemed to melt away in the California sunshine. He marveled at the hundreds of beautiful girls who flocked to Hollywood. They were as lonely as he was, it seemed, and easy to befriend. Soon he discovered their vulnerability and played the part of a guy who knew his way around. As he did at Yellowstone National Park, Frank acted as a tour guide, this time to the star-struck innocents. He pointed out the major studios and the stars' homes, but he also brought them to the abandoned buildings that were once temporary sites for shooting movies. A close friend said, "Gary joked about making love to these girls. They wanted to believe anything, and were so caught up in the excitement they responded to him. He didn't go into detail, but I know Gary made a habit of this. As I recall, his favorite building was where John Gilbert or Valentino made a film. That's where he made his subtle pitches."

In January 1925, Frank began looking for odd jobs. He used his skill with a camera as a portrait photographer, and also worked as a real estate salesman and as a milkman (his childhood ambition) for the Adohr Dairy, until he was fired five months later. By getting up before dawn to make his milk deliveries, Frank was able to make the rounds of the casting offices during the day.

Finally, quite by accident, he met an actor at the rooming house who knew Jim Galen.

"Been lookin' for him," Cooper said calmly. "What's he doing?"

"Making quickie Westerns on Poverty Row."

"Never heard of it."

"That's a stretch on Gower Street in old Hollywood."

Frank became disillusioned when he got there. It reminded him of the Bar-Nine, but worse—cowboys and Indians on dusty horses, impatient cameramen, and bums sitting in mud waiting to be hired. He got directions and found Galen, who greeted his friend with a hearty handshake. "Where ya been?" Jim asked.

"Lookin' for you," Cooper said, smiling. "Need another guy to ride?"

Galen laughed. "They're desperate around here, but don't pay much."

"Ten bucks a day's not so bad."

"That's for stunt ridin'. There's an extra five a fall."

"Why would I fall off a horse?" Frank asked.

" 'Cause you got shot."

"What about acting?"

"Fallin' off a horse without getting trampled to death is the only actin' I know, Frank."

"I was sorta thinking about Tom Mix."

"Hell, he got here first. The guy's no phony. Matter of fact he was in moving pictures before William S. Hart."

"Ever seen him?"

"Tom Mix?" Galen grinned. "Hell, I've been in some of his movies. He earns about $20,000 a week."

"H-h-how much?" Cooper gulped.

"C'mon, Frank. Let's get you a job."

Cooper, who weighed only 160 pounds, went for the falls and the additional money. He couldn't remember how many movies he appeared in as an extra. In one film he rode both with the bad guys and the good guys. Neither could he recall how often he was injured. "But if I was bleeding," he said, "the director wanted retakes. They might use my bruised arm a hundred times without showing my face."

Once he even fell on his head, but got up unassisted and walked away. His left hip took a pounding; it was either numb or throbbing with pain. But Frank never complained and he showed up for work every day. To get through a day's stunts he taught himself how to hit the dirt on his right side. Still, Cooper's days as a stuntman took their toll on his thin frame, and his hip never mended properly.

Galen told his friend to ease up. Instead the limping cowboy volunteered for the next fall. "Do your parents know what you're doin'?" Jim asked.

"Nope."

"They gotta find out sometime, Frank."

"I'll tell 'em when they get here."

"I'm goin' back to Montana for a while," Galen said.

"You comin' back?"

"Not sure."

"Givin' up already?"

"Frank, I don't wanna be an actor. No one famous ever came from Poverty Row. This is where they end up."

But Cooper never changed his mind about staying. The warm weather was worth all the sacrifices he had to make for a few dollars. And he was thrilled to work as an extra in a Tom Mix movie. Just hearing that the King of the Cowboys actually made $20,000 a week made Cooper more determined to be an actor. Frank watched Mix in a love scene with Billie Dove and, although a devoted fan, commented to another extra, "He's not *that* good." Cooper concluded there was more to acting than riding horses and that if Tom Mix could earn so much money so might Frank Cooper.

When Alice and Charles finally arrived in Los Angeles in 1926, Frank told them the truth. He was sorry if they were disappointed. "I'm ridin' horses," he said, "but not always in Westerns. Valentino's makin' *The Eagle* and I'm gonna be a Cossack."

"Valentino?" Alice cooed.

"Yep," Frank said proudly. "And I rode with Jack Holt and Noah Beery, but you have to look real close to see me."

When he showed them the boardinghouse on Romaine and the tiny room where he lived, Alice hung her head. "If you're this serious about the movies, son, I want to live in Hollywood, too." Before Charles even had a chance to think it over, Alice rented a house on Franklin Avenue, convenient to the studios.

Frank preferred to live by himself, but his mother persuaded him otherwise. Apparently Charles had very little to say about it. He had a long talk with his son, however, and explained the facts. "I know it's been tough to get this far," he told Frank, "but to be an actor means having an agent. You need someone who has influence, someone to pave the way. I might be able to help you."

Charles succeeded in getting his son into a two-reel quickie Western called *Lightin' Wins*. It was a worthless film that only proved that the elder Cooper had friends who owed him a favor. Alice was one of the few to see *Lightin' Wins*. Of course, she thought her son was beautiful on the screen. Charles concealed his disappointment and arranged an introduction to Hubert Bruning, a businessman who had once sought legal advice from him. His daughter, Marilyn Mills, was a trick rider in films and her husband, J. Charles Davis, was producing a series of feature-length Westerns. They reluctantly agreed to use "Judge" Cooper's son in *Tricks*.

Marilyn Mills said, "My father never asked for a favor, but when I saw the skinny kid, it was a disappointment. I didn't want to be bothered. I never saw so much humanity in one piece. He said the closest he'd ever been to a studio was waiting outside a casting director's office. He had some photographs . . . hair slicked down like Valentino and holding a pipe. He was trying to be sophisticated. I felt sorry for the kid even though we were the same age. When we got on location, the director refused to use him, but I insisted. We made him wear five extra shirts because he looked like a string bean. Frank played the villain. He did just fine and I suggested him for my next film, *Three Pals*."

Marilyn introduced him to agent Nan Collins, who thought Frank had possibilities. She suggested that he change his name to Gary.

"Why?" he asked.

"Because a Frank Cooper is being tried for murder and we don't want you to be confused with him."

"Why Gary?" he said, wincing.

She laughed. "Because my hometown is Gary, Indiana."

"Good thing you don't come from Poughkeepsie," he said.

Nan attempted to get her new client a screen test, but all she could scare up was a walk-on in *Watch Your Wife* at Universal. Meanwhile, the newly dubbed Gary worked on Poverty Row for $10 a day. Alice pleaded with her son to concentrate on real acting jobs. Every night he came home bruised, bleeding, and tired, but refused money from his parents. He borrowed their Buick to take out girls. When his mother asked why he didn't bring them home, Gary shrugged at the question.

"Who are they?" she asked.

"Secretaries and clerks," he replied. "Most of 'em work at the movie studios."

Gary changed the subject when Alice questioned him further. "I'm gonna do some stunt ridin' at Paramount in a Jack Holt Western called *The Enchanted Hill.* Seems to me Gary Cooper doesn't need an agent, Mother."

"You'll always be Frank to Dad and me. I don't like—"

"Gary?" he interrupted. "I spread the word around so I'm stuck with it—for a while, anyway. I met a guy at the studio . . . name's Dick Arlen and he calls me 'Coop.' That suits me fine."

It was lack of money that forced Gary to take matters into his own hands. He hung out at the studios and dated script girls, finally graduating to Sam Goldwyn's personal secretary. She bragged that they were going steady. Knowing he had made the right contact, Gary invested $65 to make his own screen test—riding a horse toward the camera, dismounting, removing his hat, and smiling. When Gary heard about a supporting role in a class-A Western, *The Winning of Barbara Worth* at Samuel Goldwyn Productions, he asked his girlfriend about it.

"Vilma Banky and Ronald Colman are the stars," she said. "Why?"

"I thought maybe . . . well, I have my own test ridin' a horse and thought maybe I'd have a go at the supporting part."

"Do you want me to make sure Mr. Goldwyn sees it?"

"That would be swell."

"How much do you want the part?" she asked.

"I'd give my left ball," Gary replied.

An uncertain Sam Goldwyn showed Cooper's screen test, along with others, to a group of girls working at the studio. The gaunt Cooper got the sighs and the job, which paid $50.

Frances Marion, a successful screenwriter, was working for Goldwyn at the time. She wrote in her autobiography, "I was working on the *Barbara Worth* project and one day Sam's secretary asked me to take a look at her beau who was standing outside. Through the window I saw a tall, lean, cowboy slouched against the wall. I said, 'That's our man!' Then I spoke to the director, Henry King, who said he'd look the boy over."

Unfortunately, the name of Goldwyn's secretary has been lost over the years. It didn't take long for Gary to forget her. He fell in love with Vilma Banky, who was friendly but aloof. Perhaps her ignoring Gary helped him portray the movie's lovesick cowboy. At the end of the film his character dies in Ronald Colman's arms after his heroic attempt to save their lives during a flood.

Goldwyn looked at the rushes and demanded retakes. Cooper said he would never forget the look of annoyance on the mogul's face. Almost in tears he told Vilma, "I'm a failure." Goldwyn told his staff, "That cowboy has no talent!" and was so angry he didn't invite Gary to the premiere on October 14, 1926. But to everyone's surprise, *The Winning of Barbara Worth* was a success at the box office. Reviews applauded Cooper's first screen credit. *Variety Weekly* said, "An outstanding performance by Gary Cooper."

But Sam Goldwyn did not offer him a contract.

"So I moseyed on over to Paramount," Cooper said, "and they were kinda glad to see me. I sat around talkin' to the big shots and they offered me a contract for $150 a week in November 1926." The contract had escalation clauses, but Paramount had the option to drop him after one year.

Goldwyn was dumbfounded when he heard that his brother-in-law, Jesse Lasky, head of Paramount Studios, had signed Cooper. He rationalized, "I'm a busy man and assumed someone on my staff signed him." Sam went to speak to Gary personally. "If things work out at Paramount," Sam said, "we'll talk."

Cooper knew he had to prove himself. He knew Goldwyn was right about his lack of talent. Sure, he could ride a horse and take a fall. But filming indoors in a studio was something else. While his parents were bursting with pride, Gary was nervous. He worried that *The Winning of Barbara Worth* was a stroke of sheer luck and that his next attempt would be a disaster.

Meanwhile, his parents bought the house they had rented in Hollywood, but they held on to the Bar-Nine. Their settling in California was another reason for Gary to worry. Suppose he let them down? After all, they had rearranged their lives because he wanted to break into movies. Every day he would go to the studio for photo sessions and meetings with the publicity staff, nervously awaiting his first assignment. When he found out it was a Western he was relieved.

In December 1926, Gary attended his first Paramount party, accompanied by his friend, Richard Arlen. The reason for the party was to let the top brass scrutinize the new contract players. Gary and Richard wanted to leave early. The morbid chatter about Valentino's sudden death a few months earlier bothered them. Hollywood had still not recovered from the shock. Everyone speculated on a replacement for "the sheik." Cooper was about to leave when the "It Girl" flew through the front door. She was a sprightly redhead with bobbed hair, perky lips, saucer eyes, and a vivacious personality.

Gary stood by, riveted. "Who's *she?*" Cooper whispered to Arlen.

"The bee's knees. The cat's pajamas," Arlen said with a grin. "That's Clara Bow."

Suddenly the party came alive, transformed by Clara's electric presence. Impish, she bounced from man to man, touching, pinching, patting, cooing. When she got to Cooper, he broke out in a sweat. She looked him right in the eye, and straightened his tie, and said, "Let's scram. This party is takin' the snap out of my garters!"

Arlen watched them get into her red Kissel convertible. He knew he wouldn't be seeing Coop for some time.

Clara Bow was the ultimate jazz baby. In 1926, she was the hottest property in Hollywood. "She lingers in the eye long after the picture has gone," *Variety* wrote. Women everywhere gave their lips the "bee-stung" look and bobbed and dyed their hair red in imitation of Clara. Paramount counted over forty thousand fan letters in one week addressed to the "It Girl."

Author Elinor Glyn's books, *This Passion Called Love* and *The Philosophy of Love* were best-sellers in the twenties, but her most sensational novel was entitled *It*. The question on America's lips was "What's 'It'?" Madame Glyn replied, " 'It' is a strange magnetism which attracts both sexes. There must be a physical attraction, but beauty is unnecessary."

Paramount decided to make Glyn's novel into a movie and began looking for a star. The author declared, "There are only three in Hollywood who have 'It'—Clara Bow, Tom Mix's horse, and the doorman at the Ambassador Hotel." They chose Clara.

The Brooklyn-born girl took such recognition in her stride. The victim of an abused childhood, her father was always either unemployed or away from home, and her mother would lock Clara in the closet while she "entertained" her boyfriends for a fee. On one of Daddy's rare visits home, he entered his seventeen-year-old daughter's picture in a magazine beauty contest. "My mother was nuts," Clara said. "When she found out about the contest, she snuck into my bedroom one night. I woke up with a cold butcher knife pressing against my throat. I cried and talked her out of it, but I never slept through another night again."

Clara won the beauty contest. The prize included a screen test and a small part in the 1922 film *Beyond the Rainbow*. Fourteen Clara Bow pictures were released in 1925. A year later she achieved stardom in *Mantrap*. In *The Great Movie Stars: The Golden Era*, David Shipman wrote, "The twenties would have been quite different without Clara Bow; she was totally representative of the era. She was gay and vivacious, as befitted the new emancipated woman; she had enormous enthusiasm for life. How typical of the period that having or not having 'It' was almost a cause célèbre." On the screen she played the shop girl, waitress, dance hall hostess, and manicurist with an innocence so titillating that audiences succumbed to her thoroughly believable effervescence.

Fan magazines flashed photos of Clara driving her red Kissel convertible with her seven chow dogs and a monkey, all dyed flaming red to match her hair. "The rapid success of Clara Bow has furnished Hollywood with almost as much conversation as the recent economy wave," one Los Angeles newspaper said in 1926.

If the public loved Miss Bow, those with whom she worked in Hollywood adored her even more. Clara was ever generous, fun-loving, and sincere. She was outspoken about not getting married and frank about her independence. Perhaps this was part of her attraction offscreen. Men fell for Clara, but she preferred a variety.

Clara liked to kiss and tell. To her, chatting about the day at the studio was "boring as all hell!" After dark was the day's real attraction. The five-feet, four-inch, 115-pound vixen had an insatiable appetite for sex. When she heard that Al Jolson claimed he had never gone to bed with her, Clara thought for a moment and then asked, "How did *he* get away?"

She was engaged at various times to the suave Mexican actor Gilbert Roland, and to director Victor Fleming. Supposedly, she was also engaged to Broadway singing star Harry Richman. She gave him a $2,000 ring after aborting his baby. Harry used Clara to further his career but lost his heart. "I almost fell for him," she said, but to her Harry was like all the others. "They want me on their terms. The trouble with men is that they all want to make you over into something else. It burns me up. Especially since it's me as I am that they fall for. The more I see of men, the more I like dogs."

Yale football star Robert Savage told the press she kissed him so hard his lips bled. When she refused to marry him he cut his wrists and dripped the blood on Clara's photo. Savage wrote love poems to Clara that were published in newspapers from coast to coast:

> A haunting voice came in the twilight whispering soft and low,
> Telling of a beautiful creature, telling of Clara Bow.
> And I lie in my bed by the window to happily, happily scan
> The heavens so star-filled above me, grateful indeed I'm a man.

Clara wasn't impressed. When a reporter asked why she wasn't more sympathetic toward Savage, Clara said, "All I can say about Bob is that as a lover, he's a wonderful poet. Jesus Christ!" she exclaimed. "He's got to be kidding! Men don't slash their wrists. They use a gun!"

Clara lived modestly in a Beverly Hills bungalow but her Chinese Den bedroom was famous for its candlesticks, incense, Buddhas, Sivas, and scarlet velvet window shades, and for the famous lovers who shared with Clara the round bed that occupied most of the room—Richard Arlen, Buddy Rogers, Eddie Cantor, boxer Slapsie Maxie Rosenbloom, Bela Lugosi, Charles Farrell, John Gilbert, and Fredric March.

Frequently she entertained the UCLA football team. In fact, her neighbors became accustomed to seeing nude football games on her front lawn. Clara admitted to taking two or three players at a time. It wasn't unusual for her to make several dates on the same night without getting caught. She couldn't care less. Her friends said there were few men who could satisfy Clara. But the night she stole off with Cooper, she had no way of knowing that the stunning Montana cowboy was a champion in bed who could outlast even her. She nicknamed him "Studs" and told Hedda Hopper, "Gary's hung like a horse and can go all night!" She went on to describe to Hedda their lovemaking on the beach, in public parks, in the backseat of her convertible, in swimming pools, in the woods, and in her dressing room. Anywhere and everywhere and anytime was Clara's motto.

Clara's fans suspected she was a "mantrap," but they had no idea to what extent. In later years she confessed her deep love for Cooper: ". . . but he was like the others—jealous and too serious. They say I was engaged to lots of men, but I wasn't officially. I never told the truth to the press about Gary and me, but we came very close to marriage. It was never printed anywhere that we were engaged, though. Everyone thought it was just a physical attraction, but there was more. A lot more."

Although Clara had already finished filming *It,* she marched into Paramount's executive offices and demanded that Cooper be given a bit part in the film. B. P. Schulberg, the associate producer, considered the request highly unusual but gave his consent, knowing Gary would only benefit by appearing in a Clara Bow movie. He arranged for Cooper to play a newspaper reporter in two scenes.

It was a smash. The critics were unanimous: "Clara Bow really does it all, and how!"

Clara earned only $3,000 a week in *It.* Three years later she would earn no more than $5,000 a week, which was far less than other major stars were pulling in. In truth, money and fame meant very little to Clara Bow. She worked hard, but was much more interested in having a good time.

After the Christmas holidays, Cooper emerged from Clara's Chinese Den and was assigned to his first movie at Paramount, *Arizona Bound,* a class-B Western. He was to play a young cowboy accused of robbing the stagecoach, who escapes lynching and gets the girl, played by Betty Jewel. He was happy to see his old buddies from Poverty Row back him up as stuntmen. But he blushed when they referred to him as the "It Boy." Worse still, some members of the crew called him "Studs." Cooper said nothing, turned his back, and walked away. He was labeled, regardless.

When the film opened, *Variety* said, "Cooper is a tall youth with a boyish smile and enough swagger to give him character. *Arizona Bound* will give him a respectable introduction to his future public."

After Gary met Clara, Alice and Charles saw very little of their son. Gary by now owned a new red Chrysler roadster and no longer needed the family car. When he did visit his parents, Alice wanted to know if the rumors were true. Was he living with Clara Bow? He said, "Sometimes I fall asleep there." When he tired of the questions, Cooper told his parents it was all a publicity stunt. After all, Miss Bow was dating other men. But his explanations did not include why he rarely came home, why his name kept popping up in fan magazines and gossip columns. It didn't matter to him that he basked in Clara's reflected glory. But when Clara demanded Gary play opposite her in her next movie, *Children of Divorce,* the word got out around town that Cooper depended on her to advance his career. It appeared as though he were a gigolo. The more Clara bragged about Gary's powers in the bedroom, the further she advanced his status as an actor. He didn't mind. From the moment he set eyes on her he was completely in her thrall. He took the teasing and razzing in his stride because it was all true—Coop fell hard for Clara.

* * *

Children of Divorce was to be Clara's first attempt at dramatic acting and a turning point in her career. James Hall had originally been cast as her leading man, but Clara was set on Cooper. Frank Lloyd, the director, tried to change her mind. "I'm here to concentrate on you," Lloyd told her. "How can I do that with an unknown fumbling around?"

"I want Gary," she insisted.

"He's scheduled for *The Last Outlaw*."

"That can wait."

"But, Clara, he's a cowboy."

"Do it my way or I'll find another director," she said impatiently.

Frank Lloyd shrugged. "Have it your way, Clara."

Not bad for a girl from Coney Island with only an eighth-grade education.

Children of Divorce was the story of a young couple (Gary Cooper and Esther Ralston) who are reluctant to marry because their parents suffered through divorce. The vamp (Clara Bow) takes advantage of Cooper in the film by getting him drunk and tricking him into marriage. On the rebound, his sweetheart marries a man who proves unfaithful. Clara has a change of heart and commits suicide, whereas Esther divorces her adulterous husband and finds happiness with Gary.

Hedda Hopper, who later became a columnist, acted in the film and commented, "Poor Gary was miscast as any guy could be. He was far from the wisecracking sophisticated playboy. One of the first scenes we did called for him to breeze into a cocktail party, mix with the crowd, have a drink, and light a cigarette nonchalantly while he made his way across the room. It was terrible. He spilled champagne all over me. He tried it twenty-two times. Twenty-two times! He told me that room got longer and longer every minute!"

Clara, in her first dramatic role, was under pressure. Cooper was mortified. He had no conception of how to be a straight actor, how to walk, how to stand and, above all, how to romance a woman outside of the bedroom. During rehearsals, Gary managed fairly well, but when he dropped the tray of champagne, his confidence was shattered.

Frank Lloyd gritted his teeth. He assumed "Studs" would do better holding a woman in his arms for the camera. What Lloyd did not know was that Cooper had proposed marriage to Clara, who replied, "Hell, that would take all the fun out of it!" Hopelessly in love, Gary was despondent and in a state of nervous tension. He wanted to do his very best in *Children of Divorce* to impress Clara.

The day he was to romance Esther Ralston for the camera, Gary was a complete disaster. He froze.

"What's the matter now?" Lloyd grumbled.

Cooper shrugged. "I'm not sure what to do," he mumbled.

"Hold her! Kiss her!"

"Well, you see, sir . . . well, ya see, I don't know the girl very well."

Lloyd fired him on the spot. Cooper jumped into his car and disappeared. "I sped through the Mojave Desert," he said, "slept in a rundown hotel, and drove back along the ocean. I had to think. I wanted to go fishin'. I wanted to quit."

Meanwhile, Lloyd called the front office and requested a replacement. But when he saw the rushes, he changed his mind. If Cooper was a clumsy bore on the set, he didn't come across that way on film. Lloyd had to have him back.

The Coopers, who hadn't heard from Gary, were sick with worry. The police were summoned to search for him. Hedda Hopper was furious. She told Frank Lloyd, "It's your duty as a professional to get a good performance out of an actor!" The director accepted the challenge and a few days later found Cooper in his favorite restaurant. "I'll make an actor out of you, cowboy!" Lloyd exclaimed. "What we have on film is not bad. Why the hell don't we finish the damn thing!"

"It's real hard for me to smooch with a filly I hardly know," Gary said with a scowl.

"Then you should have no problem tomorrow," Lloyd said, "because you'll be kissing Clara."

Legend has it that Cooper was found at the railroad or bus station, depending on the version—that he was actually packed and returning to Montana. After he became a star, this was the type of publicity the public gobbled up. But Cooper *had* made up his mind to get out of the movies when he was seen going into the restaurant. Obviously, he wanted to be found and reunited with the woman he loved. Being recognized as an actor was secondary.

Lloyd was optimistic, but when Gary tried to kiss Clara while the camera was rolling, his knees wobbled and his hands trembled. It was noticeable on film, too. Lloyd was exasperated, but Hedda Hopper hinted he was not only a quitter, but unable to direct a newcomer. He overheard her saying, "I guess we can be certain Frank Lloyd will never discover a star."

Clara had given up on Gary, too. She told the technicians, "Studs makes love to me on the set as if I was his horse!"

When Hedda Hopper became a columnist she took credit for saving Cooper's career. "I teased and ribbed Frank Lloyd," she said. "He had no choice but to finish *Children of Divorce* with Gary."

Lloyd's solution was clever, embarrassing, and amusing. After the awkward love scene with Clara, Lloyd motioned to Cooper and pointed to a chair. "Come over here and sit!" he commanded as if training a dog. "You might as well get comfortable because we're going to finish this damn thing with you sitting on your ass!"

The film was completed with the leading man seated. When the movie flopped, Clara blamed Cooper. She began seeing director Victor Fleming again.

Children of Divorce was doomed from the beginning, because it was not the kind of picture Frank Lloyd did well. His aim was to concentrate on Clara's dramatic acting. Instead, he wasted time on Cooper who was miscast in the first place.

Esther Ralston was hailed by the critics, however. She admitted her attraction to Gary. "But he wanted only Clara, I thought he was a sensitive gentleman and always well-groomed. While we were working he told me how much he loved Clara, who simply referred to him as a wonderful man 'because he always lets me take my dog in the tub when he gives me a bath in the morning.' Clara was a little untamed minx. She described her wild nights using language that shocked most people. She chewed gum and had a Brooklyn accent, but I adored her."

Cooper was lost without Clara, but he found another girl with the same salty tongue, energy, and sexy sense of humor. Carole Lombard was only nineteen when Gary began dating her occasionally. Carole was hell on wheels—strong-willed and frank. The first time she rode a horse she said in front of a crowd. "I don't know why the hell everybody thinks this is so great. It's like a dry fuck!"

Though not as promiscuous as Clara, Miss Lombard was vivacious, uninhibited, and never wore a bra or panties. If any girl could substitute for Clara, it was Carole, who was very open about her affair with Gary even after she married Clark Gable.

If Hedda Hopper takes credit for saving Cooper's career, it was Paramount mogul Jesse Lasky who was responsible for giving the cowboy the best advice he ever got. Gary knew he was to blame for the extra time and money spent on *Children of Divorce*. When Lasky wanted to see him in his office, there could only be one reason.

"I knew you were all wrong for that movie," Lasky began. "But I understand the circumstances. However, if by now you haven't realized you should be cast only in Westerns, then you aren't aware of your talent."

"Thanks," Cooper muttered.

"*Arizona Bound* is doing well and I'm anxious for you to start *The Last Outlaw*."

"Gee . . . thanks . . ."

"And, by the way, I'm doubling your salary to $300 a week."

To this day no one has succeeded in figuring out why Cooper got first prize for being a flop. But if there is an explanation, it was Lasky's keen intuition that this cowboy belonged on a horse.

In *The Last Outlaw* Gary appeared again with Betty Jewel and "Flash," the wonder horse. Cooper portrayed a sheriff who must arrest Betty's brother for murder, but in the end he gets the girl. *Variety*'s review sounded as if Gary had written it himself: "Gary Cooper is Paramount's new Western star whom they are trying to put over. Paramount can stand a Western star and has a personality bet in Cooper, but they're not doing right by him. He does some good work, rides fast and flashy on his horse and impresses with his gun totin' generally. Screen mechanics are against him. He labors against story shortcomings and creaking directorial machinations."

But Cooper's riding and roping were once again interrupted because Clara Bow could not live without him for very long. He was the only man who could satisfy her in bed. Their reconciliation presented only one problem for Clara, and that was Gary's desire to marry her. She tried to discourage him by admitting she couldn't have children, " 'cause I don't have all my parts down there." Clara pouted. It wouldn't be fair to him, after all. He was the kind of fellow who deserved a family. Cooper didn't change his mind about Clara, but they were no longer inseparable.

At this time, 1927, Paramount was going all out with a $2-million budget for *Wings,* a World War I aviation spectacular with Buddy Rogers and Richard Arlen, both beginners with only three movie credits. The cast was all-male until Lasky decided it was crucial that he feature one woman. For box-office insurance he chose Clara Bow. Her contract allowed her the right to refuse any script she didn't like, and *Wings* was one of them.

"It's a small part," she told Lasky. "Who needs it?"

"*Wings* is a man's picture, granted, but you'll be outstanding as the only woman, and we'll give you top billing."

Clara snapped her gum and smiled coyly. "You trying to boost Rogers?"

"Frankly, yes."

"Arlen, too?"

"Maybe. We hope so, of course."

"Gary's had more exposure."

Lasky felt a headache coming on. "What are you trying to say, Clara?"

"I might consider doing the picture if Gary's in it."

"He's not finished with *The Last Outlaw* and I have another Western lined up for him."

"Gary and me or nothin'!"

"Swell . . ."

Cooper wasn't unhappy to be out of the saddle. He wanted to travel to San Antonio and see the Alamo, anyway. Besides, he'd have the chance to work with Arlen. Another incentive was having Clara all to himself far away from her Chinese Den. The more he thought about it, the more he looked forward to the idea. As for Miss Bow, she couldn't get enough of Gary and hoped to change his mind about marriage. Her addiction to him was enough without bringing in the white picket fence, two-car garage, and baby carriage.

Twenty-nine-year-old rookie director William Wellman was assigned to the airplane epic. A former pilot, actor, and Foreign Legionairre, Wellman later became famous for his direction of *A Star Is Born, Call of the Wild, The*

Story of G.I. Joe, and *Battleground,* to name a few. *Wings* was Wellman's first major accomplishment. Years later he recalled: "Clara was in her glory. She was the center of attention and the only woman on location. She and Cooper took off when they weren't working, but when Clara was filming she divided her time between Arlen and Rogers and Cooper, who was jealous as hell. There were others 'in her tent,' too. Her timing was unique. Clara was concerned, however, when she found out her boyfriend, Victor Fleming, was directing a Western nearby. She managed to keep him happy, too, but didn't like seeing Coop and Vic becoming good friends on the set. Fleming was a man's man and I'm sure they were discussing hunting and fishing. Clara seemed more at ease when Vic returned to Hollywood."

In *Wings* Cooper had only one major scene. "I played the veteran flyer," he explained. "Dick and Buddy were cadets. The camera picked me up munching on a chocolate bar in their tent. I kinda salute, throw the half-eaten candy aside, and take off for some test flying. I'm killed, but all you see is the shadow of my plane. Then the camera focuses on the unfinished chocolate. I always gave credit to Arlen and Rogers for their swell reaction to my death. They made me a hero."

Wellman shot the scene and was satisfied. Cooper was stunned when Wellman yelled, "Cut and print!" the first time around. Richard Arlen recalled, "Coop's mouth actually dropped open. I think he ran through it with such ease expecting to do it again." Wellman was surprised when Cooper came to his tent later that day to plead for a retake. "I didn't know the camera was rollin' and want to do it again," he asked.

"It was perfect," Wellman said. "What's the problem?"

"Well, ya see . . . I mean . . . well, I was pickin' my nose . . ."

"You rubbed your nose two or three times with your thumb."

"No, sir. I was . . . uh . . . pickin' my nose."

Wellman laughed. "You go right on picking your nose and you'll make yourself a fortune!"

Years later, Wellman tried to describe the effect Cooper had on the screen. "I think one is born with it," he said. "Gable with his ears had it. Bogart lisped, but he had it. Tracy wasn't handsome, but he had it. They all played themselves, mind you. If Cooper was clumsy or mumbled or picked his nose, it didn't matter. Like the others, he had what I call motion-picture personality. I wish someone could describe this chemistry. These guys became top stars and made millions."

Wings won an Oscar for best picture the first year of the Academy Awards, 1927. Warner Brothers received a special one for *The Jazz Singer,* the first talking picture, which revolutionized the industry.

Charles "Buddy" Rogers became popular for a short time, but was not the leading man Paramount expected. Richard Arlen was established and Gary Cooper received some fan mail. Clara Bow as an ambulance driver was adorable in uniform, but none of the major players were acclaimed. The

Literary Digest said it was a fine picture largely by virtue of its success in reproducing scenes of actual combat in airplanes.

Cooper was relieved to know his next movie was a Zane Gray Western, *Nevada*, starring twenty-two-year-old Thelma Todd and William Powell, who began his career as a cowboy villain. *Variety Weekly* wrote, "Paramount has Gary Cooper now riding the plains, tall, two-fisted, gun-toting and lightning fast on the draw, who has done his darndest to step into the shoes of Jack Holt. Cooper does well but the stories seem to be getting thinner . . . Cooper improving in his work and serving his masters well in everything but his lovemaking." *Photoplay* noted, "*Nevada* has thrills with suspense, dazzles with a fine performance, glamorous outdoor photography and a hero with a sense of humor, Gary Cooper."

His costar, Thelma Todd, was a "hotcha baby" with the face of an angel and the body of a goddess. She would make eighty films in only ten years, then die mysteriously in 1935 at age thirty. She was found in the front seat of her car, the apparent victim of suicide from carbon monoxide poisoning. Some thought there was foul play involved.

When Cooper met her in 1927, Thelma was available, but there was no mention of a romance. Clara Bow stayed close by, and although she wasn't faithful to Gary she kept her watchful eye on him.

Alice Cooper worried that they were living together again. She and Clara met once, maybe twice—Gary tried to keep them apart. Miss Bow was not exactly the kind of girl a fellow takes home to meet his mama. Clara was bored to death with such domestic gatherings, anyway. She did not try to impress anyone. "I hate people who put on the dog," she said, "and that goes for Hollywood bigwigs, actors, and their mothers. Whatever I got, I got on my own and I don't throw it in people's faces. Everyone wants to know why I don't live in a big fancy house with servants. I have a maid and that's all. Who needs a crowd getting underfoot? Besides, I don't have to prove anything to anybody. And that goes for snobs who want to look me over and decide if I'm good enough for them."

For his next film, Cooper was honored to be chosen for *Beau Sabreur*, the sequel to Ronald Colman's *Beau Geste*, based on Christopher Wren's best-selling romantic novel about the French Foreign Legion. Gary knew he would be on location in Arizona and had no illusions about Clara's capricious ways. But he also knew she would take him back, because ". . . you outlast 'em all, Studs."

3

THE "IT BOY"

Evelyn Brent made her first movie in 1915 in Fort Lee, New Jersey, at age fourteen. For ten years the raven-haired beauty acted in films and appeared on the stages of Europe. Then, in 1922, Paramount signed her to a movie contract. She became known as "Queen of the Underworld" because of all the gangster films she made. But her star status was fleeting. "I had no guidance," she said, "and no ambition."

Underworld, a 1927 gangster melodrama in which she starred, was such a success that Paramount decided to team her with Cooper in *Beau Sabreur.* Evelyn was mature for her age and bore a slight resemblance to Clara Bow, but she had many faces and her talents were compared with Joan Crawford and Greta Garbo. Her fine performance as "Feathers" in *Underworld* opened doors in Hollywood. She was invited to elite dinner parties.

Cooper fell in love with Miss Brent and took her home to meet his parents. The four enjoyed quiet evenings at home playing bridge. Soon Gary proposed marriage to her, but she turned him down. They were seen together at the best parties and social gatherings. When Cooper was in love, it showed on his face. He was puppylike, adoring, and attentive. He was sure he had found the right girl. His mother thought so, too. Evelyn loved him in her own way, but getting to know Gary, she said, was difficult because he retreated too often into his own world.

Cooper reflected, "In Evelyn Brent I found the companionship of a woman who was wise and brilliant. I was first attracted to her as a woman who had her feet on the ground and was not riding the clouds." Miss Brent remarked, shortly before she died in 1975, "Gary and I had something going for a while."

Alice Cooper once said in an interview, "I like Evelyn and shall always appreciate the good influence that she had on Gary."

Beau Sabreur was popular at the box office. Paramount took full advantage of the Cooper-Brent romance. *Underworld* had made Evelyn a hot property, and she could only benefit Gary's career. Their "engagement" seemed like the real thing, but Evelyn was too wise to consider marriage to an actor who was constantly surrounded by women who literally threw themselves at him. "I think it was his shyness that fascinated the girls," she said. "He gave the impression of backing off. Gary didn't know how to handle himself. He brought out the mother instinct in women."

Cooper's friends were convinced that he was not mature enough for Miss Brent, that he tried desperately to live up to her expectations but was distracted by other concerns.

Hollywood was going through a transition from silents to talkies. When M-G-M's resident boy genius Irving Thalberg declared, "Sound is just a fad," it was one of the few times during his meteoric career that he was wrong. Paramount was preparing to release films that were partial talkies. The studio was having difficulty accepting the fact that ninety percent of their players might be ruined. Diction coaches flocked to Hollywood. Talent scouts invaded college campuses and legitimate theaters in search of potential stars.

While sound equipment was being set up at Paramount, production of silents continued at a rapid pace. Cooper's leading lady in his next picture, *Doomsday,* was King Vidor's former wife, Florence. She was six years older than Gary and the age difference was apparent on the screen. Another problem was the title, which was misleading. *Doomsday* didn't refer to apocalypse but to the name of Cooper's farm. The story appeared to be the same old movie theme—poor man proposes to poor girl who marries a rich man. In *Doomsday,* however, she returns home and offers to be her former boyfriend's housekeeper for six months to prove she'll work hard for her man (Cooper). He accepts.

The movie did very little for him, but Paramount thought Gary was improving as a screen lover and decided to keep him out of the saddle temporarily.

The studio chose newcomer Fay Wray to play opposite him in *Legion of the Condemned.* Critics rightly compared it with *Wings.* In fact, leftover footage from *Wings* was used in *Legion of the Condemned.*

Paramount promoted Fay Wray and Gary Cooper as the "Glorious Young Lovers," but the public didn't buy it. Fay did not take her relationship with Cooper seriously. "We went out together," she said, "but I was just another date as far as he was concerned." Cooper confirmed this twenty years later. "I liked Fay a lot. She took our relationship as one of those things." Paramount costarred them in four movies but the spark just wasn't there.

Cooper was still linked to Clara Bow, who, in a national poll, was voted one of the most popular female stars of 1928. A year later she would be number one.

Gary's next screen appearance was in *Half a Bride,* with Esther Ralston. Cooper played a yacht captain hired by Ralston and her much-older husband. The boat sinks while at sea and the husband drowns. The survivors, Cooper and Ralston, make it to land where they are the only inhabitants of a desert island. They enter into a three-month trial marriage and when they are finally rescued, the couple remain together "until death do us part." Though flimsy and silly, *Half a Bride* somehow clicked with audiences. The fan mail addressed to Gary Cooper poured into Paramount.

* * *

Jesse Lasky was determined to team Paramount's "Glorious Young Lovers" in *The First Kiss,* a familiar story of a rich girl and a poor boy. During filming on the Chesapeake Bay, Fay accidentally fell into the water and Gary saved her. The studio gave the incident enormous publicity and the public was sold on the film months before it was released. *The First Kiss* was a charming movie, according to the critics. Cooper's fans responded with a thousand letters a week, but they wanted him in another Western despite his success as a lover.

Paramount was willing to costar him in a Zane Grey epic opposite Fay Wray, but Colleen Moore, at that time a top box-office draw, requested that Cooper costar with her in *Lilac Time* at First National Pictures.

Colleen Moore began her career in 1917 and six years later found fame in the movie *Flaming Youth.* Her Dutchboy hairdo and spunky style singled her out as one of Hollywood's first flappers. Naughty and nice, she could play a variety of roles well. When she married John McCormick, production head of First National, she became powerful as well as popular. "I was filming on Catalina Island," she said, "and we went to the village theater one evening. *The Last Outlaw* was playing. I decided then and there that Gary Cooper would be my leading man in *Lilac Time.*"

Cooper again played an aviator. His plane crashes and as he lies dying in a hospital, his French girlfriend, played by Moore, sends him lilacs. Love overcomes all obstacles and he, of course, lives. *The Los Angeles Times* critic wrote, "Gary Cooper is a sincere and manly lover. I have never seen him to better advantage."

But *Motion Picture Classic* disagreed: "Gary Cooper, had he been less restrained and colored his role more, would have added considerably to the film's appeal. But he is too restrained—and the best part of the sentiment misses some necessary heartbeats."

Cooper himself complained about the project. "There was too much commotion goin' on during *Lilac Time,*" he said. "McCormick almost switched to sound. Colleen disagreed and I guess she was the boss. I knew I had a voice, but it was frightening knowing this might be my debut in talkies. I had enough problems in my love scenes with Colleen while her husband glared over my shoulder. As far as I was concerned, *Lilac Time* was a disaster. Every day people were shoutin' and askin', 'Should we add music? Voices? Yes? No?' I was sweating. Every other actor in town was rehearsing for his first sound movie and I had to wake up each day wonderin' if I was going to make an ass of myself without any warning."

Colleen Moore fondly described working with Cooper: "Gary was a long, lanky, kind of sleepy young fellow. He couldn't act at all. He was pure Montana. He didn't talk much and when he did, Gary spoke about himself and Evelyn Brent. He was not intellectual or worldly. He didn't have to be. Cooper was natural. With all the drawbacks, I knew he'd be successful because all the girls working at the studio came down to see him. I never saw this happen before. They weren't watching a film being shot. They wanted to see him. These girls were accustomed to handsome movie actors and yet they hung around to take a look at Gary Cooper who, at the time, wasn't a top star. I do recall his parents visiting the set. Naturally, I expected the typical midwestern type who owned a ranch and all. On the contrary. They were very, very British."

Colleen Moore's salary during *Lilac Time* was a whopping $12,500 a week. Yet her future in talkies was uncertain and John McCormick knew *Lilac Time* had to succeed, so he added a sound track for the theme song, "Jeannine, I Dream of Lilac Time," which became the most popular tune of 1928.

By the time Cooper had returned to Paramount, he was quite worried over the rumors filtering back about the editing of the film. When he received an invitation to the premiere, he told his mother, "I'm not going."

"You must."

"I don't have a tuxedo," he mumbled.

"Buy one!"

"Mother, it would be a waste of money."

"Why?"

"I'm not kiddin' myself. Without stage experience, I'm not gonna make it in talkies."

"You have a fine voice, son. Otherwise why would the studio ask you to make *The Shopworn Angel* with Nancy Carroll?"

"I don't know," he said, scowling. "She's from Broadway, and . . ." as his voice trailed. Alice begged him to buy a tuxedo, but he rented one instead. She advised him to take Evelyn Brent to the premiere, but he showed up with Clara Bow.

The Shopworn Angel was Gary Cooper's first talkie. It had only seven lines of dialogue at the end of the picture. Nancy Carroll sang, "Precious Little Thing Called Love." It was the touching story of a spoiled girl and a lonely soldier who marry before he goes to war. Officially Cooper's first words on screen were "I do," spoken during the wedding scene. Twenty years later he said, "All I remember saying was 'I do' after almost two hours of acting in silence." Nancy Carroll was tremendously relieved that *The Shopworn Angel* was a success.

"We were nervous," she recalled, "but Gary didn't show it. We had to do several takes of our falling asleep on the beach and when the director finally shouted, 'Cut!' Gary was sound asleep for real. I understand this became a habit of his. Everyone thought he was tired out from the night before, if you know what I mean. He was known for his hot relationships with women. But I think Gary just had the ability to fall asleep, much of it from boredom. He is my favorite leading man. I could have gone for him, but I knew I'd lose him to someone else."

Paramount was satisfied with Cooper's sound debut. Hedda Hopper said,

"His monosyllabic Montana speech matched his screen image, which hadn't been established as yet, but the voice went along well with the gaunt face and lanky frame."

The critics did not comment on his voice, but they praised his performance. *Photoplay* applauded, "Gary Cooper's charming boyishness is an effective foil for the scintillating Nancy Carroll." So did *The New York Herald Tribune:* "Gary Cooper is engaging and ingenuous." *The New York Daily Mirror* wrote, "Gary Cooper amazes fans. He gives a great performance."

It is almost impossible to fathom how anxious the public was to hear their favorite movie stars talk for the first time. They laughed at John Gilbert and Charles Farrell. Norma Talmadge, Mary Pickford, and Colleen Moore quietly "retired" from films. The pantomimes of Douglas Fairbanks, Sr., and Buster Keaton became irrelevant. Ninety percent of the silent stars were ruined.

The first words spoken on the screen were by Al Jolson in *The Jazz Singer* on October 6, 1927—"Wait a minute. Wait a minute. You ain't heard nothin' yet, folks. Listen to this."

Hollywood studio moguls disagreed about whether sound was a fad or here to stay. It took them three years to get prepared. Sound equipment was expensive, bulky, and complicated. The tragedy of ruined careers is a worn-out bit of history. What about the directors who had to change their methods? And the technicians? And what about the surviving stars who had to learn the art of talking into a hidden microphone?

Director Frank Capra said, "Suddenly we had to work in silence. When the red light went on everyone was in a sweat. God forbid if we coughed or belched or sneezed. I had to stop often and remind an actor that the microphone was in the flower pot. 'You can't turn away,' I repeated over and over. First came dialogue, then sound effects, and finally, music."

Considering the fact that Gary Cooper was trying very hard to learn the basic techniques of shuffling around on the set, it is miraculous he was able to remember what to do, how to do it, and where to do it, and still know where the microphone was hidden. Cooper was not the only star who had to adjust; he just found it more difficult than most. The fact that he made the transition was attributable to his voice, of course. He was not trained for the stage as were so many of his peers, but Gary didn't lisp, talk through his nose, or have a thick foreign accent.

As a result, in 1929 the studio doubled his salary to $1,200 a week—a fair sum, he reckoned, but not as much as some other stars who did not have Cooper's drawing power. He took matters into his own hands, just as he had done with his screen test, and refused to sign the new contract. He demanded $5,000, but eventually settled for $3,700 with substantial increases over seven years. Cooper later found out that he could have gotten $5,000 or more if he'd held out or had an agent to guide him. He had, however, found the courage to negotiate a seven-year contract without options. The soap-opera success story was just beginning.

Guadeloupe Velez de Villalobos was born in San Luis de Potosi, Mexico, on July 18, 1908. Her mother was an opera singer and her father was a colonel in the Mexican Army. She attended a convent school in San Antonio, where she learned to speak English. Lupe was nineteen when Douglas Fairbanks, Sr., spotted her in the courtyard of Hollywood's Egyptian Theater in 1927 during a sightseeing tour. She was given the small role of a beautiful mountain girl in *The Gaucho*. Her accent, however, was a drawback during the transition to sound. Following an insignificant part in *Lady of the Pavements,* Lupe was advised by Fairbanks to be patient until the pandemonium of talkies subsided.

Lupe Velez was a shy young girl but appeared on the screen as an exciting vixen who would become known as the Mexican Spitfire.

It was director Victor Fleming who suggested her for the part of the fiery Mexican girl kidnapped by a wandering trapper in *Wolf Song.* After a spat with Clara Bow, Fleming was dating Lupe and looked forward to being with her on location in the high Sierras. Paramount thought Coop would be perfect as the roving swain in *Wolf Song,* and another important phase of his life began.

According to Lupe, when she saw Gary it was love at first sight. Fleming took advantage of the fireworks on film. He was even criticized by *The New York Times* for "prolonging a violent kiss until it became more absurd than passionate." Fleming capitalized on the torrid lovemaking between Lupe and Gary.

Crooner Russ Columbo, who sang a few Mexican love ballads in *Wolf Song,* had been dating Lupe also, but she barely took notice of him. From the moment she laid eyes on Cooper, he was it!

In the meantime, Evelyn Brent married her old beau, Harry Edwards, a director who produced slapstick films for Mack Sennett. Despite his busy love life, Gary was shocked and hurt. Evelyn had given him no indication she was serious about Edwards and he felt betrayed. Cooper expected women to be faithful, but where Miss Brent was concerned, it went deeper than egotism. She was his mama's favorite. Alice considered her son the greatest thing since Valentino and was sure Gary would change Evelyn's mind about marrying him. Instead, he followed Clara like a puppy dog. If his beloved mother was aghast over the "It Girl," the worst was yet to come.

When *Wolf Song* was finished, Cooper moved into Lupe's Beverly Hills mansion on Rodeo Drive. Alice was distraught. Charles was, too, but for a different reason. His wife made it very clear she would not leave her son alone and defenseless with "that Mexican thing."

Lupe told the press that Cooper had given her a ring and that she was shopping for a trousseau. Gary denied buying the ring. A few days later scratch marks were visible on Cooper's face. He confided to a friend, "I'm a little black and blue, too, but I let her have it."

"You hit her?"

"Well, no . . . kinda slapped her."

"So, it's all over between you two?"

"Nope."

"You're going back for more?"

". . . happens all the time," Cooper said, shrugging.

"You're not going to the studio looking like that, are you?"

"Sure. Makeup does the trick. I'm gettin' used to it."

Despite their bloody battles, Cooper might have married Lupe had his mother approved. He was almost thirty years old, but was a mama's boy. He was an unassuming guy who yearned for a beautiful young lady with breeding, but instead fell in love with a nymphomaniac and a hot-tempered Latin, each of whom he could control only in bed. With both feet on the ground, he was an easy target.

Unlike Clara, Lupe was faithful to Gary. After they fought and separated, she did not go out with other men. He knew that good bed partners were plentiful in Hollywood, but a faithful woman was hard to find. When Alice chided him about Lupe, he said, "At least she's true to me. That's more than I can say for the others."

Miss Velez confirmed that to the press. "I make loff when I am in loff!" she exclaimed, but Cooper soon found out he had to pay a high price for her loyalty.

Wolf Song was a huge box-office success because Lupe and Gary's off-screen romance was exploited by Paramount. Lupe and Gary agreed to a full-scale publicity campaign and appeared together at the openings in cities across the country. Aside from the passionate love scenes, there was a rumor that the studio had cut out a nude swimming scene that was too steamy. Actually, the scene was of Cooper and his trapper buddy bathing in a hot spring. But Paramount benefited from the mistake. Modestly, Cooper said, "The Depression hit pretty hard and people needed love and romance, I guess. They wanted to believe in happiness. Seeing us in love on the screen and then in love in person was proof that movies are not all make-believe."

Lupe Velez was only five feet tall and weighed a mere 109 pounds, but her figure, 37-26-35, was more voluptuous than that of most taller women. Reporter Adela Rogers St. Johns wrote, "Strange, how up to a given moment it seemed so funny—tiny, tempestuous Lupe Velez and six-foot-three, slow-moving Cooper; her firecracker Mexican accent and her sparkling laughter against the slow drawl and slower smile of the big cowboy; Lupe's public demonstrations and declarations of love and Gary's embarrassment and adoration. Hollywood history has never had another like Lupe . . . so kind, so merry, so warm-hearted. Hollywood to this minute has no more vivid memory than that of Lupe Velez at the Hollywood Legion fights. Visiting celebrities were always taken there not to see the bouts, but to see Lupe rooting, putting on a better show than the one in the ring."

Mrs. St. Johns remembers once seeing Lupe at home, kneeling beside a couch watching Cooper sleep. "Is he not beautiful?" she sighed. "I have never seen anyone so beautiful as my Garree."

When Gary opened his eyes and grinned, Lupe stood up in a rage. "You laugh at your Lupe now?" she snarled. He covered his face with his hands while she reached for a hunk of his hair. Mrs. St. Johns said, "I find Cooper the most attractive man, but snoring with his mouth open?"

There was speculation that Gary and Lupe were secretly married. Regardless of how Alice felt about the Mexican Spitfire, she had no choice but to put up with her company when Gary brought her home. Charles got a kick out of Lupe's wild sense of humor and zany attitude. She might pretend to be mad when he laughed at her antics, but when she sat on his lap he was putty in her hands.

"In Lupe," Gary remarked to a reporter, "I find a girl who takes the same joy out of primitive elemental things that I do."

Newspapers were filled with stories about the couple. They were photographed painting her swimming pool, at nightclubs, at premieres and dinner parties. Just when the press thought Lupe and Gary were about to get married, he'd return to his parents' home a bruised and confused man. He would stay there until Lupe cooled off.

A famous story about the couple concerned a pair of live golden eagles Gary received from a fan in Montana. Because there was no room for the birds at his parents' house, Gary presented them to Lupe.

"What do I do with them?" she asked.

"We'll train 'em."

"Not we. You!"

"Would ya mind keepin' them here?"

"Where here, Garree?"

"In the backyard."

"Sheet!"

Cooper eventually got his way. Reporters picked up the story and sardonically referred to the eagles as "lovebirds," a gift Gary gave to Lupe. "Ha!" she screamed a few years later. "Garree always ask Lupe for favors. He'd come to my house and say 'Hello' to birds first. Sometimes he played with them for too long and I have to drag him in the house. I told him, 'Garree, you clean and feed them!' So he did, and was at my house all the time. People tell his mother we're married and she hates me. I said, 'Garree, all your fault that your mama spits when she sees me. I tell her about those vultures and she say that they were my idea to get you.' Ha!"

"Of course I love him," she told the press one day. "Marry him? Well, who will know what I do until I do it, eh? Maybe tomorrow, maybe next month, maybe never. But I think maybe."

On another day, in another mood after another bloody argument, she cursed at reporters and exclaimed, "I don't love Gary Cooper! I don't love anybody! I will never marry. I stay Lupe. I am sick of love!"

Paramount was concerned about Gary's blatant love affairs. They did not want him to see Lupe on a steady basis. The public viewed him as a quiet and sensible guy. Clara Bow had proven otherwise, and his foolish fights with Lupe in public made Coop look like a frightened sissy. He told friend Richard Arlen no one was going to make him give up Lupe Velez—not Paramount and not his parents.

He was nuts about her. "You couldn't help being in love with Lupe Velez," Cooper admitted, "or as much in love as one could get with a creature as elusive as quicksilver. She flashes, storms, and sparkles, but she objects to being called 'wild,' which is a word that reporters seem to favor."

But wild she was. In February 1929, *The Los Angeles Times* reported, "Cooper was at the Santa Fe Railroad station in Pasadena to see Lupe Velez off on the train heading east. The scene was one that will not easily be forgotten. In that last frantic moment of good-bye, not being able to open the window to give Gary another farewell kiss, Lupe decided the thing to do was to break the car window. Only the restraining hand of those with her prevented this catastrophe."

Some of the crew members at Paramount recall Cooper's reaction to Lupe's frequent obscene phone calls to him on the set. Sometimes he blushed, they said, but more often he got an erection. "But he didn't blush when he got an erection," one crew member said.

Paramount should have costarred Cooper and Velez in a romantic follow-up to *Wolf Song,* but they chose to ignore the affair and unfavorable publicity. Instead they cast Esther Ralston opposite Gary in *Betrayal,* Gary's last silent film, which was a gloomy melodrama of illicit romance and death. Afterward, Cooper took a brief vacation with Lupe, knowing he would return to make his first all-talkie.

Whatever he imagined might be his fate, Gary was stunned to learn that his leading lady in *Darkened Rooms* would be Evelyn Brent.

"They're doin' this to me deliberately," he told Alice. "But if I refuse they'll put me on suspension."

"Get it over with, son. Besides, Evelyn has a lovely voice and is a fine actress."

"I can't work with her now, Mother. We barely talk."

"Maybe you're still in love with each other."

"Nope."

"Evelyn is a very sophisticated lady. I think once you begin, it will seem like old times."

"She's a married woman and I'm in love with Lupe."

"I thought you were supposed to leave your personal feelings at home," Alice said with a smile.

"You don't seem to understand, Mother. Most of the letters I get are from folks who want me to do a Western. The studio promised. I'm scared to death facin' my first talkie. Why with Evelyn? I feel like quittin'."

He reluctantly reported for work. Production was stalled briefly, but Gary had to remain on the set. Evelyn kept her distance; Gary snoozed. After a few days he was called to the front office. Richard Dix had broken his contract and was leaving Paramount. Rather than cancel Dix's next movie, *The Virginian,* Victor Fleming suggested Cooper take the part. Paramount had no choice.

Evelyn Brent got a new leading man in *Darkened Rooms,* and Gary, delighted with the turn of events, took his favorite director out for a drink.

"What happened, Vic?"

"Dix wanted more money. RKO Pictures gave it to him. I was told there was no one else at Paramount who could take his place in *The Virginian,* but I didn't want to shelve the film and said so."

The Virginian was Cooper's first all-talking picture and the third film version of the Owen Wister classic. Randolph Scott, a native of Virginia, was hired by Paramount to coach Cooper in the proper accent. The lovely Mary Brian was cast as the schoolteacher from Vermont, Richard Arlen as the Virginian's erratic pal, and Walter Huston as Trampas, the villain.

During the scene of a poker game in the Medicine Bow Saloon, Trampas grumbles, "Your bet, you son of a . . . !" Gary, as the Virginian, responds with the line that made him famous: "If you want to call me that, smile!"

Cooper got top billing on movie marquees. But the critics had more to say about the quality of the sound than about the star's performance.

Richard Arlen said this about the actual production: "We filmed near Sonora in the High Sierras. The sound equipment had to be hauled on trucks and the microphone close to the actors but out of camera range. We had to contend with the wind and outdoor noises. Coop got flustered occasionally but managed very well except in the scene that I get hung. Trying to react as his best friend gets a rope around his neck and remembering lines wasn't easy for him. He kept flubbing dialogue. I came up with the idea of jotting his lines on my chaps because my back was to the camera. It worked. There was some concern, too, that Walter Huston might steal the picture, but, as usual, Coop underplayed. He never tried to shout, snarl, or rush. He didn't have to."

If Cooper's steamy personal life contributed to his box-office fame, he had yet to hit his stride. While Lupe was out of town, he spent time in Clara's scarlet-draped bedroom with the benign Buddha smiling down. For a change Clara kept her perky little lips sealed. She was not a likely candidate for talkies, although her voice came across surprisingly well except for her slightly nasal tones, which were technically remedied. The problem her directors had was keeping her in one place on the set to accommodate the microphone. Clara's abundant energy was perfect for silents, but standing still made her nervous. Before long she made the transition nicely, however.

Paramount executives were more concerned with her antics off the screen. When she made headlines about unpaid gambling debts in Nevada, she exclaimed, "I was cheated!" And then there were rumors about her taking drugs and drinking too much. She laughed it off. But Clara got involved with a married Texas physician, Dr. William Earl Pearson, who had performed an emergency appendectomy on her during *Dangerous Curves*. She gave him a $4,000 watch, but when he went back to his wife Clara found herself involved in an alienation-of-affections suit. She settled out of court.

Whatever her indulgences, sex was still her favorite pastime and Cooper the only man who thoroughly satisfied her. Clara was game for anything—anything but Gary's supposed relationship with a homosexual, Anderson Lawler. That broke her cool. "The whole thing makes me sick," she told friends. "One has to draw the line somewhere."

Cooper met Anderson Lawler in 1929. At that time, the twenty-five-year-old fair-haired tobacco heir from Virginia wanted to be a stage actor, but didn't refuse Paramount when they offered him his first film, *River of Romance,* with Buddy Rogers. Cooper's friends hesitated or refused to discuss Lawler, but the two men probably met at the studio. Several technicians on the set of *Betrayal* remember Lawler sitting with Gary.

Buddy Rogers and Richard Arlen were friendly with Lawler, who was a fine athlete and sportsman. Alice Cooper was very fond of Anderson, who was charming, witty, and bright. He shared Gary's love for hunting and was interested in the arts. The Coopers accepted him as a son. When they went back to Montana for a few weeks, Lawler stayed in their house on Franklin Avenue while Gary lived with Lupe. Cooper referred to Anderson as "Nin" and Lawler called Gary "Jamey." These affectionate nicknames, and Lawler's living with Cooper caused speculation that they were involved in more than a brotherly friendship.

Lupe liked Lawler. She thought he had a delicious sense of humor and made a good referee in her spats with Gary. Hollywood insiders didn't know quite what to think when Anderson squired a woman on a double date with Gary and Lupe.

The few people who remember Lawler today claim that he was definitely homosexual and that he was very close to Cooper, who, so they say, was a "congenial fellow." Nin's wealth and social standing placed him among an elite clan who considered movie celebrities beneath them. Gary was a humble guy, but he relished the luxury and life-style of those born to wealth. He was anxious to mingle with the *Social Register* crowd. Only Lawler could open those golden gates.

One actor who requested anonymity said, "I don't think anyone knows the truth, but Gary wasn't above using people. I heard from reliable sources that a few gays who were prominent in films knew more about Cooper than they should. Nobody was blunt about it. In fact they were very discreet, but one doesn't have to be a genius to figure out what they were saying. Lawler introduced Gary to the right people, but they weren't seen at parties together unless dates were along. They went hunting together and spent weekends on Catalina Island with Dick Arlen's group of pals who liked to party with bootleg booze away from prying eyes at Paramount. It was no secret, and I know someone took pictures of them swimming in the nude and sold the photographs 'under the table' around Hollywood. Cooper wasn't queer, but he might have strayed on occasion. Very few didn't, because orgies were common in Hollywood. I do know for sure that Paramount was upset about Gary's living with Andy, but they were more liberal than Metro, who would have fired them both. Andy made only three or four films and then dropped out, but he and Coop remained close friends."

It's surprising that Lupe did not suspect anything at the time. She indicated some of her royal battles with Gary were over Lawler, but it wasn't until she and Cooper had parted that she acknowledged Andy's "loff for Garree." In the meantime, she and Lawler shared.

In Gary's next picture, *Only the Brave,* he played a Union cavalry captain who spies on the Confederacy. Mary Brian, who costarred in *The Virginian,* was his leading lady. But the big extravaganza was *Paramount on Parade,* a film to celebrate the birth of sound, starring the studio's leading players. Clara Bow sang "I'm True to the Navy Now," and Evelyn Brent and Maurice Chevalier performed an Apache dance. Gary Cooper, Richard Arlen, and James Hall sang "Let Us Drink to the Girl of My Dreams," while Fay Wray, Mary Brian, and Jean Arthur danced. In the movie Paramount showcased their top stars singing and dancing, but it was a bore compared to M-G-M's *The Hollywood Revue of 1929*. That film premiered the song "Singin' in the Rain" and featured John Gilbert and Norma Shearer as Romeo and Juliet, Joan Crawford singing and dancing, as well as Marion Davies and Buster Keaton.

Cooper was more interested in *The Texan* with Fay Wray. As Quico, the Llano Kid, he gives up his life as a bandit for the love of a beautiful Spanish girl. *Screenland* wrote, "*The Texan* will please the Cooper addicts, win new friends for Fay, and pass a pleasant, if not too exciting evening. Gary steps and speaks out, spouting Spanish most acceptably and cutting a dashing figure as a bold hombre. This big boy is becoming a real actor."

Seven Days Leave, released in 1930, was of little importance. Gary resented "giving the picture away" to fifty-year-old British actress, Beryl Mercer, who plays the ghost of his dead mother. Cooper wore a kilt in the film and has a few fistfights before getting killed. "About all an actor can do sometimes," he said, "is hold his own and hope for a better role." It was much the same story with the next two pictures.

The Man from Wyoming sounded like a Western, but it was the story of a World War I soldier who was mistakenly presumed dead. Gary's girlfriend in the picture was stunning June Collyer, who shed many tears over the loss of her sweetheart. *Screenland*'s critic wasn't touched, but added, "If you like Gary rehashing the war and June's dimples, you may be pleased."

An Alaskan saga, *The Spoilers,* with Kay Johnson and Betty Compson, was praised for its fast action and pace. Critics applauded the fistfights. *Motion Picture News* thought Cooper did his finest work in the 1930 film. Then finally, after six mediocre movies released in quick succession, Paramount presented Cooper with a plum—*Morocco.*

And a new flame—Marlene Dietrich.

Back again in the Foreign Legion, Gary this time fought his own war with Germany on the set. He tolerated the German story and Fräulein Dietrich, but he could not tolerate her mentor and the film's director, Josef von Sternberg. The two men disliked each other intensely. Gary objected to von Sternberg's attitude. Dietrich's phenomenal success in *The Blue Angel,* which was produced in Europe and distributed by Paramount in the United States, was von Sternberg's work. He now expected and demanded the same success of *Morocco* and insisted on directing his masterpiece in German. Cooper watched as von Sternberg gave Marlene every camera advantage, as the spotlights focused on her while von Sternberg coached her alone, ignoring the other cast members. When it was Cooper's turn in a scene von Sternberg spoke German or broken English, concentrating on the beautiful Marlene as if Gary did not exist.

Finally, the cowboy from Montana went into a violent rage. During the café scene in which he sat at a table listening to Dietrich sing, Cooper stood up and walked toward von Sternberg, who tried to wave him off. Cooper stepped up to the director (who was about a foot shorter) and put his hands around von Sternberg's neck, hoisted him up in the air, and said, "You goddamned Kraut, if you expect to work again in this country you'd better learn the language we use here!" He released the gasping von Sternberg and returned to his seat in the scene. Dietrich was amused and watched her director storm off the set. He returned a few days later speaking fairly good English.

Cooper and Dietrich had an affair, though one has to wonder how they had the energy and time, because he was making films in rapid succession. Lupe was working, too, but wasn't too busy to hear the rumors about "my Garree" and his romance with the German actress.

Married in 1924 and never divorced, Miss Dietrich would have many affairs—John Wayne, John Gilbert, Eddie Fisher, and Frank Sinatra among them. Fiercely dedicated to her career, she had no intention of putting anything or anyone above it with the exception of her daughter, Maria. Cooper revealed very little about Dietrich other than he thought she was one of the most fascinating and irresistible women he had ever met.

Lupe suspected that something was going on, but had no proof. She teased Gary by doing a wonderful impersonation of Marlene at parties. He cringed when she got so much knowing applause and laughter, and she took pleasure in doing it over and over again.

Dietrich and von Sternberg received Oscar nominations for *Morocco* but neither won an award. Cooper didn't think much of his own work in the movie. At the time, however, the critics didn't agree with him. *The New York Herald Tribune* declared, "The understandably popular Gary Cooper, who underacts more completely than any other player within memory, never has been as effective and certainly never as expert an actor as he is in the role of the hero." *The New York Evening Post* said that Gary Cooper gave one of his best performances in the picture, ". . . a restrained and telling piece of work." *Picture Play* raved, "The success of Miss Dietrich is vastly aided by Gary Cooper, as the American, perhaps his best performance so far."

Morocco became a classic.

When the Coopers returned from Montana, Alice found it impossible to put on a good face for Lupe any longer. Each was more snappish than the other. Gary was forced to sit through their tiffs and afterward listen while each would corner him into listening to how horrid the other was. The gossipmongers were soon theorizing that Cooper, abused and nagged by too many women, had finally switched to men—"Nin" in particular. Gary talked about finding a place of his own to get some peace and privacy.

To this day, fifty years later, rumors still persist about the nature of Cooper's friendship with Lawler. He was not the only macho male star who would be labeled as a bisexual or homosexual. Cary Grant and Randolph Scott lived together in the early thirties. After a brief marriage to Virginia Cherrill, Grant went back to Randy, who had taken a wife, Cary moving in next door to the newlyweds. A year later Scott divorced and returned to Grant.

When Clark Gable used his influence to get director George Cukor fired from *Gone With the Wind,* insiders knew the real reason had nothing to do with George's private coaching of Vivien Leigh. Cukor, like Cole Porter and Noel Coward, was a discreet gay, and Gable was sure the director knew about his 1925 "friendship" with handsome leading man William Haines, when Clark was a starving extra in *Pacemaker.* (Haines was eventually fired by M-G-M because he was a homosexual, and later made a fortune as an interior decorator to the stars in Hollywood.)

When Cukor called Clark "dear" on the set, Gable stormed to the front office and had George replaced with Victor Fleming. According to Joan Crawford, the Gable-Haines incident was ". . . just one of those things and unimportant because the King of Hollywood (Gable) adored women. I should know. We had an affair for over thirty years."

Shortly before his death in 1983 Cukor finally confirmed the real reason for being replaced in *Gone With the Wind.* Ironically, he lived with Anderson

Lawler briefly in 1931 and tried to save the actor's fading career by casting him in *Girls About Town* at Paramount. But "Nin" was ignored.

The Grant-Scott relationship, which spanned five years, and the Cooper-Lawler friendship that spanned three years are as intriguing today as they were in the Golden Era. We know now that gay men married lesbians to protect their careers and that the studios arranged marriages for gay actors to save their images. Rock Hudson said it all in an interview with Boze Hadleigh. Boze asked, "How many top actors in Hollywood do you think are gay, Rock?"

"Whew! Too many for us to name," came the reply. "If you mean gay, or 'bisexual,' whatever that means, then maybe most. I guess if one came out, the crowding from the closet would be so strong, several would be *pushed* out. Trust me, Boze, America does not want to know."

In 1930, Cooper rented Greta Garbo's old house at 1919 Argyle Avenue and Lawler helped him to get settled. Lupe was deeply hurt that Gary did not move in with her and they fought bitterly. Reporters said the affair was over, but Hedda Hopper claimed that only Gary knew the truth and he wasn't talking. He didn't have to. Within the week he was seen going into Lupe's house. They attended parties together but Cooper didn't introduce her to the elite set he now socialized with in Hollywood. She sometimes went to Pickfair, Douglas Fairbanks' and Mary Pickford's palatial home, but that was because Fairbanks had discovered Lupe, not because she was an accustomed member of sophisticated society.

During the twenties, Cooper became a regular at Pickfair, the Buckingham Palace of Hollywood, where dinner occasionally consisted of eight or ten courses. Guests were expected to have perfect manners. There one had to be socially sophisticated, but Cooper learned quickly. Besides, he was pleasant to have around. If he didn't talk, he couldn't say the wrong thing or accidentally insult anyone. And remembering names was no problem. A good firm Montana handshake and a shrug were sufficient—and mysterious. Guests found him refreshing.

Mary Pickford adored Gary and wanted him to costar with her, but by 1933 America's Sweetheart had faded from films. Cooper was fortunate to have met the Fairbankses before their divorce, because at Pickfair they entertained dignitaries and European royalty, among them the Count and Countess di Frasso. They invited Gary to "drop by" their sumptuous villa outside Rome anytime he was traveling through Italy. Gary would soon accept their gracious invitation.

Paramount wanted to team Dietrich and Cooper in *Dishonored,* but Gary refused to work with Josef von Sternberg again. He got his way, but paid for it by filming two pictures at the same time—*Fighting Caravans* with Lili Damita (who would become Mrs. Errol Flynn in 1935) and *City Streets,* with his beloved Clara Bow.

Zane Grey's *Fighting Caravans* was a popular Western. *Motion Picture Herald* said, "The role of the hero, a young scout, is designed to fit Gary Cooper perfectly. No great demands are made upon him but he gives an interesting characterization, something more than the stereotyped western hero. And he looks and acts like a frontiersman rather than a Hollywood actor trying to resemble a cowman."

Paramount expected *City Streets* to be a blockbuster. Cooper said he was looking forward to working with Clara again, who at the time was involved in a court suit against her secretary, Daisy DeVoe, for stealing $35,000 worth of clothing, furs, and jewelry.

Daisy was a former studio hairdresser whom Clara had befriended. She shared Clara's bungalow and her bank account as well. When Miss Bow confronted her, Daisy didn't deny anything but threatened to expose Clara's love letters and her erotic activities if Clara didn't keep mum. Bow pressed charges and before Paramount could intercede Daisy told all. Clara's boyfriends were exposed—a list so long it was impossible to remember all the names. Daisy identified Cooper as "Studs" and even described the night Clara took on the entire UCLA football team.

"I was more than a secretary to her," Daisy told the court in January 1931. "I was almost a sister to her. I did everything for her. I hennaed her hair, fitted her clothing, paid her bills, bought her liquor, and everything."

"If she wanted to buy whiskey"—Clara fought back—"she bought it and I knew nothing about it. That's why I'm so sore. I trusted her. I never looked at the books."

"It was her own fault," Daisy insisted. "If she had paid attention to business, I never would have taken a dime from her. She put me in a position to take anything I wanted. I was going to tell Clara about it later on. It's hard to see a girl like Clara with everything and no respect for anything."

The jury found Daisy guilty. Bow asked for leniency and DeVoe received only an eighteen-month sentence. But Clara's reputation was ruined. Earlier, she had managed to get through the scandal of being a codefendant in a divorce of a wealthy Texas doctor by paying the wife $30,000 hush money. Paramount helped her hide the truth about her gambling debts, abortions, booze, pill and dope taking. But how could Clara's fans accept a football team standing in line outside her bedroom? How could they forget Gilbert Roland, Richard Arlen, John Gilbert, Eddie Cantor, Charles Farrell, Frederic March, Maxi Rosenbloom, Buddy Rogers, Bela Lugosi, Gary Cooper, and Rex Bell—and the male prostitutes hired in between?

An old lady leaving the courtroom apparently thought Daisy had lied about the men in Clara's life, but she hissed, "While people are starving in this country, it makes me sick to think Miss Bow overlooked $35,000 when a loaf of bread is sacred!"

* * *

Cooper's affair with Clara had been no great secret, but being one of so many men was not exactly a tribute. Lupe Velez blazed with fury. She resented hearing the details of Gary's love for Clara and she began to see Anderson Lawler in a different light. Why, he was "in loff with Garree," too, she wailed. Anyone could see that.

Cooper's typical silence was again a blessing. He muddled through the scandal with the same expressionless face and lazy eyes, but beneath his calm exterior he was ashamed. Seeing his Clara publicly humiliated and her reputation tarnished hurt him deeply. Clara had been his first love and she was truly a generous, if misguided, girl with talent, beauty, and zest. Most important, Clara was not a phony. In bed she was a little girl with a natural quality that contrasted with her vibrant sexuality. She and Cooper had never formally parted and the truth was they had never fallen out of love.

Paramount was willing to take Clara back, but women's clubs and religious groups picketed the theaters where her movies were playing. Still, the studio thought the scandal would simmer down. Gary was told she would be his leading lady in *City Streets* as planned. Clara, on the verge of a nervous breakdown, did not report for work. Her lover, Rex Bell, took her to his Nevada ranch. They were married in Reno and spent their honeymoon in Europe. "Perhaps I should have paid Daisy and saved myself many heartaches," Clara told reporters. "I took it on the chin and my health suffered. But I'm only twenty-five and will make a comeback." She never did.

The "It Girl" suffered a series of breakdowns and was in and out of sanatoriums. Rex stuck by her through it all. They had two sons and opened the "It" Café on the corner of Hollywood and Vine. Clara, whose weight blew up to over two hundred pounds at one point, stayed home to care for the children. In 1954, Rex was elected lieutenant governor of California. While running for governor in 1962 he died suddenly of a heart attack. Just before her death in 1965, Clara told a friend, "It wasn't ever like I thought it was going to be. It was always a disappointment to me."

In her will she chose her former lovers as pallbearers: Maxie Rosenbloom, Richard Arlen, Jack Oakie, Harry Richmond, Buddy Rogers, and Victor Fleming.

After the Clara Bow scandal Alice and Charles refused to talk to their son. Lupe was still insisting Gary had given her an engagement ring. Lawler hung around to lift everyone's spirits.

Clara's replacement in *City Streets* was newcomer Sylvia Sidney. The gangster melodrama was difficult for Gary. He was exhausted from overworking, concerned that his career was in jeopardy because of Daisy's testimony, and depressed over Lupe's public accusation that Alice refused to allow her little boy to get married. Cooper lost twenty pounds, and the strain began to show on his long face. His doctor diagnosed it as hepatitis and suggested a vacation. But Paramount wouldn't let him go until *I Take This Woman,* his next film, was finished. "Somehow I got through it," he said, "and I have Carole (Lombard) to thank. She was perfect as the rich brat who married a cowhand. As sick as I was, she made me laugh and took good care of me, too."

Carole Lombard, then Mrs. William Powell, stood by Cooper as he got weaker and thinner every day. He confided to her, "I'm worried about *City Streets.* After what they did to Clara, I might be next."

"If those stupid saps out there want to ban her boyfriends," Carole said with a laugh, "they're gonna have to picket every theater in the United States!"

"Think so?"

"You're doin' a pretty good job of trying to kill yourself. How many speeding tickets have you gotten recently? Be honest."

"Three . . . four . . . I don't know."

"Don't you read the papers?"

Cooper turned white.

"By now you should know if you want to find out what you did yesterday, pick up the newspaper," she teased.

"I'm gonna get as far away from this town as possible," he moaned. "Carole, I gotta get outta here . . ."

He wanted to go to Europe, with no fanfare. Tired, ill, and confused, Cooper asked Paramount to make all travel arrangements so that he would not be bothered with rail and shipboard accommodations. Above all, he demanded complete secrecy as to when he was leaving Hollywood. It was common practice for reporters and fans to watch the Twentieth Century Limited's comings and goings, so it was not easy for a popular actor like Cooper to depart without being hounded for interviews or autographs. The studio was more than willing to assist him under the circumstances. Aside from his needing plenty of rest, the publicity people at Paramount did not want the public to know Gary was ailing. The press was famous for building up a head cold into pneumonia.

He arrived at the railroad station with a few close friends. If Cooper was recognized, no one approached him. As planned, he and his party did not intend to linger. They came along to make sure he wasn't bothered and merely to say a quick bon voyage!

Despite the carefully planned cloak-and-dagger departure, Cooper was being watched by someone who wanted to know why he was leaving, where he was going, and why she wasn't with him. How she managed to find out Gary was sneaking out of Hollywood isn't known. How she discovered that he was catching that particular train is also a mystery, but it had to have been at the last minute; otherwise she would have confronted him beforehand.

Raving mad, she grabbed her gun from the night table in the bedroom, put it in her pocketbook, and raced to the station just in time. Cooper, who towered over everyone, was not hard to find. He was standing by the train chatting with friends. She cleverly maneuvered through the crowd standing on the platform, took out the gun, and shouted, "Garree, you son of a bitch!" Then she pulled the trigger. He leaped on board the train and closed the door behind him. She cursed to herself, turned around, and disappeared.

But Lupe Velez almost got him!

4

THE COWBOY AND THE COUNTESS

Paramount executive Walter Wanger sent a letter to Gary in Venice reminding him to visit the Count and Countess di Frasso. Chances are Cooper had every intention of visiting Villa Madama, the di Frasso's magnificent estate with its priceless murals, marbled walls and staircases, electric elevators, and precious paintings.

En route to Italy he made a brief stop in Algiers, where he was recognized by several Arab children. They pointed their fingers and said laughing, "Boom! Boom!" Gary found it hard to believe that these so-foreign youngsters tried to imitate him. "I kinda felt good about it," he recalled.

In Venice, however, he was just another guy sunning himself on the Adriatic beaches. When Gary wasn't sleeping he was girl watching. The highlight of his trip was riding in a gondola. "This was somethin' I wanted to do all my life," he said. Cooper claims he hitched a ride to Rome but did not do any sightseeing. Instead, out of courtesy, he telephoned Walter Wanger's friend.

Gary wasn't prepared to meet "royalty." His wardrobe was limited and wrinkled. But Wanger said his lady friend was a "good egg." She would understand.

The Countess di Frasso was born to wealth and she married nobility. Born Dorothy Taylor in Watertown, New York, in 1888, her grandfather had been a New York governor. Her father was a leather-goods manufacturer and Wall Street tycoon who amassed a fortune of $50 million. In 1912 Dorothy married Claude Graham White, the British aviator best remembered for having landed his plane on the White House lawn during their courtship. They were divorced in 1916, shortly after Dorothy came into an inheritance estimated between $10 and $15 million. Her brother, Bertrand L. Taylor, Jr., a member of the Board of Governors of the New York Stock Exchange, inherited the remainder of the estate.

In 1923, when she was in her midtwenties, Dorothy married the impoverished but distinguished nobleman Count Carlo di Frasso, thirty years her senior. Dorothy spent over $1 million restoring the count's sixteenth-century Villa Madama, transforming it into a favorite gathering place for Europe's elite. She was renowned for giving elaborate dinners for two hundred guests or more. Her two dearest friends were Elsa Maxwell, the international hostess and columnist, and Mary Pickford.

The di Frassos were a devoted couple and were discreet about their extramarital affairs. When asked to describe paradise, Dorothy said, "The English writer Max Beerbohm said that Paradise to him was a four-poster bed in a field of poppy and mandragora. I say it depends who's between the sheets." Author Ben Hecht and gangster Bugsy Siegel were among her many lovers.

When Cooper called the villa, he was told the count and countess were on vacation and would be returning soon. "But," the servant said, "you're expected and we were instructed to make you comfortable in the meantime."

Elsa Maxwell and Dorothy di Frasso found Gary Cooper waiting for them in the reception hall. His clothes were rumpled and hung like a burlap bag. But the countess was entralled with the young movie star. There in the opulence of the palace stood a timid, half-smiling, pathetically thin Adonis. Dorothy promptly fell in love and set out to turn him into her well-dressed and debonair escort. She took him to an expensive tailor in Rome, where he was fitted for a new wardrobe; Dorothy footed the bill. He had his pick of sports cars and limousines, which were often seen parked in front of exclusive jewelry stores while the countess chose the proper gold cuff links, watches, and tie tacks.

"Dorothy taught him social protocol," Miss Maxwell said. "He became a wine connoisseur and learned enough French and Italian to get by. Gary fell in love with her, though he wasn't as comfortable about the situation as the count, who thought nothing of it.

The countess was rich, but she was also vivacious and beautiful. Her black hair, blue eyes, and voluptuous figure were the envy of debutantes twenty years younger, and the objects of desire of men.

Cooper was an outstanding lover who far exceeded Dorothy's expectations. When Paramount sent telegrams regarding his return to Hollywood, Dorothy was frantic. "What can I do to keep him here?" she asked Elsa.

"Well, he loves horses, guns, hunting . . ."

"That's it!" the countess cheered. "I'll arrange for him to ride with the Italian cavalry."

Elsa paled. "I don't know if Gary can jump."

"He rode in the steeplechase in England. He told me about the fox hunts."

Cooper had no choice but to accept. "It was a challenge," he said. "The cavalry officer was testing me and I knew it. Instead of wooden bars on the hurdles, the Italians used solid stone walls. It was grueling and only a few of us made it through."

Although newspapers published tidbits about Gary Cooper's new wardrobe and the elegant dinner parties at Villa Madama and his suspected romance with a countess, reporters splashed the cavalry episode on the front pages. Paramount sent a telegram, instructing him to return at once. If he was strong enough to jump hurdles, they reasoned, he was capable of making movies. When Cooper did not answer the studio took him off salary.

"Who cares?" Dorothy said with a laugh.

"I kinda wanted to work with George Cukor," Gary stammered. "He's one of the best directors in Hollywood and is doing a comedy called *Girls About Town* with Kay Francis."

"Aren't you a cowboy?" she asked innocently.

"Yep . . . and nope. Too late, though. Cukor got Nin."

"Nin?"

"Anderson Lawler, a good actor and friend of mine."

"If you've been replaced, why do you worry?"

"They're givin' me another chance in *His Woman* with Claudette Colbert, and I think I'd better do it."

The countess thought he was innocent and adorable. "You don't have to work," she said, smiling. "Stay in Italy. I will give Carlo a fair settlement and then you and I can get—"

"Married?" he gulped.

"What else, Gary?"

"I gotta go back."

"But you don't need the money."

"I haven't made it big yet."

"You're *famous!*" she gestured with outstretched arms.

"It's somethin' I have to do. I have to go all the way to the top before I quit."

Dorothy realized her pleas were of no use. Elsa tried to cheer her up. "Why not give him a royal send-off—one he'll never forget?"

The countess casually invited the usual crowd: His Royal Highness Prince Umberto, Crown Prince of Italy, the Earl and Countess of Portarlington, Prince Charles of Greece, the Duke of York (later King George VI), Woolworth heiress Barbara Hutton, and her Prince Girolamo Rospigliosi. A hundred other guests came in attendance.

Marjorie Merriweather Post, Barbara Hutton's aunt, asked Dorothy to introduce her niece to Prince Rospigliosi. The prince was so taken with Barbara that he proposed marriage a minute later, but she wasn't interested. Barbara had her eye on Cooper; he made the prince look dreadfully dull. "I was very impressed by Gary Cooper," Miss Hutton said. "He was handsome, calm, laconic . . . in many respects the quintessential American."

In July 1931, the press incorrectly announced that Countess di Frasso was divorcing her husband and marrying Gary Cooper. Paramount frantically telegraphed him again. When he told Dorothy the time had come for him to leave Italy, she didn't try to stop him. The countess had her pride, too. After a tearful farewell she went into seclusion. But she had not yet given up the fight.

* * *

Cooper arrived in New York that August by ship. All he told the press was "The countess is a very dear friend. So is the count." He was relieved to find out that *His Woman* would be filmed at Paramount's Long Island City studio. It was a dull picture, but the public clamored for Cooper and his face appeared once again on the silver screen after a six-month absence.

While in New York he was seen dining with Anderson Lawler and Tallulah Bankhead, but Gary really preferred café society. Lupe Velez was in New York then, too, although it's not clear that they saw each other. The reporters who hounded him were shocked when Gary confessed, "I proposed to Lupe and she turned me down."

When Lupe arrived back in Hollywood the press insisted that she confirm Cooper's statement. The Mexican Spitfire obliged: "I don't love Gary Cooper," she said. "I turned Cooper down because his parents didn't want me to marry him, and because the studio thought it would injure his career. Now it's over. I'm glad. I feel so free. I know men too well; they are all the same, no? They fall in love with Lupe, very much, with the way Lupe is. Then quick they want I should be somebody else . . . the doormat . . . they wish to conquer the fiery one, to tame Lupe. I die first." Several days later she volunteered, "I'm not good enough for him, but I did make him happy. His mother! I hope she never cries the tears that I have cried. I hope she never knows the suffering I have known. I didn't hate her, but she told Gary I was seeing other men . . . that I wasn't faithful to him."

Alice joined her son in New York for a brief visit and granted an interview to reporters. "I have no ill-feeling toward Lupe Velez," she said. "I wish her continued success. I think she is a fine little actress. I wish her happiness. My only regret is that she finds it necessary to talk so openly and so violently for publication. Her love for Gary, I should think, would make her want to keep it a secret thing rather than to allow it to become public property.

"It shocks me, of course, to read in headlines that I have invaded Lupe's home to get personal knicknacks belonging to Gary. I have not been in her house since before the break. She demands of Gary that I be kept from bothering her. I haven't seen Lupe for months.

"And those preposterous stories that I threatened to kill myself if Gary married her! And that she was unfaithful to him and wasn't good enough for him—I have never set down any dictates about the kind of girl my son should marry. It will not be the duty of his father or myself to select his wife for him.

"Perhaps I have not entirely approved of any of the women with whom Gary has been romantically associated, but does any mother entirely approve of her son's choice? Very seldom."

Lupe scorned Mrs. Cooper's replies and tried to bow out gracefully. Gary had gallantly and openly declared his marriage proposal had been turned down. That would have ended it in Lupe's favor, but apparently Alice wanted the last word. As a concerned mother she might have kept her eye on Tallulah

Bankhead, who was then making a play for Gary. One New York columnist wrote that Tallulah had confirmed being engaged to Cooper; he had merely spent the night at her place.

Meanwhile, at the Villa Madama, the Countess di Frasso was lovesick and frustrated. Not one to believe in petty gossip, all she wanted was to have Gary back. The only way she knew to accomplish that was by inviting Gary along on the greatest challenge any outdoorsman could experience—an African safari.

Dorothy got in touch with Jerome Preston, a wealthy horse breeder who lived in Kenya and who just happened to be staying with his wife at the Plaza Hotel in New York. Over dinner they invited Cooper to join their hunting expedition to Tanganyika. Barbara Hutton's playboy cousin, Jimmy Donahue, was going along, too, they said. There was no mention of the countess. Cooper thanked them but declined. "I have to get back to Hollywood 'cause they're holdin' up a picture for me."

At the last minute, however, he changed his mind. Paramount was furious and immediately took him off salary again. He told a friend, "I'm usin' what money I have left to go on safari." All of Hollywood knew the countess was his sponsor. A well-known studio mogul said, "I've always wanted to go to Europe on the Countess di Frasso." Some accounts have her surprising him by arriving a few days after the others, minus the count. After all, Dorothy had had to shop first for a stunning safari wardrobe in Rome and Milan. Everyone pretended the setup wasn't planned.

On safari Cooper bagged eighty animals. One of his greatest experiences was shooting his first lion. The walls of his small Hollywood home would soon be covered with heads and skins. At night he shared a tent with Dorothy until the party returned to the Preston ranch in Kenya. Cooper might have abandoned Hollywood, but he was regaining his health and putting on weight.

The countess loved Gary with all her heart, but regardless of where he was or with whom, beggar or king, Cooper was Cooper—all of Cooper's women expressed frustration with his implacable cool. Dorothy di Frasso was no exception. She loved to tease him at parties with stories about their African safari. One of them was particularly funny. "The sun was setting. Gary was sitting by himself with an elbow on his knee . . . looking down at the ground. It was one of the most beautiful pictures I had ever seen. 'Oh, darling,' I said, 'what are you thinking?' He looked at me for a minute and said, 'I've been wonderin' whether I should change my brand of shoe polish.' "

The countess and the movie star returned to Rome in February 1932, with Gary carrying Tolucca, his new pet chimpanzee, off the boat with him. Gary Cooper's return was pictured in the newspapers, but all he said was that he would rest at Villa Madama with the count and countess before heading home.

Dorothy had reconciled herself to Gary's career in the movies, and she revised her tactics accordingly. "Before you go back," she said, "why don't we go on a Mediterranean cruise?" Cooper liked the idea, and so did the count. Reporters were astonished to find the three of them—husband, wife, and boyfriend—disembarking at Monte Carlo. Elsa Maxwell rose to their defense: "Europeans are open-minded. It seems to me the Americans could learn from them. After all, this is 1932, not the dark ages!"

Cooper was not worried about his career. His last film, *His Woman,* was faring well. If *The New York Times* called his performance merely competent, and the *Times* of London wrote that they thought Cooper was miscast, the amount of publicity he was receiving far outshone that of other film stars. If media attention was any indication of his popularity and worth, Cooper was a red-hot property. With the count by his side on the Mediterranean cruise, Gary allowed reporters to follow them at a safe distance. He later said he thought it was all rather amusing.

While gambling in Monte Carlo—compliments of the countess, of course—Gary received word that Jesse Lasky had been replaced at Paramount and there had been other major changes. Victor Fleming, fed up, had gone over to M-G-M, and several actors had been dropped, including Buddy Rogers. But Gary didn't bat an eye until he heard rumors that a newcomer was being groomed to take his place. "Cary Grant—who the hell is Cary Grant? That guy has my initials in reverse!" he told Dorothy.

"Coincidence," she assured him.

"Nope. I'm being punished for stayin' away so long."

Cooper was obviously concerned about where he stood at the studio and was anxious to find out more about Cary Grant. Gary decided to make tracks for the States, and Dorothy di Frasso made up her mind to return with him. She consulted with the count, who thought it would be a great idea to see Hollywood. The di Frassos accompanied Cooper as far as New York but no further. "I kinda want to slip into town and see what's goin' on without a lot of publicity," he told them. "If I travel by myself I know how to do it." Dorothy was upset, but didn't show it.

"We'll follow in a few days," she said.

"Can I borrow some money for fare?" he asked. "I'm plum broke."

The countess kissed him good-bye and immediately called Elsa Maxwell. "I want you to look after Gary," Dorothy said. "Pack your bags."

"Spy on him, you mean?" The columnist laughed.

"He's renting another house in Beverly Hills and I want you to offer to help him get settled. He has to mount those beasts he killed on safari and heaven knows what else has to be done."

"What on earth does he need two houses for?"

"You know Gary," the countess sighed. "He never talks much but I gather his friend, Anderson Lawler, is living in one with none other than that wench, Tallulah Bankhead."

Elsa Maxwell howled with laughter. "Don't worry, darling. I'll take good care of your Gary."

And care for him she did. Gary invited her to be his houseguest, and Elsa didn't move out until the countess arrived in Hollywood several weeks later.

Cooper managed to sneak around very quietly and very discreetly, however. His first visit was to Clara Bow.

"He was a different man," she said in an interview ten years later. "Gary wasn't as shy. He had changed. He usually wore open-neck shirts and Levis except on very formal occasions. I saw right away his whole manner of dressing was part of this new man. He told me all about Africa, but never mentioned the countess. He didn't have to. I'd read all about it in the newspapers. Actually, Gary came to see me because he needed $5,000. Could I loan it to him? He explained his predicament at Paramount, but he wasn't frightened. 'I'm prepared to fight,' he said. This was not the Gary I knew! In the meantime, he needed cash and I loaned him the $5,000. He was very sweet and wanted to know if I was happy with Rex (Bell). I told him Rex saved my life when the whole world turned against me. Gary looked very sad when I said that, but quite frankly I was not referring to him because he had called me faithfully. I understood his career had been at stake, too. We talked about *City Streets*. He was so disappointed that I was too ill to costar with him and he felt even worse that he wasn't able to help. Who knows? Maybe if I had been up to it, my career might have been saved, but I doubt it. I told Gary the truth about my shattered nerves. Another career setback might have put me in a padded cell. He kissed me and said he'd pay me back soon as he could. When Gary left I knew he was going to get what he wanted. That countess gave him confidence. I'm sure of it."

Cooper wasted no time in confronting his new bosses at Paramount. Without the aid of an agent or business manager he began negotiations for his new contract. He did not like the next film they proposed, a naval picture. "*The Devil and the Deep* isn't for me," he said forcefully. "I know you're tryin' to help Miss Bankhead make a name for herself in pictures, but can't you find someone else?"

Paramount offered Cooper a contract calling for two films a year and $4,000 a week. It would allow him to choose his own director and have script approval, provided that he did *The Devil and the Deep*. He agreed reluctantly. What bothered him most was Tallulah Bankhead's attitude. She was telling everyone in Hollywood, "I'm here for the money and to fuck that divine Gary Cooper." She was a determined woman who didn't care what people said about her, the type who might barge through the front door nude.

Not only did Elsa Maxwell try to keep an eye on Gary, she got rid of the fans who lingered on the sidewalk near his house. Elsa spoke graciously with reporters on his behalf while he was off making love to Lupe, who wanted to see him under any circumstances. Cooper told Richard Arlen, "This is a bad time for all of us. We gotta keep our noses clean. Lupe knows it. If we could go on like this . . . well, it might work out. I can't get her outta my system."

Maxwell thought she was doing a splendid job as chaperone. When she found out about Gary's contract victory at Paramount, she put her chubby arms around him. "You worried needlessly. The studios have lost their male stars to sound. Straight leading men are as scarce as hens' teeth."

"I shoulda turned down that submarine thing," he said, frowning.

"Nothing can hurt you now. Who else is in *The Devil and the Deep?*"

"Charles Laughton and that new guy, Cary Grant."

"And Talloo . . ."

"Yep."

"Dorothy's livid with jealousy. *Do* be discreet, Gary. Tallulah is another Clara. She has no secrets. That's why Mayer refused to offer her an M-G-M contract. He didn't want a bisexual on his star roster. God knows he has several under contract, but they don't flaunt their preference. Tallulah isn't particular. She had an affair with Lord Napier Arlington but was really in love with his mother! Did you meet Lady Arlington?"

"Nope."

"I'm telling you this for your own good," Elsa exclaimed. "Maybe she hasn't been on cocaine for seventeen years, but her bragging about it does nothing for her reputation. Dorothy's planning to have elegant dinner parties here in Hollywood. I'd be very disappointed in you, Gary, if there's any gossip about you and Tallulah."

Cooper smiled and shrugged.

"But then you and she have already . . ."

"Yep."

Elsa Maxwell threw her head back and laughed. "Why were you trying to get out of making a film with her?"

" 'Cause she doesn't give up."

"You don't run very fast."

The Devil and the Deep was Charles Laughton's first big picture, the one that made him a star. In the film Tallulah plays his faithless wife, who has an affair with a young lieutenant assigned to the same submarine that her husband commands.

Andy Lawler hung around the set every day and even appeared as a sailor in a few scenes just for the fun of it. Cooper was relieved to see Nin pampering and amusing Tallulah. If she and Gary were intimate during *The Devil and the Deep,* it was a guarded secret. Once at a party, Talloo called the Countess di Frasso "an old whore," got a glass of wine thrown in her face, and repeated the insult. The two women mixed in the same social circles for several months, barely speaking to each other. If Gary failed to show up at a party Tallulah told the other guests, "He's probably worn to a Frasso!"

Elsa Maxwell found a suitable house for the count and countess. It was within walking distance of Gary's home and he was not happy with the arrangement. He hired an interior decorator to fix up his place "bachelor style," with mounted animal heads covering the walls and skins scattered everywhere. Elsa was appalled; she called it a jungle. Then Dorothy di Frasso suggested another safari and Gary began packing. But this time she was unable to tear him away; it was only the idea that intrigued him. The count made things easy for his wife by going out of town on business, and soon Gary was spending more time at Dorothy's house than at his own. But he was, by now, searching for a tactful way to end the affair.

On the sly, Cooper dated Lupe Velez, who in turn was seeing M-G-M's Tarzan—Johnny Weismuller. Lupe, who hated the countess, would ask Gary in front of friends, "How's your grandmother, Garree?" If she had only kept her jealous mouth shut the romance might have continued. Hedda Hopper remarked, "There was still a spark between Lupe and Gary, but she was a bitter girl. We all thought they might elope eventually, regardless of the consequences."

Elsa Maxwell knew Cooper wasn't in love with the countess, but all the same she tried to keep them together. She told Dorothy, "You're in glamorous Hollywood. Everywhere we go there are beautiful young girls. Lose some weight, darling. You're downright frumpy. Maybe Gary doesn't mind a few extra pounds in bed, but he doesn't appreciate them in an evening gown."

Dorothy took her word, went on a diet, and wore daring dresses and entertained lavishly. Gary's parents did not voice their opinion of the countess. Though she was impressed by di Frasso's life-style, all Alice Cooper wanted for her son was to settle down with a stable wife his own age.

Charles Cooper spent his time looking at and investing in property, and he had encouraged his son to do the same before his trip to Italy. Even though Gary had to borrow money from Dorothy to get home, he found himself in good shape financially. With his new Paramount contract escalating to $7,500 a week before expiring in 1937, he could afford to live more than comfortably.

After a guest appearance in *Make Me a Star* with Stuart Erwin, Cooper starred in one of eight segments of the multistory film, *If I Had a Million.* He played a tough marine who gets a check for a million dollars, thinks it's a gag, and gives it away. He received top billing over Jack Oakie, George Raft, and Charles Laughton.

With his new contract Gary now took a greater interest in his future roles. He asked for the lead in the film version of Dickens' classic *A Tale of Two Cities,* but Ronald Colman got it instead. Gary admitted he had read neither the Dickens novel nor *A Farewell to Arms,* but he had heard so much about the Hemingway book being made into a film that he could almost taste the part of the ambulance driver, Frederic Henry. So he put in a bid. But Fredric March, who had won an Oscar for *Dr. Jekyll and Mr. Hyde,* was offered the part and accepted. Cooper told March, "Gosh, it all looked good on paper and I figured all I had to do was speak up. I'm gettin' nowhere."

"They have their minds made up, Coop. Be careful. *Hot Saturday* and *Madame Butterfly* are so bad you shouldn't even consider them."

"What about De Mille's *The Sign of the Cross?*" Gary asked.

"That's better than the Hemingway project."

Cooper shrugged. "Let's switch. My knees are too bony to be a Roman soldier anyway."

March went after the De Mille spectacular and Cooper requested *A Farewell to Arms*. Paramount executives had signed Helen Hayes as the leading lady and considered her far superior to Cooper. Miss Hayes had been lauded for her stage work and in 1931 had won an Oscar for Best Actress in *The Sin of Madelon Claudet*. She herself was reluctant to costar with Cooper for several reasons, not the least of which was his reputation for extending his onscreen romances off the movie set. Miss Hayes considered Cooper a spontaneous actor, one more himself in front of the camera than the character he was portraying. There was also the fifteen-inch difference in height.

Director Frank Borzage noticed their awkwardness on the first day on the set, so he decided to shoot some stills. The photographer, John Engstead, asked them to lie down on the floor. "By posing Hayes and Cooper closer together gradually, I got some great love pictures. It broke the ice. Borzage realized what a beautiful couple they were, but filmed them sitting down." In the romantic war story, the nurse, after giving birth to an illegitimate baby, dies at the end as her soldier-lover weeps. Paramount wanted a Hollywood ending where the couple is reunited after the war is over. Borzage insisted on doing it both ways, but the studio used only the romantic version.

Ernest Hemingway said, "I did not intend a happy ending."

This was the writer's first encounter with Hollywood and he wasn't impressed. He felt that the continuity and theme of his work had been twisted to satisfy moviegoers and make money for the studios. As the years passed and many of his best-sellers were made into movies, he became accustomed to having his novels rewritten; but he fumed.

It embarrassed Hemingway when the press attempted to publicize his wartime heroism and boxing ability. He wanted to be recognized for his literary achievements and not for his private life and hobbies. It was anger, not humility, that forced him to tell reporters his books were fiction, not biographical. He said he chose to drive an ambulance in Italy because it was safer than France during World War I. Hemingway constantly repeated, "Leave my private life alone."

Cooper and the novelist would not meet until eight years later. They became very close friends, and died two months apart.

The Daily News said about *A Farewell to Arms,* "Cooper is as natural and convincing an actor as might have had years of stage training—which isn't the case. Gary is a true product of the celluloid. His performance is ingratiating." *Photoplay* thought that Cooper revealed greater emotional depth than he had ever displayed before.

A Farewell to Arms was nominated for the Academy Award's Best Picture of 1932, but Noel Coward's *Calvacade* won.

It is interesting to note that before Helen Hayes worked with Cooper she judged him on his reputation as an offscreen lover. Afterward she said, "If Gary had asked me, I would have gone away with him." Whether she actually meant that she would have abandoned her husband for Gary isn't known, but it seems Miss Hayes was waiting for Studs to make the first move.

While Cooper was filming *A Farewell to Arms,* he told a *Photoplay* magazine reporter that after the filming he would take a vacation in Europe, and did not expect to return to Hollywood. Years later he recalled, "I was unhappy with the way things were going at the studio and my private affairs had reached a crisis. I shall never get into such a state, mentally, again. Life can never do anything like that to me again. I have learned something. In the first place, I shall never be dominated by other people again as I had allowed myself to be until that time. I had drifted, taken advice, let people get at me through my emotions, my sympathy, my affections. Perhaps, through a sort of apathy, too, because I was not well . . . my attitude toward my work had changed. It isn't as important to me as it used to be. And, therefore, I shall do better at it. I am no longer blinded by the glamour of pictures. I have learned that it is no use to have ideas unless you express them. And no one will have any respect for your ideas unless you are willing to fight for them."

One of the rewards Gary reaped in 1932 was a custom-built Duesenberg automobile. When Clark Gable saw it he ordered one for himself—but a foot longer than Coop's. The two men belonged to the same country club but were not close buddies. Gable didn't feel rivalrous but Gary did. Coop would always feel upstaged by the bat-eared actor with false teeth who had been crowned "King of Hollywood." Maybe Cooper chuckled when he heard that Gable had turned down a chance to spend the night with Lupe Velez because, "She'll be all over town telling everyone what a lousy lay I am."

Regardless of his hit-and-run reputation, few women turned Gable down. Mary Pickford was one who did. Knowing that her husband, Douglas Fairbanks, was in Europe courting Lady Sylvia Ashley (later Gable's fourth wife), Clark called Mary several times on the servants' day off and asked if he could come over. She avoided him but confessed years later, "I'm sorry I didn't see him."

Gary Cooper, however, was welcome at Pickfair. Miss Pickford announced they would costar in *Secrets,* the third attempt to salvage her career. Gary was excited about the prospect of working with America's Sweetheart until M-G-M beckoned. Would he like to appear with Joan Crawford in *Today We Live?* L. B. Mayer, head of Metro, said Crawford had personally asked for him and, to make it more tempting, hinted that he would be replacing Clark Gable. Cooper had to explain to Miss Pickford, "It means a lot to me workin' at the biggest and best studio in Hollywood." She was very disappointed. British actor Leslie Howard played opposite her in *Secrets* but was hardly the rugged pioneersman the public expected. She retired from the screen.

L. B. Mayer hadn't told Gary the whole story, however. Joan Crawford had really wanted Gable in *Today We Live,* but M-G-M knew they were having an affair and tried to separate the two stars, who were forbidden by the studio to marry. (Gable later would be punished by being sent to Columbia Pictures for *It Happened One Night,* a "rotten film nobody wanted" that would go on to win five Oscars in 1934.)

Hollywood expected a blazing romance between Gary and Joan. So did Gary, who was disappointed to find out Joan was more interested in Franchot Tone, another actor in *Today We Live.* Tone was her "spare" boyfriend in case Clark refused to get a divorce as promised. "Everyone thought Cooper and I would get together," Crawford commented, "but at the time Franchot was courting me with champagne and gardenias. He was brilliant and stimulating and I was in awe. Besides, I was in love with Clark even though our future together was fruitless."

Today We Live, another wartime love triangle story, was a mediocre film. Despite the failure of Cooper and Crawford to ignite, it made money for their studios. M-G-M might have bought out Cooper's contract had it not been for the perpetual rivalry between Mayer and his production assistant, Irving Thalberg, who had taken a chance on Clark Gable and had wanted to take another on Cooper seven years prior.

Thalberg was a warm and friendly man who usually showed up on one of the sets every day. He preferred watching the shooting to sitting behind a desk. He told Cooper, "You had an appointment with me when you first came to Hollywood. Why did you walk out?"

"How long can a guy hang around?"

"Maybe I wanted to find out how much you wanted to be an actor."

Cooper shrugged. "Know somethin'? I still can't come up with an answer to that one." He didn't tell Thalberg there was no way he would endure Mayer's wrath because, ". . . he hates Gable for the simple reason he didn't discover him."

When Irving Thalberg died tragically at the age of thirty-seven, M-G-M arranged a funeral suitable for an Egyptian pharaoh. That evening, L. B. Mayer danced all night at the Trocadero nightclub.

It was good to be back home at Paramount after his stint at M-G-M. In fact, Cooper was more content than he had been in a long time. The reason was simple: Paramount was a great place to work.

Carole Lombard referred to Paramount as "the fun house." At the end of each working day, the actors got together for "the happy hour" to relax with a few drinks. Cooper's dressing room was ideally situated, because it was the center bungalow. Lombard said, "Even Gary talked." They would all sit around and discuss their present and future roles. Sometimes they made deals and swapped ideas. "It was easygoing at Paramount," Lombard commented. "M-G-M was too much like royalty . . . don't do this and don't do that. Silly, because no one over there could do anything without permission anyway. Gary found out he needed more freedom. And, let's face it, if Thalberg had signed him back in 1926, Coop would have been fired for screwing around with Clara, and The Great White Father [Mayer] would never have taken her crap about putting Gary in one of her movies. When I was married to Clark, I was banned from his set because I made his leading ladies nervous. And I mean banned! I couldn't get through the front gate."

Bing Crosby recalled, "Maybe Coop's dressing room was in the middle, but that wasn't the only reason we drifted in there before leaving for the day. Everyone liked the guy, which is more than I can say for the rest of us. He sang pretty good, too. Matter of fact, I named my first son after Gary 'cause Coop was a good guy you could trust. We had some good times together."

Hedda Hopper laughed about it. "Gary was so casual and unruffled. The door was open if he had his pants on or not. Carole, of course, was the instigator. Her dressing room was next to his and she invited everyone for morning coffee provided they had a dirty joke to tell. If not, they had to scout around for one. Carole had plenty of blue stories and she got away with it as she did with so many of her outrageous statements about Gable, who encouraged it. Coop was somewhat embarrassed because the jokes were *really* raunchy. He wasn't square and loved to exchange off-color patter at stag parties, I'm told. Carole took advantage of this and it was, as she said, a fun house. She liked to razz Gary about his dressing room. 'Did you bring all this shit from Montana?' she asked with a straight face. The sofa was covered with an Indian blanket. He hung Indian feathers on the walls and collected artifacts, anything elaborate. It wasn't unusual to find Claudette Colbert, Mae West, George Raft, Marlene Dietrich, Fredric March, and Bing sitting around in costume having a swell time. Gary played a banjo or ukulele fairly well."

Because Lombard and Cooper had shared an intimate relationship on and off she used to tease him unmercifully with the "Studs" label. Maybe this was the reason Gable was not as warm with Gary as he might have been.

On the set of *The Misfits* in 1960 Gable was drinking heavily and talking more than usual. The conversation got around to hunting, and Gary's name came up. Clark blurted out to a group of cronies, "Coop is a right guy, the kind you liked to hunt and fish with and not talk about making movies. I laid it on him one time about his romance with Carole and he got pale as hell. She told me about it during a drunken argument we had. After that, Coop and I didn't hunt together so much and when we did, we kept an eye on each other. She used to throw him up to me in my face and that was hard to take, especially since I didn't know the whole truth until years later. I got to admit I was jealous."

Gable had every right to be sensitive. After all, it was Carole who told the press, "God knows I love Clark, but he's the worst lay in town." Another time she was knitting a "cock warmer" for him and showed it to everyone in the studio. It was rather small. When asked about the size she remarked, "An inch less and Gable would be Queen of Hollywood!" Joan Crawford admitted she tried to keep Gable out of the bedroom because he wasn't the greatest lover.

Cooper's reputation as a lover bothered Gable far more than who had the best gun collection or the most expensive automobile. Lombard, of course, felt justified in getting back at the man she loved. Clark did his share of womanizing during their marriage, and she knew it. He liked to describe in detail his former sexual experiences to her. Carole waited for the right moment to pounce. Gable was relating an escapade with a girl in the swimming pool. "It's not easy to do," he teased.

"I know." Carole smiled.

"How can you talk like that?" he ranted, turning blue in the face. "A nice girl like you!"

Lupe Velez told friends she knew about Gary and Carole. "They argue a lot," Lupe explained. "Coop has a temper which no one knows about. He belted Lombard and he belted Clara. And he belted me good. Lombard thought Garree was not as you say, articulate . . . that he didn't talk right. He stuttered and was stupid in public. You know? That's why he shut up all the time. Lombard told him where to go . . . to hell or to jump in a lake. She was a tiger. I am no tiger. She was her own person . . . her own woman. I'm Lupe! I tell you what I theenk is truth. Real problem that Cooper has. He runs for women who are not like his mama! So sweet, eh? And always he is right and perfect. He gets excited when we fight, but I tell you one thing. Lupe was the only one who scarred him for life. I got him with a knife once . . . in the arm, and he sweat and bled. Boy, he sweat. We were cooking dinner and Garree could not duck this time. He has the scars. Lombard told me Cooper was too dumb to fight with the words and she was right. If you can't fight with the mouth, you fight with the hands. The press calls me 'wild.' Ha! They do not know the real Cooper. They will never know the real cowboy. Never! I know him and love him. Lombard never did. She like to have fun."

Carole might have been a screwball, but she was a true friend. If she teased Cooper it was her way of keeping him in line. "Gary's got it all in front," she said, "and no ass to push it with." No one laughed louder than the man himself.

On Easter Sunday 1933, Cooper attended a party given by M-G-M's brilliant art designer, Cedric Gibbons (the man who designed the famous Oscar statuette), and his exquisite wife, Dolores del Rio. Irene Gibbons, married to Cedric's brother Eliot, was there, too. Irene was an attractive brunette with short cropped hair, elegant posture, and a sophisticated air about her, and, like Cooper, she was most comfortable in wide open spaces. She had grown up on her father's ranch in Montana and was an avid hunter. Irene had attended design school and opened a modest dress shop in Los Angeles.

One day Dolores del Rio dropped in to the boutique and was so impressed with what she saw that she told all her friends. Irene soon became famous for her soufflé creations, and designed screen wardrobes for Loretta Young, Barbara Stanwyck, Joan Crawford, Katharine Hepburn, and many others.

Gary and Irene would become involved in a relationship that continued over the years. In 1962, a year following Cooper's death, she cut her wrists and jumped from a fourteen-story window. Though she and Gibbons lived separate lives, it was not loneliness that drove her to the bottle and window ledge. "Gary Cooper is the only man I ever loved," she told a friend.

But it was not Irene who changed Cooper's life on that memorable Easter Sunday in 1933. Cedric Gibbons gave the party in honor of his niece from the East, twenty-year-old debutante Veronica Balfe, whom Gary had met previously at a social gathering in New York City. Veronica was tall and stunning, with dark hair, ivory complexion, and gray-green eyes. She had come to Hollywood to pursue a career in movies under the name of Sandra Shaw.

The Countess di Frasso had stayed home because she deemed daytime parties too "glaring." How fortunate for Gary!

5

SOCIETY WEDDING

Veronica Balfe's father was the millionaire Harry Balfe. Young Veronica attended the exclusive Bennett School for Girls in Millbrook, New York, lived on Park Avenue in Manhattan, and spent the winter holidays in Palm Beach and the humid summers mostly in fashionable Southampton on Long Island. When her parents divorced, Veronica's mother married multimillionaire Paul Shields, a governor of the New York Stock Exchange.

Hedda Hopper said, "Veronica was elegant, poised, and aloof. She was a striking girl who often appeared snobbish. Gary was a clod around her in the beginning. Little did he know she was very taken with him, but gave the impression she wasn't interested beyond a few casual dates.

"Cedric kept an eye on his niece, though she was quite capable of taking care of herself. In my opinion, Veronica set her sights for Gary. She played hard to get. She didn't fall all over him and she went out with other men."

"Sandra Shaw" signed a movie contract with RKO. She played a bit part in *Blood Money* with Judith Anderson and Frances Dee. And although she showed a degree of talent, she wasn't at all ambitious or dedicated. Elsa Maxwell hinted that Veronica used her interest in films as an excuse to stay in Hollywood. "Gary's frequent dates with her were very upsetting to Dorothy," the columnist said. "Dorothy was twice Veronica's age and still married to the count. There was a serious discussion about making a safari movie on location in Africa sponsored by Dorothy. Gary liked the idea and I think he was serious, but on a professional basis only. There was no doubt in my mind that he wanted to end their romance. Dorothy was desperate."

In July 1933, the countess announced she was going to establish residency in Reno and divorce Count Carlo di Frasso. "Garree got himself into a beeg fix this time!" Lupe Velez announced to her friends. But it was merely Dorothy's final gambit, obviously planted in the newspapers. She never got to Nevada.

Cooper didn't want any more damaging publicity. He knew Veronica's parents were wary of his spicy past and he was seriously thinking of asking her to be his wife. There was only one problem: Cooper was afraid to get married. As much as he wanted to settle down and have children, he worried about his ability to remain faithful. What love was everlasting? He envied his parents and admired their survival of hardships, separations, and adjustments. Yes, he had been willing to give Clara Bow the sincerity and devotion she needed, and he had been willing to give her his love. Yet, looking back, it had all been so hopeless. And what of loyal Lupe? And Evelyn Brent whom he adored?

Dorothy di Frasso had played a unique role in Gary's life. She had nursed him back to health when he was sick and depressed; she had bolstered his confidence and eased his loneliness. She taught him to appreciate fine art, fine wines, and fine cuisine. She even guided him on how to dress, how to host a formal gathering, and how to be sophisticated with ease. What else did he want from her life?

Elsa Maxwell was once again thrust in the middle. "Gary told me he wanted very much to retain a friendship with Dorothy," she said. "He hoped she would welcome him at Villa Madama and maybe they could pursue the safari movie. I didn't mince words with him. She was deeply hurt. Gary didn't say much other than his career was going well and he wouldn't have time to loaf on the Riviera or take extended vacations. I asked him about Veronica and he grinned and said, 'I nicknamed her Rocky 'cause some people here in Hollywood call her Sandra and some call her Veronica.' That's all he said."

The countess was seen with the count. Rocky was seen with Gilbert Roland. Gary was seen with a young German actress, Wera Engels. Lupe married Johnny Weissmuller. Rocky dated Gary, who was seen visiting Dorothy di Frasso. Innocently he went out with Judith Allen, a stunning Paramount starlet, only to find out she was married. Reporters pressed him, "How come you didn't know she had a husband?"

"Guess I forgot to ask," he said with a shrug.

It turned into a small scandal that annoyed and embarrassed Gary. The incident was ballyhooed in the newspapers. But everyone's reaction was, "What else is new?" and, as always, Gary walked away from it and quietly concentrated on his work.

In his next film, *One Sunday Afternoon,* he costarred with Fay Wray for the last time. Cooper's performance as a dentist who marries on the rebound and finds unexpected happiness was just fair, nothing more. The 1941 remake entitled *The Strawberry Blonde,* with James Cagney and Rita Hayworth, was much better. But *Variety* thought *One Sunday Afternoon* was underrated: "It seems a little astonishing to find this player of many formal leading-man roles suddenly blossoming into a very human character, as though he had been playing home-spun people all his life. Cooper has for years been playing a procession of stuffed-shirt polite roles and somehow giving them a human touch that they didn't intrinsically have, by virtue of some subtle awkward masculinity, suppressed in polite roles, but vaguely sensed."

But the big news of the day was not this movie but the Countess di Frasso's departure for Italy via New York. "It's only a vacation," she told reporters. "Gary plans to join me as soon as he can get away."

Cooper was, however, busy organizing his life. In August 1933, he legally changed his name from Frank to Gary, and bought a new house on ten acres of land in the Hollywood Hills in Van Nuys. The landlord of his "bachelor jungle" sued for damages but the matter was settled out of court. For almost three months Rocky saw very little of him, but when he did attend a party she was his companion.

Few people took the relationship seriously. Gossip columnists claimed he was brooding over Lupe's marriage to Weissmuller. Or that he missed the countess. Or that the studio was angry with him over the Judith Allen publicity. Yet by the end of September 1933 the press was reporting a serious romance between Gary Cooper and "starlet" Sandra Shaw, not yet identified as Veronica Balfe. Alice and Charles approved of Rocky, but the Balfes weren't sure about Cooper.

So Cedric Gibbons used his influence over them, emphasizing Gary's education in England, his father's judgeship, and tried to explain the gossip as fan magazine hokum. Veronica's mother wasn't entirely convinced, but she valued her brother's opinion. Gary begged Cedric to keep trying.

Noel Coward's *Design for Living* was a very successful Broadway comedy about two men and a woman in a ménage à trois. The bisexual theme was ahead of its time, and Lunt, Fontanne, and Coward carried it off with class and aplomb. Paramount asked German director Ernst Lubitsch, acclaimed for producing films that were risqué without being vulgar, to take charge of the film version. In Hollywood this was referred to as the "Lubitsch touch." Fredric March portrayed the playwright, Gary Cooper the painter, and Miriam Hopkins the commercial artist and third member of the trio.

The critics panned it. *The New York Times* said Coward's play was "butchered" on film. *The Village Voice* thought Cooper and March were too masculine for the effete implications of the plot, and added, "Where Coward took the sex lightly for laughs, Lubitsch took it seriously for pathos, and Coward's wit thereby dissolved on the screen." *The New York Herald Tribune* said, "You could hardly expect Mr. Cooper to be properly at home as a witty sophisticate and I fear that he isn't."

Coop never did master the art of portraying a playboy. His diction was slow and he dropped his *g*'s. Like Gable, he was overly conscious of his big hands and tried to hide them by stuffing them in his pockets or curling his fingers into fists. In love scenes, he cupped the lady's face with his long fingers, extending from her chin beyond the ears. It was spontaneous and touching. Alice thought her son was film perfection. She rationalized, "He sprouted fourteen inches in one year. I don't think he ever got used to being so tall though he carries himself very well. In certain roles I'm sure he prefers sitting down."

Cooper next portrayed the white knight in *Alice in Wonderland,* another roundup of Paramount stars. He volunteered for the part and appeared on the screen for only five minutes, but he had a good time with W. C. Fields, Cary Grant, Jack Oakie, and Richard Arlen.

Reporters asked Cooper about his next picture.

"Don't know," he replied. "I'm goin' huntin'."

"Do you miss ranch life, Gary?"

"Yep."

"If you had a choice, would it be Hollywood or the ranch?"

"The ranch, but I'd have to take two things with me—my bathroom and my car."

Gary and Rocky, accompanied by John Gilbert and his wife, Virginia Bruce, left for Kaibab in Arizona to do some hunting. Columnist Louella Parsons hinted that Cooper and the debutante had eloped. When they were tracked down, Gary said only a few words. "We have no intention of getting married here." But when they returned to Hollywood, on November 6, 1933, Veronica Balfe was wearing a fifteen-carat diamond engagement ring. It was official. She told reporters they had not set a date for the wedding. Cooper was shy and proper, but his eyes sparkled when he looked at his future wife. "Rocky is the ideal girl for me," he said. "She can ride, shoot, and do all the things I like to do."

On November 17 they attended the premiere of *Design for Living.* Leaving the theater, Cooper was mobbed by fans. They tore his clothes to shreds before police intervened. Hedda Hopper mentioned it in her column, but said in private, "That was the sort of thing Rocky had to get used to. She would be shoved aside while Gary got all the attention. It happens at parties, in restaurants, and on the street. At the *Design* premiere I watched Rocky who was just another spectator without a name."

Veronica would maintain her own identity, however. If she knew how to catch the most eligible and unattainable bachelor in Hollywood, she knew how to keep him.

Though her mother and stepfather were not convinced that Gary had reformed, they welcomed him into their sumptuous 778 Park Avenue apartment for Thanksgiving. On November 28, the Shieldses gave a formal dinner party to celebrate Veronica's engagement. She was dazzling in a silver lamé dress with a red velvet collar. Gary stood tall in white tie and tails. Most of the guests were friends of the family, but Helen Hayes and Cole Porter were in attendance also. Elsa Maxwell was included and ingratiated herself to Veronica. Supposedly she congratulated the couple on behalf of the Count and Countess di Frasso, but that might have been a breach of etiquette.

"When's the wedding?" she asked Gary.

"Dunno."

"What about Veronica's contract with RKO?"

"A woman's place is in the home. One career in the family's enough."

Elsa took him aside and whispered, "Do you plan to see *Forsaking All Others?* Tallulah's a divine smash and your 'Nin' is pretty good, too. They're so happy to be back on Broadway. Have you tickets?"

"Nope."

"Oh, well. We all had some swell times, didn't we?"

"Yep."

"Of course, *I'll* be in Hollywood." Elsa smiled. "I'll be working for one or two studios as a consultant, though I much prefer arranging lavish affairs for *societé*."

"You're welcome at the ranch anytime," he said.

"Ranch?"

"Our place in Van Nuys."

"I look forward to it. Call me when you buy a tractor," she teased.

"I got one," he said, grinning.

Elsa looked at the white marble fireplace framed with fresh lilacs and contemplated her next question carefully. "What about horses?" she asked.

"For the time bein' I figure a Mercedes is about the best substitute for a horse."

"The best," she sighed with relief.

Cooper admitted that it was he who rushed the wedding. "Rocky and I were talkin' about getting married in early 1934," he said. "We started makin' plans and I blurted out, 'Heck I think we might as well get it over with,' something like that."

The wedding took place in the Shields's mirrored drawing room two weeks after the engagement party, on December 15 at two in the afternoon. In attendance were Rocky's sister, Gary's secretary Jack Moss, and the Shieldses. The bride wore a gray crepe satin dress with a matching turban. The groom chose a brown checkered business suit, tan shirt, and brown tie. Gary gave his wife a diamond and ruby bracelet as a wedding present.

As requested, the Episcopalian minister omitted the word "obey."

Veronica's parents and Gary's secretary accompanied the newlyweds on their honeymoon at the Shields's winter home in Arizona. Alice and Charles Cooper joined them for the Christmas holidays.

Lupe Velez didn't take well to Gary's marriage. Frankly, she was bitter. "I was dating Garree when he was going out with that woman he would marry," Lupe said. "He introduced us in a nightclub. Sandra Shaw was who he said she was . . . an aspiring actress. Ha! I didn't swallow that one for I could see the way she looked at him and how she turned her back on me."

"I felt sorry for Lupe when Gary married someone else," Clara Bow said. "I understand the new Mrs. Cooper detested Lupe, who was the cause of many fights the newlyweds had. Louella Parsons told me Lupe and Rocky almost came to blows at the Trocadero and Gary grabbed Lupe instead of his wife. I think Lupe threw a drink in Rocky's face. Louella said she wasn't going to write about the episode. The nightclub was crowded and things happened so fast. I believe, however, that Gary held on to Lupe. Otherwise he might have been a widower instead of a groom."

* * *

Rocky and Gary settled in on the ranch, which was planted with lemon and orange trees. The trend at that time was to get out of the city and into the San Fernando Valley, where property was plentiful, spread out, inexpensive, and a place where the stars could find some privacy. William S. Hart, the Great American Cowboy, owned a ranch there. Victor Fleming, Clark Gable, Robert Taylor, and others would also become "gentlemen farmers" in the valley. They planted wheat and oats, built stables, raised chickens, and worked the soil. It was good therapy and was not a publicity stunt. Cooper looked forward to country living and to "raisin' a few head of cattle." But Veronica was a city girl; she missed the excitement of Los Angeles. For the time being she went along with it and began to decorate the house.

Most Hollywood insiders gave the marriage a year at the most. They claimed the fact that Dorothy di Frasso was back in town had nothing to do with their saying so, but they did want to remain on Dorothy di Frasso's guest list. Besides, they weren't comfortable with Rocky. She was standoffish and somewhat arrogant. And her lack of interest in those who made their money from stardust was obvious. She and Gary usually had intimate dinners at home. They did not try to ingratiate themselves with anybody, which did not go over well with Hollywood's inner circle. A few years after his marriage Cooper said in an interview, "Rocky was afraid. She was barely twenty-one and living in a strange place. She wanted to be liked, but gave the impression she was stuck-up."

One day the newlyweds were having a quiet lunch in a Hollywood restaurant when the countess showed up, alone. Hedda Hopper was there, and observed what happened. "Dorothy di Frasso walked over to their table and Gary stood up. He and Dorothy chatted while Veronica just sat there. It was very tense. Gary always had good manners, but did not ask the countess to sit down. Neither did Veronica. Interesting. These two women were both sophisticated and rich, but Dorothy had the grace and poise that comes from maturity. Rocky, of course, had youth and beauty on her side. The countess had told me she wanted to be Gary's friend and this was her way of proving it. I don't know how long they stood there talking . . . fifteen or twenty minutes. Dorothy wanted to meet Rocky, and Gary was waiting for a nod from his wife, but she had no intention of asking the countess to sit down. Finally Dorothy left the restaurant and word got around town about Rocky's rudeness. I felt sorry for Gary."

Veronica's adjustment to Hollywood and to facing Gary's former girlfriends was more of a challenge willingly taken on than an ordeal for the young debutante. It was only a matter of time before she would run into the Mexican Spitfire again. In August 1934, the Coopers attended a gala at the Little Club. Lupe and her husband, Johnny Weissmuller, were there also.

"I was married then," Lupe commented later, "and the socialite needed someone in her corner. "Garree's grandmother [the countess] was the threat. She was available and very reech. She had the nerve to come into a restaurant and embarrass Rocky Cooper. So, suddenly she [Rocky] was nice to Lupe."

An alert photographer at the club took a picture of the two couples together and should have been satisfied with that, but he asked Lupe to pose alone with Gary, who quite innocently sidled up next to her. Lupe darted away. "Eez not nice!" she hissed. The picture of the foursome was published. Lupe, Rocky, and Johnny were smiling but Gary was not. He didn't know what to do with his hands. One was under his chin and the other reaching for his wife's hand.

Talk of difficulties in the Weissmuller marriage spawned new rumors about Velez and Cooper. Rocky, however, was unusually pleasant to Lupe.

When Dorothy di Frasso saw the photo of the "happy couples," she remarked to friends, "Can you believe this? That Velez woman has no place in society! I was so sure Veronica Balfe would be more receptive to my invitation. Instead she sides with that Mexican woman."

Under the circumstances she was very surprised to receive a luncheon invitation from Rocky. Elsa Maxwell tells the story: "They were to meet at the Mocambo. When Dorothy got there she was astonished to find Lupe sitting with Veronica. Quite a frame-up. The countess had given Gary some emerald studs and cuff links. Rocky threw them across the table and said that her husband wouldn't be needing them anymore and he wanted her to have them back. Lupe had no business saying, 'That's right! Garree has no use for them now.' I don't know why Veronica chose to return the jewelry in a public place. And why did she invite Lupe? The countess felt like breaking plates over their heads, but she remained calm and left with her chin up. She said it was bad enough losing Gary to the *Social Register* because if it hadn't been for her, he'd still look like a cowboy—that she taught him everything he knew."

The Mocambo luncheon was a juicy news item. Reporters had mixed versions about how Rocky returned Gary's jewelry to Dorothy di Frasso. Some observers at the restaurant did not notice anything unusual until the countess left early. They agreed that Lupe was having a marvelous time and had a fixed smile on her face. The consensus was, however, that Rocky Cooper proved to the world she could face up to her husband's past.

Lupe kept her mouth shut about the incident. Gary called Dorothy and apologized. They would keep in touch over the years. She did not return to the Villa Madama. One reason was her love affair with mobster Bugsy Siegel, who mingled with the Hollywood elite, including Cooper and George Raft. When Siegel was slain in 1947 Dorothy was seen in the company of Anderson Lawler in New York. And when Gary was in the East by himself, he dined with them, as he did with Tallulah.

Rocky commented in an interview about the other women in Gary's life, "Gary and I should not be cemented to each other." When asked how she felt about the women who ogled him wherever they went, Rocky replied, "If I had married a businessman who lived a normal life, I would not be faced with these trials. But I did not marry an ordinary man."

Again she proved herself by giving Gary the freedom he needed. His buddies said marriage changed him for a while, that he didn't hang around the studio after work as he used to, or disappear with a script girl for a few hours. At least, not yet. A studio electrician, Ned Nugent, told me he thought few Hollywood marriages had the stamp of fidelity. Temptations, opportunities, and frivolities were always in the air. "Guys like Coop worked twelve hours a day. They were expected to be seen dancing at the best nightclubs and to get up at five o'clock the following morning and know their lines. In the early thirties we worked six, sometimes seven, days a week. The Gables, Coopers, and Tracys needed outlets—hunting, golf, or tennis, but always women. Their egos were like batteries. They needed constant recharging. They were the things dreams were made of, but they didn't believe it so they had to find their own magic. There was no way Coop could be faithful and it had nothing to do with not loving his wife. Gable worshipped Lombard, but he played around every chance he got and she knew it. When she was killed, he died, too . . . was never the same again. A lot of it was guilt because I'm told he was having a last fling while she was flying home. Cooper, too, was a man's man *and* a ladies' man. He never missed a trick. If he was born for the camera, he was born to make love. He was too good to be a rooster. He wanted to satisfy women . . . enjoyed looking at them, listening to them, pleasing them. A guy like that does not change."

Cooper rejected several scripts in succession and he might have turned down *Operator 13* in 1933 if William Randolph Hearst, owner of Cosmopolitan Productions, hadn't asked him to costar with his mistress, Marion Davies. Marion was a warm and talented woman who might have done better in films had it not been for Hearst's easy millions. He was forty years older than she, a married man who refused to get a divorce. Yet their romantic affair lasted more than three decades and was respected by the motion picture industry. Gary was friendly with the couple, and had attended parties at Hearst's castle at San Simeon, with its sixty guest rooms, on top of La Cuesta Encantata (the enchanted hill) several hundred miles north of Los Angeles. The tycoon never allowed alcohol at his lavish parties, though Marion imbibed, to put it mildly. Gary frequently slipped away with her to have a few drinks.

It's been said that Hearst had more power than the president of the United States. No one who toyed with his influence got away with it. Fatty Arbuckle tried and although he was acquitted of causing the death of a young actress at an orgy in 1921, the Hearst newspapers convicted him.

Then there was the ill-fated cruise aboard Hearst's 280-foot yacht, the *Oneida*, in 1924, when producer-director Thomas Ince suddenly died. The cause of his death was never established. His body was cremated before an autopsy could be performed. The Hearst papers attributed Ince's fatal illness to "acute indigestion," but a reliable witness claimed he was shot in the head.

Did Hearst find Marion with him, or was he mistaken for Charlie Chaplin, whom the old man suspected of making love to his mistress?

Gossip columnist Louella Parsons managed to get off the yacht without being noticed, and later denied ever being on board. Was it more than coincidence that Hearst gave her a lifetime contract with his newspapers shortly after the tragic incident? Mrs. Ince claimed she was at her husband's bedside when he passed away, but Hearst set up a sizable trust fund for her. Was her silence bought? Hollywood insiders accepted the theory that Hearst shot Ince in front of witnesses. The rumors were enough to scare any actor, including Coop, from trying to touch Marion offcamera.

Because of her busy acting career, Miss Davies did not live at the Hearst castle. She usually stayed at her house in Santa Monica, a multimillion-dollar compound with eight hundred feet of oceanfront. It had a ballroom, a theater, thirty or more guest rooms, and fifty-five bathrooms. Marion humbly referred to this mansion as "the beach house."

The ex-chorus girl from the 1917 Ziegfeld Follies was fun-loving and witty. She was also a gracious hostess and talented performer, with a stutter that could either be very cute or very frustrating. She was a natural comedic actress, but Hearst couldn't accept that. He lost $7 million trying to make a dramatic actress out of her.

Cooper adored Marion, but Hearst's gruff presence on the set of *Operator 13* made Gary extremely nervous. He did not want to give the old man any reason for jealousy. The film was set as a Civil War melodrama, and contained few romantic scenes. But, under the circumstances, one was too many for Cooper. His knees and hands shook. He mumbled and Marion stuttered, but Hearst was satisfied. After all, *Operator 13* was *her* picture. Critics called Cooper's performance "adequate."

Afterward Gary was relieved to return to Paramount and anxious to work with Carole Lombard and Shirley Temple in *Now and Forever*. When Lombard asked him about the Hearst film, Gary replied, "I felt like I was just startin' out in pictures."

"Why?" she teased. "Because you couldn't get into Marion's bloomers?"

"Nope. Well, I don't think so."

"Did you enjoy her catered lunches?"

"Yep. Hot peppers and beans."

"No caviar?"

"For a hundred people?" he yelped.

"I was joking," Carole said, taking a deep breath. "By the way, how does it feel being surrounded with blondes?"

"Huh?"

"From Marion to Shirley Temple and me."

He stretched out his long legs and leaned back in the chair. "It's good to be back," he said closing his eyes, "even if I have to play second fiddle to Little Miss Marker."

"That cute five-year-old kid knows more about acting than we do," Carole said, laughing.

She looked over at Gary, but he was fast asleep.

Cooper played Temple's widower father who attempts to sell custody of Temple to his brother-in-law until his girlfriend (Lombard) straightens out the situation. *The New York Sun* said that Cooper successfully played the role with quiet sympathy and humor. *The New York-American* wrote, "Mr. Cooper does excellently in a role that is much improved by the underplaying which is his habit."

But, as expected, the adorable Shirley Temple walked away with the film. Gary shrugged it off good-naturedly. "I've been accused of stealin' scenes all the time so I don't mind havin' it done to me."

Lombard, divorced from William Powell, was zanier than ever. She had been dating singer Russ Columbo when he accidentally shot himself in the eye with a Civil War pistol. At his funeral in August 1933, Carole said, "His love for me was the kind that rarely comes to any woman." Before she got involved with Gable, she dated screenwriter Robert Riskin, who wrote *It Happened One Night, Mr. Deeds Goes to Town, Meet John Doe,* and others.

Carole was seldom serious with reporters. She could be blunt and her remarks were often taken the wrong way. If pushed too far, she could be downright raunchy. There would be many quotable remarks from her about Gable that made most streetwise reporters blush. Full of energy and spirit, Carole was often impatient with Cooper. "In a conversation," she said, "by the time he opens his mouth it's tomorrow." She didn't think Gary could act, and added, "He's effeminate in his mannerisms." On the set she was overheard saying to him, "I like you lots, Studs." He glowed. Then she turned to a stagehand and said with a straight face, "Jesus, what a clam! He sleeps while he's acting, you know!"

Carole Lombard never got to know Gary really well, but then few did. Her comments about Howard Hughes were similar. Hughes and Cooper were well-known for their harems and for being very quiet about themselves. Lombard dated both of them, but they were not her type. "At least Howard can count to ten," Lombard said with a laugh.

Lives of a Bengal Lancer was filmed on location, which meant Cooper would be separated from his wife for a month. Rocky paid one visit to him on the five-hundred-acre site of Paramount's "Khyber Pass." When Hedda Hopper asked for a brief interview Rocky did not try to conceal her loneliness. "I know this is the first of many such separations," Rocky said. "But when Gary's home, there are times I feel as though he doesn't belong to me. People are not interested in me. My mother advised me not to ride on my husband's coattails. She said, 'Develop your own personality.' I'm only human, of course, and wanted to tell Gary how I felt being pushed aside, but he refuses to argue.

Before we got married, he told me how much he hated fighting—his way of saying he would have no part of it."

Cooper had little to say about their first professional separation other than that "Workin' on a film like *Lancer* is exhausting. There's a lot of action and dialogue and this takes all my concentration. If I were home it wouldn't be any different."

He grew a mustache for the picture and considered it very sporty. It was his own idea. The reaction was nil compared with the hullaballoo over Gable's "soup-strainer," which made its debut in 1932. Cooper did not shave his off so fast.

Lives of a Bengal Lancer, costarring Franchot Tone and Richard Cromwell, was a huge success and is considered one of Cooper's best pictures. Critics were unanimous with their praise. They called it "thrilling," "exceptionally good," "terrific," "magnificent," "superior," "splendid." Franchot Tone shared the honors with Cooper, who wasn't about to give away three films in a row, but it almost happened. M-G-M was so pleased with Tone's performance they rushed him into *Mutiny on the Bounty.* He and his two costars, Clark Gable and Charles Laughton, were nominated for Academy Awards. They didn't win, but *Bounty* was voted Best Picture in 1935 over *Lancer.*

Though *The Lives of a Bengal Lancer* gave Cooper's career a big boost, the studio considered it as only one in a series of mediocre pictures the actor had chosen. Paramount was anxious to erase the ladies' man label and emphasize Cooper's acting ability on the screen. Articles praised him for his portrayals in notable films, but always his romances with leading ladies were mentioned as the highlight of Gary's career. Paramount made plans to keep their star's name in lights with no lulls between pictures.

This busy schedule allowed little time at home with Rocky. She understood the situation, but did not want to be shut off from the world in Van Nuys. Rumors of a rift circulated around the film community. Several gossip columnists announced that the Cooper marriage was in trouble. Gary denied it. "Two years after the wedding in this town," he said, "and it's automatic divorce. The gossip about Rocky and me is not true." An old friend of Cooper's said, "Gary didn't want to move back to the city, but he had no choice. He and Rocky decided to build a house in Brentwood. While it was being completed, they rented a place in Beverly Hills. I don't doubt that they argued over this. To Gary, quarreling was not saying anything one way or the other and that can be frustrating, especially to someone as spunky and determined as Rocky. He wanted to live in the country and got his way in the beginning."

This soon became a pattern in the Cooper marriage: Life revolved around Gary, but if Rocky wasn't satisfied she bided her time and gradually got what she wanted.

Reporters were not allowed in the new house. Gary's close friend, Hedda Hopper, was a frequent guest and commented at the time, "I saw very little of Gary's taste other than his gun rack and a zebra rug in the living room. The rest of the house was richly furnished with expensive antiques and paintings. It is quite lovely, but I didn't expect the interior to be quite so feminine."

Fan magazines were allowed to photograph the exterior of the Bermuda-style house with its red doors. There was the usual swimming pool, and orange trees, weeping willows, and a tennis court, with high hedges surrounding all four acres. Elsa Maxwell cracked, "Gary doesn't have much of a chance to enjoy his new house. Rocky makes sure she gets him out of Hollywood as soon as he finishes a film. She never got accustomed to the movie crowd. She's more comfortable with her society friends in New York. The Cooper marriage is one of compromise. Rocky goes hunting with Gary, but she refuses to kill anything. He's taking up skiing because it's one of her favorite sports."

Gone were the days of wild stag parties and last-minute fishing trips with the boys. Jack Oakie said he saw very little of Gary after he married Rocky. "Most of the guys got hitched," Oakie remarked, "but we got together—all except Coop. We saw each other 'cause we worked for the same studio, but we talked about guns and cars mostly. He was the same Coop, but not as relaxed."

Sam Goldwyn invited Cooper for dinner to meet the stunning Russian movie actress, Anna Sten. Goldwyn's goal in 1935 was for the lovely twenty-seven-year-old to rival Garbo and he wanted Gary Cooper to help him do it. "King Vidor is going to direct *The Wedding Night,*" Goldwyn told Gary. "I'm willing to pay you $100,000. This project is very important to me."

Cooper gulped when he heard the offer. "Okay," he replied.

In *The Wedding Night* Gary played the part of a married author who finds the peace and quiet he needs to write on a Connecticut farm. He falls in love with a lovely Polish girl who lives nearby. The wedding night is not Gary's, however, but the one spent by his sweetheart with another man. Sten portrayed the tragic bride who dies from falling down a flight of stairs on that wedding night.

The blond beauty responded to Cooper instantly. If Gary had problems making love for the camera in the past, there were no such signs during production of *The Wedding Night.* But when it was released the picture received only lukewarm reviews. Cooper did not regret his decision to work with Anna Sten. Their convincing love scenes and their off-camera harmony leaked to the gossip mills. King Vidor would not comment on a reported romance, but he was blunt about Cooper's acting. "He had difficulty remembering more than one or two lines at a time. We had to break it up. I tolerated his mumbling because he came over so good on film."

Sam Goldwyn never forgave himself for letting Cooper slip away in 1926 and wanted to get him back. He asked Paramount to loan Gary for several other important projects. The studio politely said Cooper had prior commitments.

In his next film, *Peter Ibbetson,* costarring Ann Harding and a seventeen-year-old starlet, Ida Lupino, Gary had to fight for the title role—that of an architect who accidentally kills the husband of his childhood sweetheart and then spends the rest of his life in prison. In its review, *The New York Daily News* said Cooper had been miscast. Apparently Gary had realized this during production. He had fits of anger on the set, swore at the technicians, stormed off, and sulked alone.

Word got around that Cooper had "gone Hollywood" and was exerting his power at Paramount, but his personal problems far exceeded any existing professional letdowns. The Countess di Frasso was back in town and staying with the Fairbankses at Pickfair. Then there was the anxiety about an upcoming film with a woman he could not resist—Marlene Dietrich.

His mother was also making life difficult. She was not close to her daughter-in-law. Gary visited his parents regularly, but Rocky kept her distance. Each woman considered the other beneath her. Mother and wife were headstrong and firm in their beliefs. Alice resented her son's marriage to a Catholic; the *Social Register* meant nothing to her.

Gary worked long hours and spent most of his spare time with his wife. Alice could accept this, but Rocky's rushing him out of town after every film was an obvious giveaway: Rocky did not want to share her husband with his peers or his family.

What no one could change was Gary's devotion to his mother. He adored her and had made many sacrifices to keep her happy. Now he was obligated to do the same for his wife. Gary tried to balance his love carefully, but the two Mrs. Coopers were always a few steps ahead of him. Despite his screen image, Gary was easily influenced, and both women used this weakness to their advantage.

During this turmoil, it was typical of Cooper to worry about something inconsequential. Carole Lombard found him staring at himself in the mirror one morning. "What's the problem?" she asked.

"My mustache. It doesn't suit my image. I'm gonna shave it off."

"Congratulations," she mocked.

This was a monumental decision for Cooper, but he was beginning to understand himself and accept the fact that he was unique in his own right not only as an actor, but as a man. As his second wedding anniversary approached, he realized he could not be faithful to any one woman, including his wife. He was highly charged sexually. He needed discreet diversions and they were there for the taking.

6

SUPERSTAR

In 1935, Marlene Dietrich asked Paramount to give silent-screen idol John Gilbert another chance to resume his career in *Desire*. His screen test for the role as her jewel-thief accomplice was successful. Marlene took over and nursed Gilbert, who was in ill health and drinking heavily, back to sobriety. It was not an easy task. Gilbert had lost everything he loved—Greta Garbo, his career, and his self-respect. And as anyone in Hollywood can tell you, the best remedy for an actor's depression and physical degeneration is a good part in a good picture. Marlene made that possible for Jack, and Cooper was anxious to help. During the filming of *Desire,* however, Gilbert suffered a mild heart attack while swimming with Marlene in his pool. It was too late to stop production, so he was replaced by John Halliday.

In the film Dietrich and Cooper were deliciously matched—he as a gullible American tourist and she as a sophisticated thief. Her evenings, however, were devoted to Gilbert until Garbo drove up to his front door and he ran out to greet her. Apparently, the excitable Dietrich misunderstood his innocent gesture—she slipped out the back door of his house in a huff.

Gary consoled her and, to Paramount's delight, they were seen dining together. People assumed they had resumed their sensuous affair, but Rocky pretended not to notice. When Gilbert went on a binge and had another heart attack, Marlene blamed herself and rushed back to him. That was all right with Cooper, who was expected home for his second wedding anniversary. The holidays came and went.

On January 9, 1936, John Gilbert died, apparently of a heart attack. Marlene never forgave herself for not being there when it happened. She told Cooper, "The nurse who was with Jack gave him an injection to help him sleep. He choked to death on his own tongue. Why didn't she stay with him?"

A pall fell over Hollywood. Gilbert was one of the victims of that town's fast living. Everyone who had been touched by his life was grief-stricken. If it hadn't been for Gilbert the twenties might not have seen a romantic replacement for Valentino, or a $5 million gross at the box office for *The Big Parade,* or the magic that he and Garbo provided in *Flesh and the Devil.*

Gary went to the funeral with Marlene, who collapsed while walking down the aisle. Cooper picked her up and carried her to their seats. During the service she wept uncontrollably while Gary held her in his arms. Some attribute Gilbert's fall from the silver screen to his catastrophic performance in the talky *His Glorious Night,* where his high-pitched voice shrieked, "I love you. I love you. I love you." Some say L. B. Mayer tampered with the sound to destroy Gilbert because he was one of the few M-G-M stars who stood up to him. Others say it was Garbo's standing him up at the altar. But of course there was his drinking out of loneliness for Dietrich. Why did she desert him at the eleventh hour for Cooper? Gilbert couldn't understand it. How could she punish him for a little enthusiasm toward Garbo?

"Who in Hollywood could play honest, humble 'corn tassel poet' Mr. Deeds?" Frank Capra exclaimed. "Only one actor, Gary Cooper. Every line in his face spells honesty. So innate is his integrity he could be cast in phony parts, but never look phony himself."

Frank Capra, the brilliant director who called the then-unknown Barbara Stanwyck a "porcupine" when she walked into his office, gave her a chance anyway, and taught her the tricks of the movie trade in *Ladies of Leisure* (1930). Frank Capra couldn't convince any studio to make *It Happened One Night* until M-G-M decided to punish Clark Gable by lending him to Columbia Pictures for the expected flop with Claudette Colbert that won five Academy Awards.

For his success with Gable and Colbert, Capra was given top billing above the title *Mr. Deeds Goes to Town.* He fought the studio successfully to get Jean Arthur for the part of the newspaper woman who takes advantage of the innocent Mr. Deeds.

Cooper had never met an actor who was more jittery than he was until he met his leading lady in *Mr. Deeds.* But on screen Jean was a charm. Capra described her as "a cockroach who turned into a butterfly" when she stepped before the camera. After the cameras stopped, though, she would run to her dressing room to throw up. When called for another take, Miss Arthur wandered aimlessly out to the set, muttering and complaining until "Lights! Action!" was called. She worked well with Cooper, who walked through his part of Longfellow Deeds. Cooper's lines were unimportant. As Capra explained, "He had body instinct. Cooper was a very physical actor. He did wonderful things with that long body. He was actually very sparing of gestures but they were all sharp, definite. I don't think it was practiced. It was just natural. All of the best of Gary Cooper was natural."

Capra won an Oscar for Best Director for the film. *Mr. Deeds* was nominated for Best Picture but lost to *The Great Ziegfeld.* Cooper got his first nomination for Best Actor, but Paul Muni won for *The Story of Louis Pasteur.* Of his acting, *The Philadelphia Evening Public Ledger* wrote, ". . . Gary Cooper turns another corner in a career which has slowly developed him from a wooden-faced hero of horse-operas into a sensitive player with a reticent, but wholly American wit."

Capra explained, "There were little things we did to make Cooper a clumsy lover in *Mr. Deeds.* In one scene he read Jean one of his love poems. I knew I was playing with fire. Maybe the audience would laugh, so I had Gary run away and fall over a garbage can."

Lines such as "Nice day . . . er, nice night, uh, wasn't it, isn't it?" was Mr. Deeds, all right. It was also typical Cooper. Finally in 1936 he was voted one of the Top Ten film personalities.

The best years of Hollywood's Golden Era were from 1935 to 1940. Movie stars such as Gary Cooper became legends. So did the likes of Joan Crawford, Clark Gable, Loretta Young, Spencer Tracy, James Cagney, Katharine Hepburn, Humphrey Bogart, Myrna Loy, Henry Fonda, Bette Davis, Robert Taylor, Merle Oberon, Fred Astaire, Barbara Stanwyck, Bob Hope, Ginger Rogers, Cary Grant, Jean Harlow, Jimmy Stewart, Carole Lombard, Fred MacMurray, and Claudette Colbert. These were the best years of their lives.

There has never been a five-year period when so many stars sparkled with such grace and romance and nearly perfect harmony. Movie houses were gold mines. Nightclubs thrived, too, when booze was legalized. Between 1935 and 1940 Hollywood produced 750 movies a year on the average, and they were all pretty good. There was scandal, however.

Jean Harlow's sudden death, reportedly of uremic poisoning, in 1937 was one. Thelma Todd's death was another.

Harlow was only twenty-six years old when she died. The scandal involved her impotent husband's suicide in 1932. Paul Bern had beaten her with a cane on their wedding night. She suffered bruises to her kidneys but did nothing about it. Bern put a gun to his head and left a note apologizing to Jean. Her mother, a dogmatic Christian Scientist, allowed Jean to die without proper medical care.

Thelma Todd was found dead in her garaged car. The thirty-year-old "Ice Cream Blonde" died of carbon monoxide poisoning. Was it suicide or murder or accidental death? We'll never know. The investigation wasn't pursued, and those who offered to talk fell suddenly silent.

There were the usual marriages and divorces, abortions, affairs, orgies—gay and straight—all covered up by the studios, which had complete control over the fan magazines and gossip columnists. There was always an epidemic of the clap. If Clara Bow had "it," the male population of Hollywood did, too. Tallulah Bankhead got it from a "very famous movie actor." The studios had their own cathouses and asked their male stars to frequent them rather than take chances elsewhere. The prostitutes were beautiful, young rejected starlets, a friend of Gable said. They were examined regularly by studio doctors. Clark went there, as did Robert Taylor and others. It was a safe outlet for the male stars because they didn't have to worry about disease, gossip, or eloping while on a binge. And there was another problem for which they got help—impotency. Those gals were well trained and helped some troubled actors get through bad times.

Hollywood had learned its lesson in the Roaring Twenties. Alert publicity men from all of the studios worked day and night to rescue contract players from press coverage of auto accidents, brawls, affairs, hangovers, botched abortions, and bigamy.

Marlene Dietrich's tuxedos became a fad, and women wore slacks or satin evening pajamas on the screen and to parties in the early thirties.

In 1935, Mary Astor's husband sued for divorce when he found a description of her hot affair with playwright George S. Kaufman in her diary, where she wrote: "It was wonderful to fuck the sweet afternoon away." Mary lost custody of her daughter, but fought back and regained both her child and her pride. Moviegoers liked Miss Astor. If the rest of her diary had been revealed, many scandals might have erupted. "I jotted guarded secrets of my friends, too," she said.

That same year Loretta Young adopted a baby girl supposedly fathered by Clark Gable, with whom she had had an affair while they filmed *The Call of the Wild.* Will Rogers was killed in a plane crash, and Joan Crawford married Franchot Tone.

In 1936 Charlie Chaplin married Paulette Goddard without a license, and Joan Blondell married Dick Powell.

In 1937, twenty-four-year-old Hedy Lamarr arrived in Hollywood and Clara Bow opened the "It" Café on the corner of Hollywood and Vine. Alice Faye married Tony Martin, Jeanette MacDonald married Gene Raymond, Betty Grable married Jackie Coogan, Mary Pickford married Buddy Rogers, and Marion Davies retired from films.

In 1938, Lupe Velez divorced Johnny Weissmuller, whom she referred to as a "furniture-breaking caveman."

In 1939, Douglas Fairbanks, Sr., died of a heart attack. Ten years later, Lady Sylvia Ashley, Fairbanks's widow, married Clark Gable (who, in the meantime, had wedded Lombard while he was filming *Gone With the Wind*). Joan Crawford divorced Franchot Tone, Barbara Stanwyck married Robert Taylor, Tyrone Power married Annabella, and Joan Fontaine married Brian Aherne.

The year 1939 was the zenith of motion picture excellence: *Dark Victory, Goodbye, Mr. Chips, Mr. Smith Goes to Washington, Ninotchka, Of Mice and Men, Stagecoach, The Wizard of Oz, Wuthering Heights, Intermezzo, Gunga Din, Stanley and Livingstone, Golden Boy, The Roaring Twenties, Alexander Graham Bell,* and *The Hunchback of Notre Dame.* These were the greatest of the great. *Gone With the Wind* won ten Academy Awards.

In 1940, Vivien Leigh married Laurence Olivier, Ronald Reagan married Jane Wyman, Lana Turner married Artie Shaw, and sixty-year-old Tom Mix was killed in an automobile accident.

Joan Crawford remarked of that period: "In the late thirties, we had it made. The Depression was over and war was only a rumor. We had mastered sound and were ready for technicolor. Good scripts were plentiful. The studios renewed our contracts with big bucks and moviegoers couldn't get enough."

Mere money didn't mean everything to everybody, however. The Los Angeles Country Club barred actors. Randolph Scott, married to du Pont heiress Mariana du Pont Somerville, applied for membership and was informed of the policy. "If you've seen any of my pictures," Scott said, "you'd realize I'm not an actor." His application was promptly accepted.

The great stars of the silver screen had one thing in common other than a romance with the camera: They had a sense of humor. Director George Cukor said shortly before his death, "Talking and writing about Hollywood in the golden years will never cease. There were tragedies and tears and disappointments. They shouldn't be forgotten, but the silver on the screen consisted of pure wit that the public never saw. I tell everyone who interviews me that the only way to approach the truth about Hollywood is with a sense of humor."

When Marion Davies and William Randolph Hearst gave up their lavish entertaining for small dinner parties, one Hollywood gag went, "Marion Davies closes Beach House. Thousands homeless."

Gary Cooper had his own brand of humor. "When they say I'm just being me, they don't know how hard it is to act to be a guy like me." He was one of the few who took his innocent wit seriously. David Niven, who wrote about Hollywood with savoir faire, mentioned Cooper's intensity. Niven once asked him, "You have such great concentration. How do you do it?"

"Con . . . cen . . . tra . . . tion?" Gary asked slowly, as if trying to figure out what the word meant. "Bullshit! I'm just tryin' to remember what the hell I have to say next."

After a cameo appearance in the movie *Hollywood Boulevard,* Cooper appeared in *The General Died at Dawn* with Madeleine Carroll. He was helplessly attracted to her. Many photographers considered the British blonde with porcelain skin to be the most beautiful woman in the world. Some old-timers insist Miss Carroll was one of Cooper's women. No big affair, they admit, but Cooper and Carroll couldn't keep their eyes off each other. Studs was a bedroom legend—a temptation. The fact that he was married made him more safe to leading ladies, anxious to hang on to the security of their husbands or wealthy boyfriends. Carroll and Cooper would be teamed again in the company of Paulette Goddard, an avid admirer of Studs. According to Richard Arlen, Gary had a crush on her for a long time.

In *The General Died at Dawn,* actor Akim Tamiroff, who was nominated for an Academy Award for his performance, made up his mind not to let Cooper steal any scenes from him. Tamiroff wore himself out. "I did everything," he said, "but when I saw the film, even *my* eyes focused on him."

Director Howard Hawks commented, "It didn't matter how much action was going on in a Cooper picture because he kept us guessing. When's he going to say something? When's he going to move? It was the same thing at parties. He was the center of attention because he didn't want it that way. It wasn't the clothes because the most expensive suit usually looked rumpled except when he wore a tux. Cooper and Gable were reactors, but each had his own style. Gable gave the impression he was about to pounce and Cooper gave no impression whatsoever."

Whether Gary was filming a movie or walking into a swank restaurant, his suits rarely looked pressed. The double-breasted jackets filled out his thin frame but hung from the lapels as if he'd just grabbed them off a store rack. That was part of his charm, of course. When he was filming, Cooper often took naps on the grass, on the floor, or on a soft bale of hay, so that when he was called to do a scene he appeared disheveled. Directors were exasperated. Time was called while his clothes were cleaned and pressed, but he managed to forget again and again. Why? "When I'm not thinkin', I'm sleepin'," he said.

Gary and Rocky were hardly interesting news, whereas Gable and Lombard were grabbing Hollywood headlines. The Coopers vacationed in Bermuda, Sun Valley, and New York. They were members of the Beverly Hills Tennis Club. But who wasn't? Their home was robbed twice. No one seemed to care about Rocky's jewelry.

Even Coop's "official" visits to Montana were dull publicity. There was the usual "Welcome Home" ceremony. He was honored in Helena, and reunited with old friends. When they knew he was coming, a parade down Main Street was planned. He was not too thrilled but went along with it. Old friends Jim Galen and Jim Calloway had returned home for the festivities. Harvey Markham was another old pal who was there to greet Cooper. (The Helena crowd still called him Frank.) Alice and Charles joined Gary and Rocky at the Bar-Nine for a look around.

This kind of publicity was often arranged by the studio. According to actor Robert Taylor, it was an overbearing experience. "You don't want to go back home like a big shot," Taylor said, recalling his return visit to Beatrice, Nebraska. "I felt like a fool shaking hands with the soda jerk and some of my old schoolteachers. What I remember is the movie marquee. One of my pictures was playing and they put my real name up there—Spangler Arlington Brugh. It's an experience one prefers to forget. . . . And what do you do when an old friend asks for an autograph?"

While Cooper kept a low profile out of town, fan magazines thrived on his characteristic candor. "I think movie actin' is a silly business for a man. It takes less trainin' and less brains than any other business I can think of," he told one reporter. Paramount executives gritted their teeth.

Clark Gable's first major interview was just as bad. Soon after he became a star he said, "It isn't looks and it isn't experience. It isn't ability because everyone knows there are stars who can't act worth a damn. The public makes the stars, but they don't know what they want. You can't explain a damn thing in this business. It's a chain of accidents. When you get to Hollywood, you find yourself in lots of chains of accidents. If it turns out all right, you're a star. If you're enough of a gambler or a jackass to figure everything will turn out just fine, move to Hollywood. You want to be a movie star? Maybe you'd like it and maybe you wouldn't like it. You might not be happy at all."

That was Gable's last interview. M-G-M told him to keep his mouth shut unless he had to adjust his false teeth. The Hollywood crowd often compared Cooper to Gable because they never said much, but when they did they pulled no punches. In truth, both men were embarrassed about being actors. Gary was more natural and uncomplicated than Gable—less conniving and ambitious. He never analyzed his roles and scoffed at method acting. His instinct was far superior to his basic intelligence.

Randolph Scott said Cooper was uneasy with words. "One day I dropped by to see his new car and I asked him to take me for a drive. We must have been on the road for over an hour without saying one word. As we were rounding the last turn for home, Coop saw a bird flying overhead. He raised his arm and pointed a finger and said, 'Bang!' That was the extent of our conversation."

Isabel T., who worked as a script girl at Paramount Studios, knew Gary Cooper fairly well. "I wasn't quite twenty when I met him," Isabel said. "Gary had been a lot of fun before the Clara Bow trial. He was never much of a talker, but he wasn't as self-conscious. Some people think he got conceited when he became a big star, but actually he was scared to death and that's why he was so quiet. I knew him before and after, as they say. We used to take long walks around sunset and make love behind some bushes or on an abandoned movie set. How did it happen the first time? I like to think we were together at the right time and place, but looking back he had a line. We reminisced about love scenes. He put his arm around me and we pretended to be Valentino and Agnes Ayres in *The Sheik*. Gary was very romantic, very sweet. I heard he used to hang around some of the studios and take out secretaries, so he had entrée to the producers, and it worked with Sam Goldwyn. Maybe I was convenient after he signed with Paramount, but Gary could have had any girl he wanted, even they and I knew that. The word got around what a good lover he was . . . so warm and kind. And satisfying. I was only nineteen, but overheard Mae West and Clara Bow talking to their hairdressers about the men in their lives. Even a script girl learns fast in Hollywood.

"I saw Gary on and off for almost five years. Sometimes our meetings were planned and sometimes it just happened. If the opportunity presented itself, he never passed it up. It's a bit corny to say he made me, and from what I hear, the others feel as if we were the only women in the world. My two husbands never made love to me that way . . . though I loved dearly and totally. I think Gary appreciated women sincerely. He was a complete lover and he told me in a few brief words that he didn't like quickies. It was an insult, he thought. He admitted indulging and hating himself. For days he lived with guilt. Back then we didn't analyze everything. We didn't go to psychiatrists or sex therapists.

"When Gary was suffering through the Clara Bow scandal, he never mentioned it to me. He was haggard and in a sweat because I think he loved Clara and Lupe, too. During this time, we took our long walks, but did not always make love. We just strolled in silence."

Isabel did not discuss Cooper's lovemaking in detail. She claims he was very well constructed, ". . . but not a bull." The romantic Cooper was the real Cooper.

"He had magnificent hands," Isabel recalled. "His fingers were long and quite beautiful. He used them firmly and gently. I felt shrouded in his arms. I loved Gary, but I wasn't in love and I think that was the way other girls felt about him.

"There were many stories about Gary and Dietrich, Gary and Madeleine, Gary and Tallulah, Gary and Anna Sten—all from reliable sources. So many women, but they weren't all famous. Many were secretaries and script girls like me . . . hairdressers, wardrobe girls, and extras. I don't doubt he had a man occasionally. They wouldn't let him alone, you know."

What did Isabel think of Rocky?

"I didn't mingle in their circle, of course," she replied, "but I think she was right for him. He needed roots. He needed a mother, too. Most men do. I admit the studio crowd didn't warm up to Rocky, but she knew the man she married, believe me. The term used around Hollywood was, 'She had him on a long leash.' I saw her once or twice and she was extremely beautiful. I thought she resembled Mary Astor. Rocky was friendly in a distant fashion. She was responsible for much of the respect Gary got through the years even though he was capable of doing that himself."

In an article in *Photoplay* about Hollywood society versus Fifth Avenue society, Cooper was cited as having plowed through the dowager circle before "picking himself a peach, Veronica Balfe." According to the writer, bluebloods were taken off the lists of many socialite hostesses for playing around in Hollywood. Alfred Gwynne Vanderbilt wasn't invited to the usual rounds of gala parties because he was interested in Hollywood's Ginger Rogers. Winthrop Rockefeller was given the cold shoulder, too, for getting involved with the cellophane-wrapped and celluloid-displayed "Four Hundred of Picturedom." Lord Mountbatten was said to have been amazed that guests at Pickfair actually knew what fork to use! In Hollywood partygoers stole bottles of liquor before leaving by the back door. This would not happen on Fifth Avenue. At charity benefits in Tinseltown, the money is collected right away. New York's elite would never think of tapping anyone on the shoulder. The article concludes with: "Every day in every way the stars get swankier and swankier—but their wining and dining is to the manner bought, not born."

A young Gary Cooper in *The Virginian* (1929), the film that made him a star with ''When you call me that . . . smile!''

Above: Clara Bow with ''Studs'' in *Children of Divorce* (1927). Despite their passionate affair, Cooper froze during the filming of their love scenes.

Left: Gary and Evelyn Brent in *Beau Sabreur* (1928). She refused to marry him.

Below: ''Paramount's Glorious Lovers,'' Cooper and Fay Wray, in *Legion of the Condemned* (1928). The team never did click on the screen.

Lupe Velez with Gary in *Wolf Song* (1929). This was the beginning of their stormy love affair.

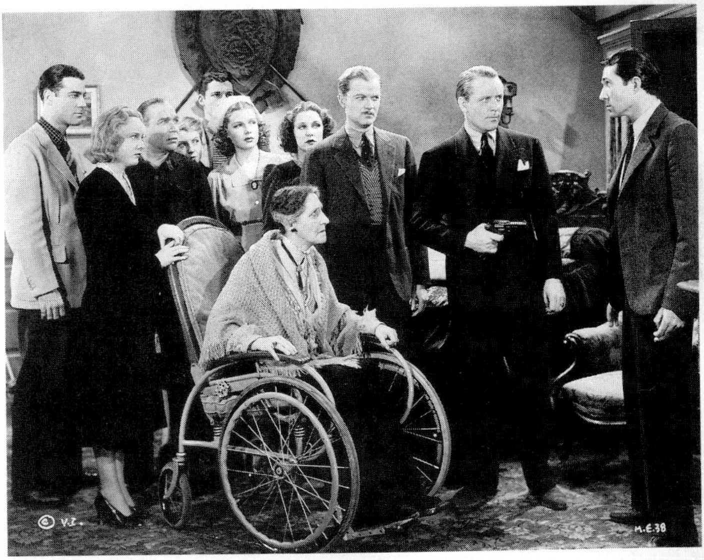

A rare photo of Anderson Lawler (the chap third from right), Coop's close friend and ''roommate,'' from a scene in *Mystery House* (1938).

Gary and the Countess di Frasso on the set of *The Texan* (1930), before their well-publicized European fling.

Above: Tallulah Bankhead and Gary in *The Devil and the Deep* (1932). Tallu said, "I'm going to Hollywood to get laid by Gary Cooper."

Right: Coop and Carole Lombard in *I Take This Woman* (1931). Clark Gable was jealous of Carole's affair with Gary.

Below: Marlene Dietrich and Gary in a scene from *Morocco* (1930). Electricity sparked between them off the set, but marriage was never considered.

Cooper in his prime (1938).

Gary and Rocky out on the town.

Gary and the two most important women in his life, Rocky and Maria.

A tender pose from *The Fountainhead*. Pat said, ''I think his hands are what I remember most.''

Pat Neal and Gary in the famous seduction scene in *The Fountainhead* (1949). They would relive their passion after the cameras stopped.

Gary with the bewitching Merle Oberon in *The Cowboy and the Lady* (1938). Their screen chemistry lasted after hours.

With Grace Kelly in the Oscar-winning *High Noon* (1957). Coop was the first of many men she would conquer.

Gary and costar Ingrid Bergman in *Saratoga Trunk* (1943). ''We were in love,'' said Gary, ''but after the picture was finished I couldn't get her on the phone.''

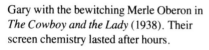

A foreign accent could stand for nobility in America, however. Charles Boyer, David Niven, Maurice Chevalier, Ronald Colman, Cary Grant, and Laurence Olivier were welcome anywhere. Their continental sophistication made one wonder whether the American Revolution was worth it. Hedy Lamarr, Greer Garson, Marlene Dietrich, and Greta Garbo had lyrical voices with foreign tones and were welcome everywhere in New York society.

But the American public paid to see their own kind. They wanted to see Joan Crawford as the shop girl, Cooper as their honest hero, Gable as the tough-guy lover, and Carole Lombard as the crazy girl next door. Regardless of their roles, they came from lower- and middle-class America and were proud of it.

Tobacco heiress Doris Duke and Woolworth's Barbara Hutton had so much money they could mingle in Hollywood's smart set and ignore Fifth Avenue. Cole Porter didn't have to answer to anyone, either. Then there was the Mafia. Bugsy Siegel was entrenched with Dorothy di Frasso in Los Angeles, and became sought-after by the crème de la crème thanks to his old friend George Raft. Siegel made half a million dollars a year shaking down studio moguls. Maybe he wasn't allowed at Pickfair, but most of the big stars mingled with him. Bugsy was a handsome blue-eyed stud who easily attracted beautiful women to his mansion in Beverly Hills. He was a smart man and a busy one—so busy, in fact, that he wasn't even aware the Mafia had a contract out on his friend Gary Cooper. It was George Raft who heard about it and very quietly intervened.

"One of the boys was in love with a young starlet," Raft told a confidant years later. "She blabbed that she was in love with Coop. They were having a casual affair and she took it to heart. Word got around and the guy who was sponsoring her put the contract out. It was no joke. As soon as I found out, I went to her apartment, packed her things, and got her out of town—fast. I don't think Coop missed her. She was just a kid who belonged to one of the boys, but she almost cost Coop his life."

Cecil B. De Mille produced and directed Gary Cooper as Wild Bill Hickok in *The Plainsman,* with Jean Arthur as Calamity Jane. Mexican-born Anthony Quinn made his film debut as a Cheyenne Indian. De Mille thought Quinn was really an Indian, and said while directing one scene, "Oh, just sing one of your old songs. It doesn't matter." Quinn grunted out words that were mumbo jumbo and got away with it. He would, ironically, become De Mille's son-in-law.

The Plainsman was a fine film and Gary got good reviews. "By the simple expedient of being himself and not acting at all, Gary Cooper remains winning and effective," *The New York-American* critic wrote.

If his reviews sounded repetitious and flat, Cooper's star status was anything but. His new contract with Paramount was scheduled to be renegotiated. Sam Goldwyn took advantage of the opportunity to steal Gary away from Paramount. "Six pictures in six years," Sam offered, "and I'll pay $150,000 each, with bonus clauses."

"That's all?" Cooper muttered, clearing his throat.

"That depends if you're interested."

"I am."

"In that case, I might go higher."

Samuel Goldwyn Productions immediately announced that Cooper had signed with them exclusively. It was not true. Paramount sued both parties. It worked out best for Gary in the end because Paramount fought with dollars to keep him under contract. The court found no reason why Cooper could not work for Goldwyn also. Gary could have his cake and eat it, too. His home was Paramount, but he never forgot Sam's giving him his first break in *The Winning of Barbara Worth*.

Goldwyn was truly a legendary character. His wit and malapropisms are famous. Among the best known ones are:

- I can answer you in two words: Im Possible!
- Anyone who goes to a psychiatrist needs to have his head examined.
- Never let that bastard back in my office—unless we need him.
- Throw everything out but make a copy of everything.
- Tell me, how did you love that picture?
- Include me out!
- About L. B. Mayer: The reason so many people showed up at his funeral was because they wanted to make sure he was dead.

He was born Sam Goldfish in 1882 in Warsaw, Poland. In 1895, he arrived in America without money or friends and worked as a glove maker, attended night school, and became a traveling glove salesman. He married Blanche Lasky, a vaudeville performer. In 1912 he convinced her brother, Jesse, to go into partnership with him in the film business. Cecil B. De Mille made it a threesome. In 1916, Sam made up his mind to go on his own. He changed his name to Goldwyn and produced several worthy films, but could not turn down L. B. Mayer's takeover bid in 1924. This was the birth of Metro-Goldwyn-Mayer, but Sam couldn't work with Mayer so he bowed out and formed Samuel Goldwyn Productions. This time he succeeded.

He continued to frustrate as well as to amuse his associates. During business negotiations he once quipped, "A verbal contract isn't worth the paper it's written on!"

When told about a newborn baby being named William, Goldwyn shouted, "Why would you name him Bill? Every Tom, Dick, and Harry is named Bill."

And so it was on the set. During one of Cooper's love scenes, Goldwyn threatened, "If this isn't the greatest, the whole picture is going to go right up out of the sewer." It was one of the few times Cooper laughed out loud. Gary also got a kick out of Goldwyn's mispronouncing names such as Joel "McCrail" (McCrea) and "Withering" Heights. Time and time again Sam was corrected, but he didn't care. Why should he worry about such nonsense when his creative genius was for making films such as: *Stella Dallas, Wuthering Heights, The Little Foxes, Ball of Fire,* and *The Best Years of Our Lives.*

Cooper's only film in 1937 was *Souls at Sea*. Paramount hoped to rival M-G-M's *Mutiny on the Bounty,* but it was a feeble attempt. George Raft was the studio's choice for Gary's tough seaman friend. Joel McCrea's wife, Frances Dee, was chosen to be Cooper's love interest. Raft said his hair was curled for the role and he wore one ring in his ear. "I didn't mind," he exclaimed, "because it was an adventure film about the slavery days. But Gary and I had a scene where we're drinking rum and he says, 'You know I love you.' Then I say, 'I know, I love you, too.' Coop shook his head and said, 'If you put that in the picture people are gonna think we're a couple of queers.' But they left it in."

Carole Lombard was sitting in a corner on the set while director Henry Hathaway was debating about changing the dialogue. She laughed out loud and motioned to an electrician. "I love this kinda shit," she cracked. "Raft's a helluva rooster with dames and Studs is going to be a father! Not that it makes any difference, but they're cackling like a couple of hens!"

7

DEEDS TO DOE

Both Gary Cooper and director Frank Capra paced back and forth in the maternity halls of the Good Samaritan Hospital, each waiting for the birth of his child. It was September 14, 1937. Lulu Capra, Frank's third child, was born first. "Like idiots," he said, "Gary and I gitchy-cooed at my beautiful daughter through the window. When I couldn't find him, there he was chain-smoking on the fire escape. I stayed with him and the next day Rocky gave birth to Maria and again we stood at the window and gitchy-cooed like two dazed dopes. Our daughters grew up as close friends and kept in touch. They were almost like twins."

Gary's relationship with his daughter, Maria, was very close and special. He didn't spoil her; Rocky wouldn't allow it. And even if she had, Gary would not have substituted gifts and money for love and affection.

Another actor might have considered the role of Rhett Butler in *Gone With the Wind* a plum. David Selznick, Mayer's son-in-law, had bought the screen rights to Margaret Mitchell's best-seller for $50,000, but he needed a major studio to distribute it. Gable was the logical choice for Rhett, but not the only actor who was qualified for the role. Mayer asked $150,000 to lend Gable, and Warner Brothers offered Errol Flynn for only $50,000. No records are available on how much money Paramount wanted for Gary Cooper because there were only verbal negotiations with Selznick. He wanted Gary to think it over, but didn't get an answer until it was too late.

Selznick did not get along with Mayer and tried to avoid releasing the epic through M-G-M. Metro wanted half the profits from *Gone With the Wind.* Publicity brewed about the forthcoming motion picture for more than two years before shooting started. Moviegoers wanted Gable and confirmed their choice in writing.

Selznick said, "The public will accept a Flynn or Cooper because they are, inevitably, anxious to see *Gone With the Wind.*" Gable didn't care one way or the other. He did not look forward to being tied down to one film for a whole year and he wasn't fond of Selznick, who went ahead with the writing of the script and production details before casting his leading players.

Cooper, in the meantime, inwardly gloated over the fact he was Gable's main contender for the part of Rhett Butler. Louella Parsons said there was more politicking in Hollywood than in Washington. "Most likely Gable will be the chosen one," she speculated, "but there isn't an actress in town who doesn't want to play Scarlett. Suddenly all the ladies have a southern accent!"

Joan Crawford tried to convince her lover Gable to demand that she play opposite him. "I can't do that," he replied, "because Carole wants to be Scarlett and I have no intention of doing the picture without her."

Lombard, who was not about to lose her man to any actress for a whole year, had her own plans with Cooper as the bait. "Tell Selznick you'll play Rhett and then cancel out," she told him.

"Why?" Gary responded.

"So I can play Scarlett."

"But I may not get to play Rhett," he said.

"Christ, you've got a thick head! Paramount hasn't got anyone to play Scarlett. I'm a shoo-in. When you back out, Selznick will have no other choice but to sign Clark."

Cooper scratched his head.

Carole smiled sweetly. "All you have to say is 'Yup' and 'Nope.' Can't you do that for me?"

"Nope."

"You've got half of it right."

"Yup."

"You owe me."

"For what?"

"Your fuckin' career."

"Huh?"

"Who the hell carried you through *I Take This Woman?* Christ, that Clara Bow mess almost killed you, Studs. You looked as if you were the one who took on the UCLA football team instead of Clara. But I got you through it, didn't I?"

"Guess so. Hey, remember our first date, Carole. You were just a kid."

"And you were cheating on Evelyn Brent."

"She kinda turned me down."

"Poor lamb. But you did all right. Let's face it. You fucked your way into Clara's movies."

"Clark didn't do so bad with Jane Cowl and Pauline Frederick on the stage," he said with a smirk.

"They took his pants off!"

"Not the way I hear tell."

"You've been jealous of Clark for a long time and I think you're playing hard to get . . . trying to make Selznick squirm and Clark wait it out."

"You tryin' to rile me?"

"How could I do that?" she said, laughing. "You're not even breathing."

"Do you really want the part of Scarlett that bad?" he asked.

"Yes, because I can do it better than anyone else. And I don't trust Clark with Paulette Goddard or Crawford or any other dame for twelve months. C'mon, Studs, tell Selznick you'll play Rhett. He doesn't want to share *Gone With the Wind* with Mayer. He'd love to release the film right here at Paramount. Clark isn't anxious to play Rhett, but he's in demand."

"M-G-M publicity."

"Bullshit."

Cooper frowned. "One and the same."

"There you go again! You hate Clark. If it isn't bigger cars, it's a better gun collection. What is it with you two guys, anyway?"

"Dunno. Ask him."

"I'll do that, because if I talk to you much longer, I'm gonna need oxygen."

"You got me all mixed up." Cooper scowled. "What do you want me to do?"

Carole sat on his lap, put her arms around his neck, and looked him squarely in the eyes, noses almost touching. "I'm giving you a chance to give Clark some competition. Think of the free publicity you'll get. Cooper agrees to play Rhett. Cooper turns down Rhett. Selznick stuck with Gable. You'll be a hero."

"And you'll be Scarlett. She's brunette, you know."

"Who says she can't be a blonde?"

"Margaret Mitchell."

"Since when does a movie follow the book?"

"I gotta go home now," he said, easing her off his lap.

"I gotta go home now," she mimicked.

"Carole, I'd like to help, but I have my reputation to think about."

"Since when?" she asked.

"I might do *Gone With the Wind* even though I think it's gonna be the biggest flop in Hollywood history."

"How would *you* know?" she yelled. "You've never read a book in your goddamned life!"

"That's another thing Clark and I have in common," Cooper said.

The rest is history, of course. Mayer lent Gable to his son-in-law, and Vivien Leigh sailed from England just in time. Carole had no reason to fret because off the set Gable and Leigh did not get along. Vivien said Clark had bad breath and wasn't too bright. He, in turn, resented an English girl getting a plum role that should have been given to an American like Carole Lombard. Several times he almost quit. Instead he had director George Cukor fired for favoring Vivien (the real reason was the Haines affair). Victor Fleming took over, but when Miss Leigh demanded he follow Margaret Mitchell's adaptation, Fleming walked out, telling Vivien, "You can stick this script up your royal British ass!" He was replaced by Sam Wood.

Cooper was relieved not to be involved. Besides, he later admitted, "I think the part of Rhett Butler was too dashing for me. When I saw Gable in the film, I knew I was right."

David O. Selznick said repeatedly that the man who should have played Captain Butler was dead—John Gilbert.

Cooper was anxious to star in the 1938 film *Lost Horizon,* but Frank Capra didn't think he fit the role of the Englishman who discovers Shangri-la. Somehow the rumor got started that Gary was perfect for the lead and that no one else was in contention. Several newspapers had announced that he'd star in the film, but Capra signed Ronald Colman. "Cooper doesn't have the intellectual capacity for the part," Capra stated frankly. "He would agree with Shangri-la, but to *lead* it was far beyond his intellectual attainments." Capra admired Cooper for his unique abilities and meant no harm. Gary was stunned nonetheless.

Sam Goldwyn came to the rescue with an offer of the lead in *The Adventures of Marco Polo.* Cooper, on the rebound from *Lost Horizon,* agreed. During the filming he was caught in another "Anna Sten-type campaign" sponsored by Goldwyn. This time the girl was "Norwegian" actress Sigrid Gurie. During production it was revealed that she was really from Brooklyn! Miss Gurie was a beauty, and though her career was short-lived, she was one of Cooper's most ravishing leading ladies. But the film was a flop. Goldwyn called it the worst picture he'd ever made. Cooper was in a daze. "We had three different directors," he said, "and they all had a different interpretation of Marco Polo. Halfway through I wasn't sure, myself." The reviews were uniformly negative. Today, however, it is a beloved classic on television. Cooper's charming and gentle Marco Polo matches the softness of Sigrid Gurie's Oriental grace.

If Cooper said little to the press about his screen roles, he was proud enough to talk with them about his daughter, Maria. "Before she was born it seemed hard to believe that somebody was coming along, walking right into the picture where there hadn't been anybody before." He was very concerned that she have a normal childhood. "Hollywood's full of spoiled brats," he said. Terrified that she might be kidnapped, Cooper did not allow any pictures of his daughter to be published. But when Maria was about five years old she was surreptitiously photographed and her picture ran in the newspapers. Gary was livid and took extra precautions to make sure it would not happen again. His obsession with Maria would last a lifetime. Bing Crosby remarked, "I told Gary if he had four kids like I do, he might be more reasonable. But he says one girl is worth four boys."

Only a few select friends were invited to the Cooper's home. Gary's cronies weren't welcome; if they picked him up for a game of golf or a hunting excursion, they would wait for him in the car. If he was going on location to film a movie the arrangements were the same. No one came to the front door.

Elsa Maxwell said, "If Gary is a national hero to his fans, he's just a father and husband at home. Rocky's the boss. He says he's glad to be rescued from the life of a playboy, but I wonder if any man can change so drastically. He built a separate building in back of the house that he refers to as his 'playroom.' This is where he keeps his safari treasures, plays billiards, and paints. Gary spends most of his time there because he's more comfortable."

The Countess di Frasso, meanwhile, had purchased a large Beverly Hills estate. On occasion her swimming, tennis, or luncheon parties would last for days on end. And she was a regular at the Friday night prizefights held in the Hollywood Legion Arena, where she out-screamed her rival, Lupe Velez. Spectators expected more blood outside the ring if a Mexican was fighting an Italian. The two women tangled verbally in both languages, neither knowing what the other was spouting. One night Dorothy took home one of the handsome boxers, but she threw him out on the night he was knocked out. No one laughed louder than Lupe.

Jean Harlow died, leaving an estate of only $28,000. Her fiancé, William Powell, paid for her funeral and crypt. That year the great John Barrymore declared bankruptcy, another reminder to a new generation of movie stars that no one was invulnerable.

John Wayne, who had been making Westerns since 1928 and had envied Cooper's success, finally made the grade in John Ford's *Stagecoach* in 1939. Originally Cooper was thought to be the only actor who could do justice to the part of the Ringo Kid, but John Ford stubbornly held fast to the new cowboy. Not only did *Stagecoach* make Wayne famous, the film increased the public's appetite for Westerns. Over the years Wayne and Cooper would not have much of a chance to be pals, but were quite friendly when their paths crossed.

If Clara Bow's *It* and *Children of Divorce* made Gary look foolish, *Bluebeard's Eighth Wife* made him appear almost as bad. Not only was he miscast but he was given second billing to his leading lady, Claudette Colbert. Cooper, an unlikely choice to play a suave millionaire, was not comfortable doing comedy. And he was apprehensive about working with a pro like Miss Colbert. David Niven, who was also in *Bluebeard,* said that he was terrified of Gary Cooper *and* Claudette Colbert. "I was the novice," he commented, "but Claudette coached me, patted my hand, and kept repeating, 'Everything's going to be just fine. Everything's going to be all right.' Coop kept to himself pretty much because he liked to sleep. Trouble was, he sprawled out on a pile of straw wearing an expensive suit. Our director said, 'He still thinks he's a cowhand! He's supposed to be a business tycoon on holiday in Cannes, France. Stop him from going to sleep in his elegant wardrobe every time he finishes a scene!' Coop didn't seem to care. He put on a pair of pajamas and said nothing. To me he was just a country boy, but very handsome. I could see why women fell head over heels for him. He was charming and natural, and he didn't miss a trick. When he looked at a girl, she was scanned like a spotlight."

In its review of *Bluebeard's Eighth Wife, The New York Times* stated: "Although it's not a bad comedy by our current depressed standards, it has the dickens of a time trying to pass off Gary Cooper as a multimarrying millionaire. Put seven divorced wives behind Mr. Deeds, each with a $50,000-a-year settlement, and it becomes pretty hard to believe that he's just a small boy at heart—which is the principal charm of Paramount's gangling hero."

Cooper was eager to put *Bluebeard* behind him and begin work on Goldwyn's *The Cowboy and the Lady.* The rumors that M-G-M wanted him to play opposite Greta Garbo in *Ninotchka* were apparently founded. Cooper casually mentioned that he knew he wasn't right for the role. "After *Bluebeard,*" he said, "I couldn't take a chance on being miscast again." Anyway, doing a Greta Garbo movie didn't appeal to him. Cooper felt, and rightly so, that he had reached the stage when his films should belong to him.

As usual, Goldwyn was anxiously promoting another beautiful starlet, this time Merle Oberon. "She's absolutely exquisite," Sam told Gary. "I don't know why she hasn't caught on. She's a Tasmanian aristocrat who was educated in London and India. Alexander Korda discovered her in England."

"Who?" Cooper asked.

"A director-producer. A son of a bitch. Merle had an affair with producer Joe Schenck, too. He spent a fortune on her—jewels, furs, and vacations on the Riviera."

"I hear tell she's livin' with David Niven."

"Not anymore," Goldwyn said. "He's crazy about Virginia Bruce, but Merle wants him in *Cowboy and the Lady.* I'll give him a small part. You know, of course, that Merle is very close to the Countess di Fatso."

". . . Frasso."

"That's what I said."

"Sam, I met Merle at a New Year's Eve party two years ago. We're not strangers."

"If you were, you won't be after working with her. She's the most exotically beautiful woman I ever laid eyes on."

Merle Oberon had almost as many affairs as Cooper. Her studio biography was all false. She was not of aristocracy, but was born a half-caste in Bombay. Her real name was Queenie O'Brien. She began her career as a dance hostess in 1931 at the Café de Paris in London, where she caught Alexander Korda's attention. Korda constructed a fairy tale about her background, but the truth came out after her death in 1979. Her marriage to wealthy industrialist Bruno Pagliai made Merle an international hostess at her palace in Acapulco, Ghalal. She would come to have it all. In 1938, however, she was a newly rising star.

One of Cooper's friends said he could always tell when Gary was "on the make" with a leading lady. "It was obvious, but one had to know him well to notice. Gary's eyes gave him away. Miss Oberon was definitely his type. No one knew much about her, though she was a regular at Pickfair and every fashionable Hollywood scene. Society adored her before she married money. Yet she could have several affairs going on at a time. She was involved with Leslie Howard and David Niven at the same time. Then George Brent and Gable. Her approach to sex was very elegant, I understand . . . champagne and caviar, soft music, silk sheets, French lingerie, incense. It was a banquet of love with no strings attached."

Gary and Merle were enthralled by each other on and off the set. The sexual merry-go-round was, as David Niven described it, ". . . a series of lighthearted uncomplicated adulterous interludes cheerfully covered up by all those involved."

The Cowboy and the Lady was one of Cooper's favorite films, and Merle Oberon might have been one of the reasons. The critics liked it, too. *The Brooklyn Daily Eagle* wrote, "Gary Cooper, the long-legged Montana boy who was ill at ease as Marco Polo and as a modern Bluebeard earlier this year, got back into chaps and Stetson to play *The Cowboy and the Lady.* That gave all of us, including Samuel Goldwyn, something to be thankful for. Gary is natural again, and with the aid of Merle Oberon, he makes an enticing picture out of an old fable."

A year later, Miss Oberon achieved superstardom in Goldwyn's *Wuthering Heights.* She won the part over Vivien Leigh, who fought desperately for the role of Cathy opposite her real-life lover, Laurence Olivier.

Gary enjoyed the company of Fred MacMurray, who was then under contract to Paramount, too. Joel McCrea was another close friend. Their group grew larger when Barbara Stanwyck married Bob Taylor, and when Annabella married Tyrone Power. The Gables had their M-G-M clique and seldom went out for fancy get-togethers. At Pickfair, Buddy Rogers held court after he married Mary Pickford. Cooper rarely joined Oakie and Arlen at these gatherings, preferring to share the quiet life with Rocky. Gossip columnists, paid off by the studios not to reveal Gary's flings, wrote about the Coopers as the ideal couple. Hedda Hopper, ever Cooper's protector, warned him that news about one of his affairs might leak out. "You'd better warn Rocky." Without naming names Gary told his wife to expect rumors in the near future. That was the end of it. The next time he would be more discreet.

For his next flick, Cooper was cast in the remake of *Beau Geste* with Ray Milland and Robert Preston. Susan Hayward and thirteen-year-old Donald O'Connor had small parts. It was shot on location in the Arizona desert outside Yuma. Preston, the newcomer, warmly recalled how famously the entire cast got along. "We sat around at night telling tall tales and drinking. Gary and I were friends right away. He was a better actor than I expected. He had his own style, and trying to learn from him was almost impossible. I watched him carefully and found out he planned every move. Most of the stories I heard about him were true. He was an irresistible flirt and he fell asleep anywhere, anytime. His ability to close his eyes for only a second or two before dozing off almost got him killed when we were filming the end of *Beau Geste*. Our director, Bill Wellman, said we could do the fire scene only once because he was actually burning down the sets. I ran out of the bunkhouse assuming Coop was following, but when I turned around I didn't see him. I ran back inside and he was sound asleep in his bunk. We barely made it through the smoke. He thought it was very funny, but Bill Wellman was livid. He shouted, 'I warned you, Cooper! I hope this will teach you a goddamned lesson!' It didn't, of course."

While filming *Beau Geste* Gary got word that Maria had been taken ill. She was with her mother in Phoenix, but there was no way Cooper could contact them. So he hopped on a camel and rode seventeen miles to the main road in a sandstorm, then hitched a ride to Yuma and called his wife. When he heard Maria was recovering nicely he hitched a ride back to the camel and reported for work.

"I didn't know you could ride one of those things," Wellman said.

"I can't," Gary said. "I mean, I couldn't, but I can now."

Beau Geste was praised by the critics. All agreed that Cooper was perfect in *Beau*. His fans noticed his boyishness developing into more mature qualities. Rightly so. He was thirty-eight years old and the highest-salaried employee in the United States—making almost half a million dollars a year.

The Real Glory with David Niven and Broderick Crawford was Goldwyn's most expensive movie to date. Over a million dollars was spent on this film epic about the Moro uprising in the Philippines during the Spanish-American War.

Henry Hathaway, one of Cooper's favorite directors, related an amusing anecdote: "We had just finished a scene and someone happened to walk past one of the windows, casting a shadow through the shutters. I told Gary to get back on the set. 'Hurry!' I shouted, 'before the guy leaves.' "

"But it's not in the script." Cooper frowned. "Who is he?"

"I don't know, but I like the effect. We'll work it in somehow. Hurry up!"

"Who is he?" Gary repeated, without moving.

"I don't care! I don't know! It doesn't matter!"

"What do I do?"

"Just sit at your desk. Do nothing but—sit there!"

"Cooper was completely frustrated and confused," Hathaway explained. "All he had to do was sit down on the set and allow me to get that shadow in the window. Everything had to be planned, written down, have meaning. He said it was impossible for him to do it."

David Niven, Gary's costar, was amused, but he was amused with life in general. One of Hollywood's most infamous ladies' men, he and Cooper spoke the same language. Niven was far more worldly and charming than Gary. But, like Ray Milland, the Scottish-born actor did not get the notoriety Coop did. All three men had a fling with Grace Kelly.

The Real Glory was Gary's last film in 1939, but not one of his best. His Hollywood pals were astonished to learn he had earned half a million dollars for two pictures. Before the New Year, his fortune was flourishing under the expert financial guidance of his father-in-law, Paul Shields.

Robert Taylor commented, "I think these few years were Coop's best. He seemed content with his career and his family. We met Ernest Hemingway and his wife in Sun Valley and did some pheasant hunting. I think Hemingway played a few tricks on Coop and me. He assigned positions to us and insisted we wait until he gave the signal to shoot. There were birds all around us and we had our fingers on the trigger, but we held off until several of the flock headed straight for where Hemingway was. *Then* he shouted, 'Shoot!' Coop and I got covered with feathers and that's about it."

Rocky wasn't interested in the hunt, though she won the 1939 Women's Championship in skeet shooting. Taylor's wife, Barbara Stanwyck, tried to be a good sport during the first two years of their marriage. Actually, she was terrified of guns and shuddered when Taylor cleaned them in the house.

Though they had very little in common intellectually, Hemingway was quite impressed with Cooper. Gary was an enigma to the writer and he may have been somewhat envious of Cooper's success on the hunt and in bed. Their friendship would last for twenty years, their deaths separated by only days. Hemingway's reported latent homosexuality has often been mentioned in regard to Cooper, of whom he was in awe.

There was talk about *For Whom the Bell Tolls*. Hemingway led Cooper to believe he had fashioned his hero, Robert Jordan, after him. The author was as good an actor as he was a writer. Still, there is no doubt that he wanted Cooper to get the starring role in the screen version. Hemingway asked him if he knew Ingrid Bergman.

"Met her at a party Selznick had in her honor," Gary said.

"What was your impression?"

"Wholesome. Doesn't wear makeup, and her hair's natural. I think she's Swedish."

"I hope Hollywood doesn't change her." Hemingway scowled.

When Walter Brennan was asked to play Judge Roy Bean in *The Westerner* for Sam Goldwyn, he first went to his friend Cooper. "You're the star, but my part's better."

"Fine with me," Gary shrugged.

When Brennan won an Oscar for Best Supporting Actor, no one was prouder than Cooper. He told Hedda Hopper, "Don't know why they needed me for *The Westerner*. It didn't require any effort on my part." The director, Bill Wyler, said the two men were such close friends that they merely played themselves, acting instinctively. "Each knew what the other was going to do," Wyler said. "Brennan had the stronger role, but we needed Cooper's name. As it turned out, Coop's reserve and instinct for human nature made a dramatic foil for Walter's rambling dialogue."

In *The Westerner,* Gary plays a roving cowboy arrested by the legendary Judge Roy Bean, whose only weakness is a beautiful actress whom he admires from a distance. Cooper gets released from jail by promising to get a lock of her hair. The heart of the film is the relationship between the crafty cowboy and love-smitten judge.

The Christian Science Monitor thought Cooper gave a great performance, but agreed with Wyler that it was Walter Brennan's picture. They added, ". . . Mr. Cooper is an economical player who can accomplish much with the flicker of an expression."

In *The Westerner* Gary was in pain every time he mounted a horse. X rays showed that he had fractured his hip years before in the automobile accident with the handicapped Harvey Markham. Alice Cooper shook her head sadly. "We won't tell Dad," she whispered.

"How's he feelin'?"

"Considering he was hit by a car, he's doing remarkably well," she replied. "Dad just walked out on the street without looking . . . in a daze."

"Anything I can do?"

"Visit him once in awhile. And it would be nice if we could see our granddaughter before she grows up."

Gary kissed her on the cheek and shrugged. After all, it wasn't up to him.

Sheila Graham, one of Hollywood's top gossip columnists of the forties, fifties, and sixties was crazy about Gary Cooper. She was so anxious to interview him that she was involved in a car accident on the way to speak with him at Paramount in 1935. There was no one in Hollywood like Gary Cooper, on or off the screen, Miss Graham claimed. "Every woman loved him and he loved every woman," she wrote.

Sheila accompanied Gary to Dallas for the premiere of *The Westerner.* Two planes were rented to fly the group of fifty on the twelve-hour overnight flight to Texas. Someone asked her which plane she preferred. "Gary's, of course!" she announced even though her lover, F. Scott Fitzgerald, was standing there to see her off.

During the flight everyone on board chatted gaily. Cooper flirted outrageously with Sheila who, unknown to him, was prone to air sickness. "My pink glow turned green. In a few minutes I was going to throw up. How awful to do this before my idol! I excused myself to lie down and Gary picked me up in his arms as though I weighed two pounds and put me in a top berth. 'Shall I rub your tummy?' he asked. I shook my head, but he stayed with me until he knew I was all right."

Miss Graham was the first to arrive at the party in a suite at the Adolphus Hotel. She repaired her makeup in the bathroom and found Gary waiting for her in the bedroom. He assumed she had arranged this on purpose. He took her hands, drew her close ("What ecstasy!"), and stood looking down at her and she up at him. Then she giggled. He took it in his stride, grinned, offered her his arm, and they went to the party. "It might have been different if I hadn't been in love with Scott Fitzgerald," Miss Graham said.

Cooper was eager to get together again with Madeleine Carroll in *Northwest Mounted Police,* his first Technicolor picture. (He didn't mind having Paulette Goddard around, either.) It was known around Paramount that Gary and Madeleine were very attracted to each other. Since she was recently divorced she had no one to report home to. Maybe Cooper was trying to confuse onlookers when he huddled with Miss Goddard throughout most of the filming. One of the supporting actors in *Northwest Mounted Police* hinted that Gary could easily have managed to see both Paulette and Madeleine after hours. "I have no proof, but I think he did. There was one very obvious thing about Coop. He couldn't conceal his feelings. He was in awe of Carroll's beauty. We all were. When I heard that she and Goddard were going to be in the same picture with Coop, I said to myself, 'That's nice. Very nice.' But if I were ever asked to list the leading ladies Coop was involved with, one would be Carroll. Goddard, maybe. She was great fun and stuck close to Coop—or was it the other way around? He said he turned down *Destry Rides Again* with another flame, Marlene Dietrich, to be with Madeleine."

Destry made Jimmy Stewart a major star and established Marlene's screen image. She played Frenchy, the tough, hot-tempered barroom entertainer who sang with gusto, "See What the Boys in the Back Room Will Have."

The New York World-Telegram praised Cooper for his performance in *Northwest Mounted Police*—"Gary Cooper plays the Texas Ranger with all the ease and charm and dry humor that have made him one of the cinema's outstanding leading men."

The picture was the sixth biggest money-maker in 1940, despite *New York Times'* critic Bosley Crowther's listing it as one of the "Fifty Worst Films of All Times."

Frank Capra, director of *Mr. Deeds Goes to Town,* said there was no one else but Cooper to take the lead in *Meet John Doe.* "I wouldn't have made the picture without him," he said. The problem was Capra had no script to show Cooper, who agreed to do it anyway. Barbara Stanwyck, Edward Arnold, and Walter Brennan also accepted Capra's offer without seeing a single line on paper.

"I had faith in Capra," Gary said. "Sometimes faith pays off and sometimes it doesn't. Take *Stagecoach,* for example. I read the script and turned it down. Can you imagine! *Stagecoach!* It made a star out of John Wayne, but it seems lots of stars were born in movies that I refused to do, but in a way I'm glad I did. They needed the exposure . . . the break. Thing is, it makes me wonder if I can pick 'em."

John Doe—Capra's sane, honest "man of the people," thrust into a confrontation with the forces of evil, wins out with his innate goodness. Even though reviews of *Meet John Doe* were excellent, neither the film nor the players were nominated for an Oscar in 1940, but Cooper did make the cover of *Time* magazine.

The year also saw Greta Garbo retire from films; Marlene Dietrich and John Wayne became involved in a long-standing love affair; Katharine Hepburn met Spencer Tracy for the first time and thought he was too short to be her costar. "I'll cut you down to my size," he said dryly. And for the next three decades he did just that, and she wouldn't have had it any other way.

Rocky and Gary entertained with great dignity. Janet Leigh referred to them as "Hollywood Royalty." Gary was fast becoming a gracious host. Though he hadn't changed in any basic sense, Cooper was now considered a pro and admired by such younger actors as William Holden, Jimmy Stewart, Ray Milland, David Niven, Fred MacMurray, Henry Fonda, and Alan Ladd. It didn't matter that he had no stage experience before breaking into films: Cooper proved to all that he was born for the camera. No one seemed to be jealous over the fact that he couldn't make a mistake, because he always played himself. He finally seemed to have it all, to be at ease with himself. He didn't drink too much or take drugs. He tried to do his own gardening, depending on his spare time. He had a tractor and raised chickens, loved kids and animals. He was one of the best-dressed men in the country, but preferred jeans. He went to Europe and dined quietly with royalty, rubbed elbows with New York society, and was thoroughly captivated by his daughter Maria, whom he put above everyone and everything else.

Although he was quiet and usually not one to share his thougths, there were times when Gary let go, and another Cooper surfaced. Once, while he was in New York with a press agent, he found out an appointment had been canceled.

"What'll we do now?" the agent asked.

"We'll go look at the tits of the pretty girls on Fifth Avenue." And that's what they did.

When he was recognized in a restaurant or on the street, he easily complied with an autograph. Sometimes, on other occasions, he refused to acknowledge his fans. At the theater or a concert Cooper usually ignored his public. If he was mistaken for another actor—most often it was for Henry Fonda or Randolph Scott—he would laugh.

Robert Taylor said, "We couldn't be normal folk, but there were times we forgot we weren't! For example, I was measuring floors on my hands and knees in a vacant house that was for sale and got so involved it didn't occur to me there were other people looking around, too. There I was with my ass sticking out and suddenly I realized I had an audience. Coop told me he was so taken with a new car in a showroom, he walked in, and got underneath to examine it more closely. In the meantime an audience gathered and when he slid out Coop said, 'I felt like a real sap!' "

Playwright Clifford Odets said Cooper knew all about cows, bulls, cars, and ocean tides. "He had the enthusiasm of a boy. He could always tell you his first vivid impression of a thing. He had an old-fashioned politeness but he said nothing casually."

Poet Carl Sandburg thought Gary Cooper was the most beloved illiterate this country has ever known.

Perhaps Ernest Hemingway said it best: "If you made up a character like Coop's, nobody would believe it. He's just too good to be true!"

8

"PAPA" AND INGRID

Warner Brothers wanted to film the World War I story of Sergeant Alvin York, the Tennessee farm boy with a deep religious conviction and an aversion to killing who was transformed under fire, killed twenty-five German soldiers single-handedly, and captured 132 prisoners.

As expected, there was only one movie actor capable of playing the humble and uneducated hillbilly—Gary Cooper. But Gary refused to do it. "In screen biographies," he explained, "dealin' with remote historical characters, some romantic leeway is okay. But York's alive and I don't think I can do justice to him. He's too big for me . . . he covers too much territory."

To escape the studio's pressure, Cooper and Rocky went to New York to see some Broadway shows. "We stayed in a hotel," he said, "and every time I turned around I ran into someone from the studio. They wouldn't leave me alone. What got me to change my mind was York, who wanted me to do the picture. Even then I wasn't convinced. When we met I realized we had a few things in common. We were both raised in the mountains—Tennessee for him, Montana for me—and we learned to ride and shoot as a natural part of growin' up." Gary consented to do the role.

He went to Tennessee and learned the dialect, and to see for himself where Alvin York grew up, to know the man he was going to portray. Director Howard Hawks said, "To understand Sergeant York was to understand Gary Cooper and that wasn't possible . . . something else they had in common."

It had been a struggle to get the young war hero to sell his story and an uphill battle to persuade Cooper that he was right for the part. Sam Goldwyn complicated things. He told Jack Warner of Warner Brothers they could have Cooper, provided Goldwyn could have Bette Davis for *The Little Foxes*. Miss Davis was furious, but the deal was finalized. Then Paramount balked because Cooper was scheduled to make *Reap the Wild Wind* for them. Fortunately they had not begun production, and Gary was replaced by John Wayne, who proved his acting ability out of the saddle.

While all negotiations were being untangled, Cooper again changed his mind. "I was scared to death. I did not want to play a man who was a living hero. When there was no turning back, I faced the biggest challenge of my life. I was terrified."

He was also uncomfortable with the age of his leading lady, Joan Leslie, who was only sixteen. "I felt like a cradle robber." Walter Brennan played the country preacher, but all his friendly encouragement during the four months of filming did nothing to improve Gary's nervous, often irritable attitude.

But the anxieties and difficulties were worth it. For his performance Cooper won the 1941 New York Film Critics Award for Best Actor of the Year. *Sergeant York* was nominated for an Academy Award for Best Picture, but lost to *How Green Was My Valley.* Gary won his first Oscar for Best Actor and accepted it in person. His speech was characteristically brief and modest. "It was Sergeant Alvin York who won this award. Because to the best of my ability, I tried to be Sergeant York."

His next picture, *Ball of Fire,* also released in 1941, was a light comedy about an absentminded professor and a burlesque queen. Barbara Stanwyck was nominated for an Oscar for her performance as Sugarpuss O'Shea, whereas Cooper stumbled over his dialogue as Professor Bertram Potts. If he worried about doing justice to a hillbilly, Gary was panicked by words that were foreign to him: "What's the difference?" Sam Goldwyn laughed.

"I don't know what they mean," Cooper grumbled.

"Neither does anyone else! All that matters is the pronunciation."

"Neanderthal bucolism?"

"You're the professor, not me."

Stanwyck stole the whole ball of wax, anyway. Cooper had only to react to her antics and seductiveness. But *The New York Herald Tribune* said he was amusing and even hilarious in a performance in which nobody expected anything of him. "Before you know it, Cooper will be a rounded actor as well as a great one."

Bugsy Siegel and one of his new girlfriends, Virginia "Sugar" Hill, attended the *Ball of Fire* premiere and party. The Countess di Frasso was reportedly busy as a paid agent of the Italian government, involved in criminal and Fascist activities. Bugsy had accompanied her to Italy a year prior to sell an explosive device to Mussolini. Dorothy had been under FBI surveillance for several years, but they could not find enough evidence to indict her. The countess apparently had no idea she was a suspect, nor did her close Hollywood friends.

Dorothy was also busying herself as a matchmaker. She thought Cary Grant would make a perfect third husband for Barbara Hutton. Elsa Maxwell said, "The countess hoped Cary would be a stabilizing influence on poor Barbara. Actually it was Dorothy who needed guidance. She was a screwball who thought Bugsy Siegel was an innocent, overgrown boy. She introduced him to European royalty who, through a misunderstanding, thought he was a baron! Dorothy's liaison with Bugsy was strange, but we loved her, anyway. She could laugh at herself and she was a very generous woman who craved adventure rather than getting old."

Cooper kept in touch with Dorothy, but it was common courtesy not to invite the countess and Rocky to the same party. After Pearl Harbor was attacked, though, Hollywood had more important things to worry about. It became just another American town, anxious to help with the war effort.

Hollywood's first fatality of war was not in uniform. On January 16, 1942, Carole Lombard was flying home with her mother after a successful war bond rally in her home state of Indiana when their plane crashed after taking off from Las Vegas. Three days later all activities at the movie studios were halted at noon as "Taps" was sounded and a tribute paid. Carole's husband, Clark Gable, was forty-one years old, but he joined the Air Corps and volunteered for several missions over Germany with a death wish in his heart.

John Wayne, who was ten years younger than Gable, chose not to enlist. As a married man with four children he was exempt from the draft. But the majority of male stars, including Jimmy Stewart, Tyrone Power, William Holden, Robert Taylor, and Glenn Ford, chose to be in uniform despite their exempt status.

Gary Cooper was classified 4-F because of his bad hip. He and John Wayne were among the few old-timers left in Hollywood as new faces appeared: Van Johnson, Peter Lawford, Robert Mitchum, John Garfield, and Cornel Wilde.

Sam Goldwyn patriotically told his stars, "Don't think of the money, think of your country!" L. B. Mayer reminded his M-G-M family, "Gable's only drawing $66 a month in the Air Corps. The least we can do is take a cut in salary!" Bette Davis founded the Hollywood Canteen, and Betty Grable became America's Pinup Girl.

Cooper took an undisclosed cut in salary and went to Washington, D.C., to testify before Congress in an effort to publicize the importance of motion pictures during wartime. "That's what the boys overseas want," he said. "Our films bring them closer to home. They're inspiring. This is not the time to cut down our production in Hollywood."

When asked by a government official if he was concerned about the box-office grosses, Gary said, "The more taxes an actor can pay, the more he is helping to win the war."

Within the year he would tour military bases in and out of the country. And though he would not come within any real danger as Gable and Stewart did, Cooper would be close enough to hear the bombs and console the wounded.

He was still an all-American hero who actually loved to eat a whole cherry pie with a quart of milk, then lie down on the grass and take a nap.

"That's one reason I think you'll make a fine Lou Gehrig," Sam Goldwyn said.

"Who?" Cooper asked.

"Lou Gehrig. He played first base with the New York Yankees."

"Oh?"

"You never heard of him, did you?"

"Nope . . . well, he died."

"You can hate the Yankees if you want to, but—"

"I don't hate them," Gary mumbled. ". . . just don't know anything about them."

"Jesus Christ! When I came to America it was more important to play baseball than learn how to speak English!"

"I went to a few games back home . . ."

"How many bases are there?" Goldwyn asked.

"One or two, I think."

"Ever hold a bat in your hand?"

"Nope."

"A baseball?"

"Nope."

"Ever hear of Babe Ruth?"

"Yep . . ."

"Who is he?"

"Plays baseball."

Goldwyn was speechless, but Cooper wasn't embarrassed or defeated. "They say ya can't teach an old dog new tricks, but I'm willin' to try," he said.

Retired major leaguer Lefty O'Doul came down from San Francisco to coach Gary. Lefty said Coop threw a ball like an old woman tossing a hot biscuit. Cooper was learning to swing a bat but couldn't run or field. Goldwyn said they'd use doubles. When rehearsals began at Wrigley Field, Gehrig's former teammates were invited to observe. They weren't impressed.

Goldwyn asked them, "What's wrong?"

"Gehrig was a southpaw," one of the players said.

The lessons began all over again, but Cooper could not swing a bat left-handed. The problem was solved by reversing the letters and numbers on Gary's uniforms. Then the film was processed with the back side to the front. No one seemed to notice Cooper did everything else with his right hand except when he was at the plate.

Teresa Wright, in this her third film, was cast as Gehrig's wife. She said, "I didn't learn anything from Gary's acting. He didn't like to discuss a scene or rehearse it. He knew his lines and wanted to get the job done. Between takes he liked to whittle or ride his bike around the lot. His wife was a very stylish woman and he was an elegant man. I don't believe his mannerisms were what made him quintessentially American. I think the values of the characters he played were generally the values regarded as the American ideal. He played that character so much that it became identified with him."

The Pride of the Yankees was nominated for Best Picture of 1942 and Gary was nominated for Best Actor. But James Cagney won the Oscar for *Yankee Doodle Dandy*, and *Mrs. Miniver* won Best Picture. Teresa Wright was nominated for Best Actress for her role as Mrs. Lou Gehrig and for Best Supporting Actress in *Mrs. Miniver*. She won for the latter.

The war prevented Gary and Rocky from taking their annual trip to Europe. So instead they vacationed in Bermuda or stayed with her parents in Southampton, their second home. Their visits to Sun Valley became more frequent as *For Whom the Bell Tolls* was being readied for the screen. David Selznick decided not to produce the picture, but offered his new star, Ingrid Bergman, for the part of Maria. Paramount was undecided despite the fact Cooper and Hemingway wanted the Swedish actress. Selznick threatened to lend her to Warner's for *Casablanca,* and then had no choice but to do so. When *Bell* was ready to go into production, Ingrid was making eyes at Humphrey Bogart to the tune of "As Time Goes By."

So the part of Maria in *For Whom the Bell Tolls* went to the beautiful Norwegian actress and ballerina Vera Zorina. The Spanish Civil War drama was to be shot on location in the Sierra Nevadas. Cooper had been pondering his conception of Robert Jordan for two years and felt he knew Maria's traits as well. Cooper knew that Vera lacked the strength and authority the part called for. He made his feelings known, but no one cared. It wasn't until Paramount executives saw the rushes that they realized she was all wrong. The ballerina, concerned about her legs, tiptoed around the mountains more like a tourist than a Spanish peasant. She was sent back to Hollywood, sued Paramount, and won. No one seemed to care because by now Ingrid Bergman was available and extremely eager to play Maria.

Director Sam Wood was not surprised when Cooper strolled down the mountainside and greeted his costar. "Hello, Maria," he said with a smile. Ingrid looked up at him and blushed.

"I think they had waited for this moment and thought it would never happen," Wood said. "I was certain they were drawn to each other when Coop joined Ingrid outside and offered to go over the dialogue. He never does that. Besides, he didn't have a script with him."

Thirty years later Ingrid Bergman said, "Looking at Gary Cooper, it was so wonderful! It was unbelievable that I was working with him. The personality of this man was so enormous, so overpowering—and that expression in his eyes and his face, it was so delicate. I so loved the part of Maria. All she is thinking about is the man she loves. What she means to him. How she can make him happy. She simply lives to fit his needs."

Ingrid's dialogue instructor was on the set every day and felt compelled to speak up. "Really, Ingrid, you must stop looking at him like that. You sit there just looking! I know you are supposed to be in love with him in the picture, but not too much in love with him!"

Cooper's true feelings were obvious only to those who knew him, but as one observer commented, "Gary and Ingrid were both ripe for a torrid affair and what better place than in those mountains for twelve beautiful weeks from summer into autumn. We lived in cabins. It was all very romantic and primitive. No pressure. We felt as if we were cut off from the rest of the world. You could reach up and almost touch the stars."

Cooper rarely talked about his leading ladies, but he said it was easier to work with Ingrid than with any other actress he had known. "I don't feel I am just standing there while she is wondering if her makeup is right. Or her hair right. She has absolutely no thought of it. She lifts the scene. That's because she is so completely natural."

The Bergman-Cooper romance was accepted by those on location. Both Hedda Hopper and Louella Parsons got the not-so-surprising scoop from their spies, but did not mention it in their columns. However, Sheila Graham came right out with it when the picture was finished: "Anything to the rumors about you and Miss Bergman?" she asked.

His broad smile was the affirmative response.

Before the couple parted they agreed to costar in *Saratoga Trunk*. Ingrid said, "We had so much fun and got on so well, why shouldn't we make another film?"

David Selznick replied, "Because you're Swedish! You just played a Spanish girl and now you think you can get away with being the French Cleo Dulaine?"

Ingrid was in no position to demand anything. She knew she had to rely on Cooper, who had the power, and wondered if he'd change his mind about accepting the weak role. She did have Sam Wood's support. According to Ingrid, Sam was negotiating with Warner Brothers and nagging Selznick to lend her out again. "The love scenes with Gary and Ingrid were so passionate. I didn't want them to simmer down," said Wood. What he didn't relate was his desire to film *Saratoga Trunk* before Rocky or Ingrid's insanely jealous husband got wind of the affair.

A few months after they had returned from the Sierra Nevadas Cooper and Bergman were together again for the camera. At the end of a day's work on *Saratoga Trunk* they could be seen leaving the set together and dining in public. They were an item in the gossip columns. Ingrid told friends she had never been happier. "Every woman who has ever known Gary is in love with him," she said publicly.

When Ingrid's husband, Petter Lindstrom, accused her of having an affair with Cooper, she denied it. "He thinks that about all my leading men," Miss Bergman said. Spencer Tracy fell in love with her and Humphrey Bogart admitted he had been very attracted, but did not touch. Cooper told columnist James Bacon, "Ingrid loved me more than any woman in my life loved me. The day after *Saratoga Trunk* ended, I couldn't get her on the phone."

There are several versions as to why *Saratoga Trunk* was not released for two years. One source claimed that studio executives did not want it to conflict with *For Whom the Bell Tolls*. Another source claimed it was the reported love affair that might, during wartime, upset the public. Two married movie stars carrying on in public while America's young men were being killed wasn't going to sell more tickets at the box office, they reasoned. And why weren't these two stars out selling war bonds?

Rocky must have taken the persistent rumors in her stride. Ingrid's daughter, Pia, and Rocky's daughter, Maria, became good friends. The two families exchanged dinner invitations.

So it goes. As novelist Raymond Chandler wrote, "Hollywood is wonderful. Anyone who doesn't like it is either crazy or sober."

For Whom the Bell Tolls received ten Oscar nominations in 1943. Among them were Gary Cooper for Best Actor, Ingrid Bergman for Best Actress, and the film for Best Picture. Alas, *Casablanca* won Best Picture; Paul Lucas won Best Actor for *Watch on the Rhine,* and Jennifer Jones won Best Actress for *The Song of Bernadette.*

Variety called *For Whom the Bell Tolls* one of the most important pictures of all time.

In her book, *Ingrid,* the actress provided unique insight into her performance. "I enjoyed it all so much," she wrote, "particularly Gary Cooper. What was wrong was that my happiness showed on the screen. I was far too happy to honestly portray Maria's tragic figure."

All Cooper said was that he had prepared himself for the role of Robert Jordan, but *something happened.* His mind was elsewhere.

Hemingway told Gary he saw *For Whom the Bell Tolls* five times.

"You really liked it, huh?" Cooper asked.

"Hell, no. I walked out five times!"

Hemingway adored Ingrid, too. They wrote letters to each other after she was ostracized for having an affair with Italian director Roberto Rossellini, and for having his son before divorcing her first husband. Hemingway addressed her as "daughter" and offered to face the press and the world with her. "I'll defend you," he exclaimed.

By this time of the war Gary's colleagues had already started to tour the military bases, entertaining troops. Hedda needled him by telling him they had gotten a head start on him. "They wanna see fillies," he said with a shrug. "Don't know what I can do, anyhow."

"Sing and dance. Talk to the boys."

"Sing?" he gulped.

"They don't expect a Nelson Eddy," Hopper said, laughing.

"Dunno . . ."

"You'd better get in this fight, boy! My God, just to see a movie star of your stature in person is enough. What's wrong with having fun at your own expense? Everyone's doing it."

"Dunno . . ."

"It's fun, Gary."

"Okay, but I won't sing." He scowled.

So in November and December 1943, he volunteered for a tour of New Guinea with actresses Una Merkel and Phyllis Brooks. Cooper would mumble answers to questions and join in during "Mairzy Doats." When a GI asked him to recite Lou Gehrig's farewell speech, Gary looked dumbfounded. He made sure to get a copy for the next performance.

Gary later said that his five weeks in the mud and rain with shell fire nearby was the greatest emotional experience of his life. "The boys are appreciative of the slightest little thing," he said.

Cooper was not aware until a year later that he had picked up an amoebic infection in New Guinea. It surfaced during an attack of influenza a few months after he returned home. It would continue to plague him for the rest of his life.

Ingrid Bergman entertained the troops, too, but instead of the South Pacific she chose Alaska. "I don't like insects and snakes," she said. Though she and Gary were away at the same time, and on opposite sides of the equator, it was their romance that weakened both their marriages. Cooper's friends agreed that his obvious involvement with the Swedish actress confirmed that he could not be tied down. Reporters rumored his separation from Rocky—who refused to answer press inquiries. Gary ignored questions, too, and raved about his daughter. "I missed Maria when I was away," he said. "I want to be around to watch her grow up. Life's so darn short and kids grow up so darn fast."

Cooper agreed to do *The Story of Dr. Wassell*, but said he wanted to stop making biographical pictures. He thought he was pressing his luck. "I've done Wild Bill Hickok, Alvin York, Marco Polo, Lou Gehrig, and now Dr. Wassell. I'd sorta like to do a comedy next time."

In the film he played the heroic naval doctor who rescued a group of wounded soldiers from Java in 1942 after they had been abandoned. But his acting was too low-key. *The New York Times* said, "Mr. Cooper's performance as the good doctor is familiarly shy. Except for an occasional 'Good gravy!' and a startled look, you'd hardly know he was pressed." Gary's costar, Dennis O'Keefe, went on to a brilliant career after *Dr. Wassell.* Some critics even thought he stole the movie from Cooper—no great feat.

In 1944, after eighteen years with Paramount, Gary decided not to renew his contract. He was under no obligation to Sam Goldwyn, but the two men hoped to work together again.

Writer-director Nunnally Johnson, producer William Goetz, and former RKO mogul Leo Spitz had organized International Pictures. Johnson convinced Cooper to play the lead in *Casanova Brown*—the story of a man who learns his wife is pregnant after their divorce. Gary asked for director Sam Wood and Teresa Wright as his costar. He also expressed his desire to produce one of his films and was given more leeway as Casanova Brown. Miss Wright thought Gary was rather fussy. Gary commented on her posture and the importance of body movement. He also insisted on changing "Mommy" in the script to "Mama," which was difficult since Miss Wright had memorized "Mommy." Cooper was persistent about "Mama" and she wondered why. What Miss Wright did not say was how the cast and crew reacted to Gary's fetish and the well-known fact that he was a mama's boy.

Casanova Brown was labeled by the critics as delightful nonsense, an old-fashioned unimportant bit of fluff. *The New York Times* thought Cooper was somewhat obvious and ridiculous clowning over a baby. But in 1944, even a silly film featuring the costars of *Pride of the Yankees* was worth seeing. And International Pictures realized a profit on their first picture.

Cooper was eager to produce their next movie, *Along Came Jones*, a fun Western. Why had he decided to mount a horse again if it pained him so? "I got to thinkin' that I get the itch every so often. Besides, I hurt myself pretty bad fallin' off a bicycle in the last picture. A horse is safer."

Now, as coproducer of his films, he had his own plush office and was responsible for every detail. His signature was needed on all papers pertaining to the film. Usually he had no idea what he was signing. When he was presented with the bill for Loretta Young's ranch wardrobe, he studied it carefully.

"A simple cotton dress costs $175?" Gary guffawed.

"Yes, sir," the designer replied.

"What would this thing cost in a store?"

"Oh . . . maybe ten bucks."

"So, go out and buy that."

"It's not as simple as all that, Mr. Cooper. These dresses are more durable and they're wrinkle-resistant."

"Too expensive, damn it! We have to cut our budget."

"Yes, sir."

"Tell Miss Young we'll get her clothes directly from a store."

"It's not my job to tell her, Mr. Cooper."

"Whose job is it?"

"The producer's."

"Oh . . ."

Gary initialed the designs. He didn't want to tangle with a star of Loretta's magnitude. "I wasn't cut out for a desk job," he said, "but I have more respect for producers now that I've tried it. All I saw day and night were dollar signs. I began to wonder if I could afford myself!"

Though Loretta Young had been linked with many men in the 1930s, among them Clark Gable and Spencer Tracy, when she appeared in *Along Came Jones* she was a happily married woman. During filming she found out she was pregnant by her second husband. If she was radiant, it wasn't because of Gary Cooper.

Gary and Loretta complemented each other on the screen. Considering his heavy load of production duties, Cooper had every excuse to give a bad performance. Yet both the critics and the public liked his performance as Melody Jones, the stumbling, fumbling cowboy who allowed his woman to take advantage of him. After the picture Cooper said many of his Hollywood friends thought he had damaged his career by playing a fool. "I was just a guy who couldn't hit his hat if he was wearin' it," he said. "We played that up, and the picture made money."

On December 14, 1944, Lupe Velez committed suicide in the Beverly Hills hacienda she called "Casa Felicitas"—Happy House. Since her divorce from Johnny Weissmuller in 1938, precipitated by, among other things, his dumping a bowl of salad on her head in Ciro's, Lupe had had a series of unhappy love affairs. Yet she was still popular at the box office in a series of Mexican Spitfire films costarring Leon Errol. They made her a household name. She was certainly not Oscar material, but was working steadily and, at age thirty-six, still an attractive woman. One of her handsome beaus was Clayton Moore, America's Lone Ranger, a suitable substitute for Weissmuller. Lupe was in love with the handsome Mexican leading man, Arturo De Cordova, but when the affair ended she was deeply hurt. On the rebound, Lupe became involved with French actor Harald Ramond. When she became pregnant he refused to marry her and Lupe broke their engagement. A devout Catholic, she would not consider abortion, and having a baby out of wedlock was unthinkable.

The suicide she planned is one of the most bizarre in Hollywood history. First she ordered dozens of flowers and candles for her bedroom, then had her hair done, donned a silver lamé gown, and sat down to a hot Mexican feast. For dessert she swallowed seventy-five Seconals with her favorite brandy. Finally Lupe lay down on her silk sheets and, like Cleopatra, waited for a dramatic and glamorous death. But sometime during the night her dinner erupted. She stumbled to the bathroom and drowned in the toilet bowl. Ironically, Lupe might have survived had she not gone into the bathroom. According to police, she had regurgitated the pills with her spicy dinner.

The suicide note she left to Harald:

> May God forgive you and forgive me, too, but I prefer to take my life away and our baby's before I bring him shame or kill him. How could you, Harald, fake such a great love for me and our baby when all the time you didn't want us? I see no other way out for me so goodbye and good luck to you.
>
> Love,
>
> Lupe

In her column, Louella Parsons did not print the truth about how Lupe really died: "Lupe was never lovelier as she lay there, as if slumbering . . . a faint smile, like secret dreams . . . looking like a child taking nappy. Like a good little girl. Hark! There are the doggies! There's chops, there's Chips, scratching at the door. They're whimpering, they're whining. They want their little Lupita to take them out to play . . . "

There was another secret known to a very few. Robert Slatzer, at the time a young newspaperman from Ohio, interviewed Lupe a few weeks before her death. "She was very sweet," he told me. "I recall she made pitchers of Margueritas and we finished several because her telephone rang all afternoon. One call came from her mother. Lupe spoke in Spanish, but I knew the language fairly well. She said, 'I have to have the baby. It's too late now.' Then Lupe pleaded with her mother not to call Coop. 'I think it might be his baby,' she said, 'but I'm not going to tell him.' "

Slatzer had heard enough. "I knew I had a scoop," he said. "I played dumb and asked Lupe where her child was . . . that I didn't know she'd had Coop's baby, trying to get her to open up. She realized I understood Spanish and the cat was out of the bag. Earlier in the interview Lupe said she thought I was very young and didn't understand many things, and that was her approach to her pregnancy. She admitted being in love with Coop and that he knew about the baby. 'He tells me it belongs to my boyfriend.' That was Harald Ramond. Lupe believed it was Coop's baby. Maybe she wanted to believe it. I told her I wouldn't print anything and called a few days later to read my interview and get her okay over the telephone. She thought it was good and thanked me for not mentioning our side conversation.

"Over the next few years I became friendly with Coop and brought up the subject of Lupe's baby. He wanted to know what she told me and he swallowed hard. Then he asked me a very peculiar question. 'You're not a newspaperman anymore, are you?' He knew I was a screenwriter, but I shook my head. Coop said he didn't know if Lupe was carrying his child. 'Coulda been,' he said. I asked if he went to the funeral and he told me, 'No, but I sent a nice display of roses.' "

Slatzer interviewed Clara Bow often, too, and considered writing her autobiography at one time. He didn't print what she had to say about Gary calling her when Lupe was found dead. "He was in complete shock . . . babbling, crying and screaming that he was going to kill that son of a bitch (Ramond) who got Lupe pregnant," Clara said. "I told him she was so grateful that he had called her often when her spirits were so low. Personally, I never thought the baby was fathered by the foreign boyfriend because he didn't mean that much to Lupe. I think she blamed him to protect Gary. Lupe died believing he wasn't happily married. She thought he was the most humble, caring, sensitive man she had ever known. But he was controlled by his mother."

Myrna Loy, who, like Gary, was born in Helena, Montana, said in her autobiography that Cooper often used to visit her at her mother's house in Hollywood during his affair with Lupe. "Once he turned up depressed and tipsy," Loy wrote. "I consoled him before leaving the room to make some coffee. He was gone when I returned, which worried me. I found him slumped on the sun porch, staring into space. He looked so forlorn and vulnerable with that long body sort of crumpled, those fine eyes clouded. I spontaneously laid my hands on his shoulders. He stirred, murmuring like a lost child: 'Mother?' "

As Lupe had told Louella Parsons in happier days, "Sometimes my Garree is like a little boy and then I want to mother him. Other times, he is like a big strong man and then I bite his ears."

Cooper needed a quality film like *Saratoga Trunk* to pick him up in 1945. The public did not know it had been shelved for two years. *The New York Herald Tribune* said, "Cooper is perfect as the backwoodsman who tried unsuccessfully not to become entangled with the scheming spitfire." *The New York Times* thought Cooper was pleasantly roguish. "Saratoga Trunk, however, is a piece of baggage labeled solely for its two stars."

How did Bosley Crowther know that?

Gary next agreed to sign with Warner Brothers for *Cloak and Dagger*. The fee was $300,000. His leading lady, English actress Lilli Palmer, was making her American debut in films. She was accompanied from England by her husband, Rex Harrison, costar of *Anna and the King of Siam* with Irene Dunne. Lilli told the press that Hollywood was a great strain on any marriage, ". . . particularly for two people who came out of the blackout of England as we did. Suddenly all the ladies threw themselves into Rex's arms." Like Rocky Cooper, Lilli kept her husband on a long leash and was reluctant to accept his infidelities "because they were purely physical." Lilli did, however, find Gary Cooper very attractive. "I couldn't keep my eyes off him," she said. "The camera didn't exist. I tried to praise him, but he said, 'It's a cinch. I just learn my lines and try not to bump into the furniture.' Gary Cooper was like hanging a lollipop in front of a baby. But from there to wrecking my marriage . . . I was, I hope, a little too wise to throw it all away for the sake of a fling."

Unfortunately, Rex Harrison did not feel the same way. Harrison's blatant carryings-on with actress Carole Landis may have been a factor in her tragic suicide from barbiturates in 1948.

After *Cloak and Dagger* Lilli went on to do *Body and Soul* with John Garfield. Cooper stepped back and took a good long look at his choice of pictures. Producer Cecil B. De Mille came through with a $5 million spectacular, *Unconquered,* with Paulette Goddard, who referred to Cooper as "my hero."

It took De Mille a year to complete his epic. He was tense throughout production, complaining about the dark circles under Paulette's eyes and hinting an actress who was thirty-six years old should be getting more sleep. De Mille also had to conquer an age problem with his leading man. Cooper was now forty-six and he did not fall easily into the dashing role of the Virginia militiaman. So De Mille told the film editor to pick shots based not on Gary's acting ability, but on his appearing youthful.

De Mille refused to use a double or Paulette's stand-in during a scene that involved firebombs being hurled on the set. When she refused to do it De Mille shouted, "Get her out of here before I kill her!"

Miss Goddard fought with De Mille throughout. She burst into tears at his wrath. Her double and thirty extras suffered minor burns from the firebombs that day. But Cooper did not stand up for Paulette, or for any of his leading ladies, for that matter. He was criticized for not defending Lilli Palmer when director Fritz Lang was rude and insulting to her. Apparently someone in the cast thought Gary should say something to Lang. Instead Cooper waited until filming was finished and hemmed and hawed with a boyish apology. "Ya know, kid," he mumbled, "I'm sorry 'bout . . . well, you know . . . Lang and all. I shoulda spoke up or somethin', but well . . . ya see . . . I'm not very good at that sorta thing. Can't find the right words and all. Without a script . . . well, guess . . . hope you understand."

Time magazine called it "Cecil Blount De Mille's florid, $5 million, technicolor celebration of Gary Cooper's virility, Paulette Goddard's femininity, and the American Frontier Spirit." *The New York Times* praised the picture, adding, ". . . isn't the chance of watching Gary Cooper, in a colonial costume and tricornered hat, acting the gallant frontiersman sufficient for anyone? If it isn't, there's Paulette Goddard as the red-headed, flashing-eyed slave, exhibited in numerous situations, from a bathtub to an Indian torture stake."

Unconquered was the last film Cooper would make for Cecil B. De Mille.

9

GOOD SAM

In 1946, at age eighty-one, Charles Cooper died from pneumonia. The judge had never fully recovered from his automobile accident. Myrna Loy indicated in her autobiography that Charles had never been happy in California. "Gary's mother transplanted the poor judge from Montana to Hollywood, where he always seemed lost and lonely. I used to invite him later on, for tea and comfort by the big fireplace in my Hidden Valley house."

Alice Cooper was, however, very happy in Hollywood. She was an active member of a club for mothers of stars—Motion Picture Mothers, Inc. The organization sold tickets to fund-raising social events and afforded her entrée to elite gatherings everywhere in Hollywood. Perhaps the few times Alice got to see her son was in nightclubs when she was raising funds.

Alice told Hedda Hopper that she was very sad that her granddaughter, whom she rarely got to see, was being raised a Catholic. "And I know that Gary's wife is trying to convert him," Alice fretted.

Hedda Hopper wrote fondly of Gary's marriage in the forties: "Rocky has a fine chiseled profile, big dark eyes, a queenly air. She's Gary's queen and he loves pleasing her slightest whim. It's a marriage that's been perfect from the start. Gary has fitted himself into the life his wife likes—the top-drawer, smart Hollywood life of unending parties and quiet luxury living. Rocky's a social sparkplug. This sort of life is not really Gary Cooper's natural style. He's not a party boy or greeter. He's shy, built for open skies and a saddle, not drawing rooms and Hepplewhite chairs. Gary has never cared about cocktails. He hates like fury to dance. Small talk and clever conversation aren't his strong points. Fluttery, flirtatious society girls scare him to death. Yet, he likes it because Rocky does . . ."

Hemingway enjoyed teasing Cooper about being henpecked. Their Sun Valley hunting jaunts were often cut short because Rocky wanted her husband home on time for dinner. Another member of the hunt thought Rocky was a very domineering woman. "We had to rearrange everything according to her wishes," he said. "I wouldn't have taken that from my wife. Coop used to say that he was the puppet and Rocky pulled the strings. I mean, he actually came out and said it. Maybe that's what he wanted her to think."

Meanwhile the Countess di Frasso was in the news again to remind the world who she was; her name was linked with Gary Cooper's past. After divorcing the count she had hired a yacht for a four-month treasure hunt in the Coco Islands off the coast of Costa Rica. Among her guests on the voyage were Bugsy Siegel, Jean Harlow's stepfather, Marino Bello, and his girlfriend. The trip ended in charges of piracy and mutiny and suits for assault, and the delivery of an illicit cargo to Louis (Lepke) Buchalter, a gangster on the lam, who was later executed.

Dorothy appeared before a federal grand jury. When asked why she was in the company of a well-known gangster, she said innocently, "Mr. and Mrs. Bello were there to chaperone me!" What she failed to mention was that Bello had married his girlfriend on the last day of the trip. The details are sketchy, but Dorothy walked away from the grand jury in a huff. They had, after all, interfered with her social life.

On June 20, 1947, Bugsy was shot in the head while reading a newspaper in his Beverly Hills home; three bullets penetrated his skull. Dorothy di Frasso was heartbroken. Bugsy was, she said, the love of her life.

Paramount's *Variety Girl* was a musical extravaganza. Though he was not under contract to Paramount in 1947, Cooper made a guest appearance on a merry-go-round horse. Alan Ladd sang "Tallahassee." The stars were billed in order of importance: Bing Crosby, Bob Hope, Gary Cooper, Ray Milland, Alan Ladd, Barbara Stanwyck, Paulette Goddard, Dorothy Lamour, Sonny Tufts, Joan Caulfield, William Holden, and so on. Seventeen years earlier, Cooper had had a marvelous time on the set of *Paramount on Parade*. Now he did not look like a happy man. Nor did he look well. Observers thought he was bored with life in general.

Parties, parties, parties. The same socialites blended with Hollywood elite. Oleg Cassini, who was married to actress Gene Tierney, recalled the large garden parties held almost every Saturday night—by someone or other—in a big tent with dinner and dancing for several hundred. "I remember one such party at Cobrina Wright's house," Cassini wrote in his autobiography. "Gene and I were talking with Gary Cooper and his wife, Rocky. Of all the actors in Hollywood, Cooper was the man I admired most; the least affected, the least 'starlike,' a solid American man (the archetypal American man, perhaps). We were standing in the garden talking when a cinematographer, fairly well known, came up and started pawing at Gene, drunkenly perhaps, but pawing, kissing her neck. I decked him. It was a surgical strike, a quick left and he was flat on his back in the flowers. Cooper nodded, as if to say, 'Nicely done.' His wife laughed and said to him, 'You only do that in the movies. Why don't you ever do that for me in real life?' "

Director Henry Hathaway said he was amazed that Cooper had no conception of how to fight even as an actor. "I could accept his not being able to throw a baseball," he said, "but he didn't know the first thing about throwing a punch—something most boys learn on the way home from grade school. He was graceful—almost effeminate. Everything was in the face with Coop. If he couldn't swing, we concentrated on his facial expressions and he could be cruel, fierce and murderous. He clenched his teeth and every line on his face got deeper with sweat."

Instead of fighting his way back from his slump in films, Cooper chose to portray *Good Sam* with the Oomph Girl, Ann Sheridan. He hoped that by playing characters like Deeds and Doe again in light comedy his rating at the box office would be secure.

The film's plot is captured by the title. Sam gives everything he has to friends even though he had little to begin with. Down and out, he is rescued by his friends and Sam knows he did the right thing. The reviews were not favorable. *The New Yorker* said, "The picture, strung together like a vaudeville show, gives all hands a chance to do a turn with Mr. Cooper. Toward the end of the piece, he looked pretty tired to me, and I can't say that I blamed him."

Cue magazine's critic said, "It may be unkind to quote vital statistics to make a point, but Mr. Cooper is by now a grown man, and his boyish bashfulness, sheepish grins, trembling lips and fluttering eyelids are actor's tricks he can surely do without."

Time magazine was a bit kinder. "Gary Cooper is probably better qualified than most Hollywood leading men in suggesting a nice guy who cannot say no. Until he comes to share, with the picture as a whole, its air of haggard and ill-concealed desperation, he does a beautiful job."

Good Sam did not boost Cooper's career. He wasn't alone in his difficulties. After Gable hung up his Air Force uniform he returned to star with Greer Garson in *Adventure*. (He loathed M-G-M's slogan—"Gable's Back and Garson's Got Him!") The film was a disaster, and his follow-ups were almost as bad.

Robert Taylor was miscast in *Undercurrent* with Katharine Hepburn after his discharge from the Navy. He told Cooper, "I was better off in the service. I didn't want to come back." His marriage to Barbara Stanwyck was falling apart.

Gable socialized with the Coopers in New York while he dated the twice-divorced Standard Oil heiress Millicent Rogers, who had a home in Southampton. Millicent wanted to marry Clark; her mistake was to have him followed. He was dating so many women she bowed out. Then there was Dolly O'Brien, the delight of New York and Palm Beach society, who received a $5 million settlement when she divorced yeast millionaire Julius Fleischman. She agreed to marry Gable if he would live in the East, but he said it was too long a drive to the M-G-M studios. They remained a happy couple at the Stork Club in New York until Gable got drunk and married Lady Sylvia Ashley, the widow of Douglas Fairbanks. Three years later Gable would pay dearly for a divorce.

Oddly, Gary felt secure in Clark's company. A mutual friend commented, "Cooper and Gable had many things in common besides hunting, guns, and cars. They were modest men who pursued the best in life—fine clothes, elegant women, expensive automobiles, and money. Lots of money. Clark carried his with him; Gary's was invested. They became close friends in New York. Cooper was accepted by the crème de la crème, who looked down on actors, because he was married to Rocky. Gable mingled a little easier in Gary's crowd. I can't imagine anyone turning the King away, but society has its barriers. They were both very private people and short on talk unless one of them just got back from a fishing or hunting trip. If the Queen of England was being coronated, they would find a corner to gab about the big trout he caught or a pheasant he shot. Gable could take a car apart and put it back together. I'm not sure about Coop, but he'd never walk away from a conversation about high-powered machines. They liked speed. Coop was always trying to break the record driving to and from Sun Valley. Clark was involved in a few accidents; he drove out to the desert and pressed the gas pedal all the way down to the floor."

Life in the Hollywood of 1947 was not a round of parties. The Motion Picture Alliance for the Preservation of American Ideals was striking back at Communist Party members who were infiltrating the unions and guilds. Among the Alliance's founders were Sam Wood, Robert Taylor, Victor Fleming, Clark Gable, and Gary Cooper. All agreed to testify before the House Un-American Activities Committee in Washington. George Murphy, Ronald Reagan, and Adolphe Menjou also volunteered. Although most named names or cited films they were forced to do or scripts they labeled as "pink," Cooper was reticent. He answered in generalities—"I believe so," or "I don't recall exactly," or "Overhearing has been my observation, yes." Often his voice was barely audible as he swallowed between syllables. Obviously he had no intention of getting any suspected communist sympathizers in trouble, as his peers did. Lending support seemed to be enough. Cooper admitted not knowing what a communist was, but he said the Party should be outlawed.

Sam Wood said, "He came across badly. Stupidly. He emphasized hearsay and couldn't remember the names of scripts he turned down because of an un-American theme. He was just as opposed as the others, but could not get himself to label anyone. Maybe it was a mistake to let him testify, but they were suspicious of anyone who didn't and Coop hated the Reds as much as the rest of us did. All and all, it was not a happy time for him. He looked tired and he wasn't sure what direction to take in his career. He hadn't done a good picture in quite a while and he told me, 'I wonder if they're getting tired of seeing the same old me up there saying the same old thing.' "

On October 31, 1947, Cooper signed a contract for a minimum of six films with Warner Brothers that guaranteed him $3 million in five years. The only studio that did not try to sign him was Metro-Goldwyn-Mayer.

Warner's roster included such superstars as Bette Davis, Humphrey Bogart, Lauren Bacall, James Cagney, Olivia de Havilland, Errol Flynn, Ida

Lupino, Dick Powell, Eleanor Parker, and Dennis Morgan. But the Golden Era had ended. Hollywood was different. Contracts were expiring and not being renewed. The standard seven-year arrangement no longer applied. The big stars had out-priced themselves and were aging. When Bette Davis threatened to quit it took Warner fifteen minutes to draw up the appropriate papers. Errol Flynn was bloated from booze and dope. He would go adrift on his yacht, *Yaca,* and die an old man at fifty. Spencer Tracy went on his last drunken binge on location in Arizona. When M-G-M fired him, he sat down on a rock and wept.

Jane Russell, however, signed a twenty-year contract with Howard Hughes for $50,000 a year, whether she worked or not. He guided her career faithfully. Miss Russell's contract was unique, as was her platonic relationship with Hughes.

When Clark Gable heard that M-G-M was not going to renew his contract, he quit. It wasn't long before they went to him about a movie. Gable reportedly told his agent, "Get all the money you can out of them and then tell them to shove it up their ass!" Robert Taylor was the only star who remained at M-G-M, with the longest running contract of any actor or actress in history—twenty-four years. His career was revived in *Quo Vadis* and he became America's Knight in Shining Armor. Despite his million-dollar pension he said to Cooper, "I should have left three years ago, but it's hard when you've been with one studio for so many years."

Union strikes became frequent and films were fewer. European movies flooded the market and television loomed on the horizon. Jimmy Stewart started the trend of taking a minimal salary and receiving 10 percent of the profit from *Winchester '73* made in 1949. It now seems almost unbelievable that the contract players were on straight salary while making movies that made millions for the studios. Gable did not get a percentage for *Gone With the Wind,* which by 1953 had grossed $100 million. The stars deserved their rightful share under the new system, but the studios were forced to reduce the number of pictures they made each year, which resulted in fewer jobs. Many scripts were available, but most were of low quality.

At the turn of the decade, the Method actor descended on Hollywood. Marlon Brando and James Dean had to "get into character" before doing a scene. The big stars were thrown off, annoyed, and disgusted. Joan Crawford said, "They put on a better act *before* the camera rolls, for Christ's sake! They run around the set getting in the right mood—crock of shit—meditate and go into some sort of trance. To each his own, but those kids looked down on us. What the hell had we been doing for twenty-five years? Raising oranges?"

Crawford stuck out her neck and said, "Any Hollywood star who appears on television is a traitor!" She left M-G-M because the newcomers were getting all the good films. "I got the leftovers," Crawford admitted. "I had to break away and begin again though it broke my heart. L. B. [Mayer] reminded me I had been with M-G-M as long as he was, from the beginning almost."

She signed with Warner Brothers and was there when Cooper moved into his new dressing room.

The rising young starlets at Warner Brothers were a different breed. They did not have the voluptuous curves, caressing voices, and sweet faces of the stars of the twenties, thirties and forties. They had class, plain features, and spoke in husky tones. They bore the sign of the New Woman and teased with the sting of a cobra. Lauren Bacall and Eleanor Parker were typical examples.

Patricia Neal was another . . .

10

TRUE LOVE

Patricia Neal was only twenty years old when she appeared in *Voice of the Turtle* on Broadway. Born on January 20, 1926, in Packard, Kentucky, the daughter of the manager of the Southern Coal & Coke Co., she spoke with a slight southern accent. At Northwestern she studied theater arts, but had a natural acting ability, composure, and maturity. In 1946 she won a Tony Award for her performance in *Another Part of the Forest.*

She was not beautiful in the classic sense. The tall willowy blonde had the wholesomeness of Ingrid Bergman and the tenacity of Lauren Bacall. Her most outstanding features were dreamy eyes, arched brows, and a throaty voice that was both seductive and commanding.

Despite her stage success Pat accepted an offer from Warner Brothers and settled into a film career. *John Loves Mary,* costarring Ronald Reagan and Jack Carson, was the screen version of a hit Broadway comedy and her first movie. While she was filming it director King Vidor came to see her about playing Dominique, the spoiled heiress with a heart of steel in *The Fountainhead,* based on Ayn Rand's best-selling novel. Vidor briefly considered Barbara Stanwyck but then decided the role required a younger woman. Ayn Rand wanted Garbo to play Dominque, so Vidor met with the retired Swedish actress. Garbo vacillated and then declined. He knew she wasn't right for the part but wanted to give her the chance to turn it down. He liked Pat Neal right away; she had the strength and vitality to play Dominique.

When Rocky read *The Fountainhead* she knew immediately that Gary would be the perfect Howard Roark, the character supposedly patterned after architect Frank Lloyd Wright. After Gary browsed through the seven-hundred-page book he decided to pursue the role. Warner's original choice, Humphrey Bogart, expressed little interest in it. Though Cooper did not have the dynamic personality of Roark, he shared with the character the quiet determination of a man who refused to accept personal compromise.

The only obstacle was a good screenplay. Ayn Rand said she would write it providing not one line of dialogue was changed without her permission. The story, a tale of individualism and integrity, centered around architect Howard Roark, who takes a job in a stone quarry rather than conform to society's expectations. Dominique Francon, a woman ruled by nothing and no one, seduces Roark without asking his name; she assumes he is a common laborer.

The next time they meet is at a cocktail party to honor Howard for the first skyscraper built to his specifications. When the press and public opinion set out to destroy Roark, he refuses to give in even for Dominique, and she marries another man. He agrees to help a fellow architect design a housing project without credit. When the drawings are changed without his knowledge he blows up the monstrosity. Roark goes to trial and is acquitted. He and Dominique are together at the end. The film shows her riding up a construction elevator to the tallest building in the world. Waiting to greet her at the top is Howard Roark, towering over the skyscraper, hands on hips.

Vidor wanted to film the quarry scene first, at the perfect location he had discovered near Fresno, California. "Gary wanted to drive us up there," Vidor said, "but I had no intention of getting into a car with him behind the wheel! So Pat, Gary, and I took a studio limousine. They had met in my office briefly. She was very taken with him. We all met for dinner and I could tell they were falling in love. I have no reason to believe their romance began in the physical sense during production of *Fountainhead.* When we returned to Warner Brothers in Hollywood, their feelings for each other were obvious."

Cooper was approaching fifty but appeared older. Pat was half his age. "He was a gorgeous man," she said. "For me it was love at first sight and that love never died."

Some observers felt that if it hadn't been for the passionate love scenes in *Fountainhead* the Cooper-Neal romance might never have been. In one sexy scene Dominique chases Howard on horseback and then slashes his face with a riding crop. In another, Howard appears on Dominique's bedroom terrace in his work clothes, with uprolled sleeves, to give Dominique what she's been desiring. They do not speak. She pounds him on his chest, but his strong arms force her into one of the most passionate kisses ever seen on the screen. When they confess their love, Howard picks up Dominique in his arms and asks, "You won't leave me, will you?" Before she replies, he reaches out his long fingers and frames her face as he gently kisses her cheeks, then her nose, eyelids, and hair. It was a devastatingly sensual scene—one Gary and Pat would undoubtedly relive in private many times.

Patricia Neal's portrayal of Dominique was sensational. Cooper's Roark was, frankly, not strong enough. Costar Raymond Massey never gave a bad performance but Neal overshadowed him as well. Financially, the picture was not the success Warner had expected. Vidor said, "Cooper was not well cast, but I knew that. He came through much better than I expected, but the public had a difficult time accepting him as Roark." Considering the fact Cooper bungled his role of Robert Jordan in *For Whom the Bell Tolls* becaue he was distracted by Ingrid Bergman, Gary should be given credit for doing as well as he did in *The Fountainhead.* He deserves more credit for not carrying their torrid love scenes beyond the set until the picture was finished. Gary knew Pat wanted him as badly as he wanted her.

Cooper originally had no intention of becoming entangled with any other woman. He was flattered that Pat, a girl twenty-five years younger, was attracted to him, both emotionally *and* physically. But soon he realized that this was not a passing affair, though Pat had no intention of discussing a permanent relationship.

Gary told her the truth about his relationship with Rocky—that they had an understanding. They had invested sixteen years of their lives to create a lasting marriage. Divorce was out of the question, because Rocky was a devout Catholic, and Gary would never do anything to hurt their daughter, Maria. Pat did not want to break up the marriage, yet she could not accept a back-street affair. She wanted a home and family of her own.

Hedda Hopper understood. "Neither Pat nor Gary were prepared for what happened," she said. "I felt sorry for them. The press had respect and did not print anything about them for a while. There were the usual 'Guess who?' items, but Rocky had seen women come and go in her husband's life. The Coopers continued on with their social life in New York and Sun Valley. Pat was seen with other men, usually Kirk Douglas. She was trying very hard to get on with her life. Gary told me it was wonderful being with her. There was no pretense or heavy discussions. She didn't press him or try to be coy. Pat was honest and straightforward—hardly the type to be hiding in downtown cafés with a man she couldn't have."

In the fall of 1948 Patricia Neal went to England to film *The Hasty Heart* with Ronald Reagan and Richard Todd. Cooper costarred with Walter Brennan and Jane Wyatt in *Task Force,* in a role more suited to him. *The New York Times* said, "Gary Cooper, after mushing the romantic scenes, does a pretty right job of imitating an air officer and then a captain in the midst of war. His scenes as the operating officer of the Yorktown at the Battle of Midway are some of the best in the picture, so far as personal drama is concerned." *Photoplay* thought *Task Force* was a magnificent movie—"Gary Cooper effectively portrays a Navy man who winds up a rear Admiral . . . A classic of its kind."

When Pat returned to New York in February 1949, the Coopers "just happened " to be there, too. Gary and Pat had corresponded by letter and talked on the telephone during her three-month stay in England. When she arrived in Hollywood, Pat was a very happy young lady. The man she loved had been there on the East Coast to welcome her back, and her career was going very well, with a seven-year contract starting at $1,250 a week, escalating to $3,750.

It is doubtful that Warner Brothers wanted to reteam Neal and Cooper on the screen in order to cash in on their affair, because it was not yet public knowledge. Their romantic scenes in *The Fountainhead* were steamy enough to propel them into the forgettable *Bright Leaf,* costarring Lauren Bacall.

The film was routine; there were no surprises or thrills. Cooper was quite good, but Lauren Bacall was restrained. Patricia Neal, on the other hand, overacted. *The New York Times* was amusingly blunt: "Her eyes pop and gleam in crazy fashion, her face writhes in idiotic grins and she drawls with a Southern accent that sounds like a dimwit travesty."

Sometime during the latter part of 1949 Rocky Cooper became aware of her husband's affair with Patricia Neal. How she found out isn't clear, but her evidence was too reliable for Gary to deny. He continued to see Pat and put up a good front at home. Cooper family photographs appeared in the newspapers. Louella Parsons mentioned in her column that the Coopers were building a new house in Aspen, Colorado. Rocky finally allowed pictures to be taken in their Brentwood home. She had never been on the best of terms with the Hollywood press, but used them to prove her marriage was intact.

One day it was a very cozy threesome—mother, father and daughter—the next, Gary was attending Hollywood parties by himself. That's when the separation rumors started. Rocky was in New York at the time and sternly denied it. She emphasized that she was Catholic and, therefore, would never consider a divorce. As usual, Gary said nothing. He and Pat were closer than ever, but rarely ventured out of her apartment.

Meanwhile another "ideal" Hollywood marriage was in trouble. While in Italy filming *Quo Vadis*, Robert Taylor took the opportunity to have a fling with an Italian bit player, Lia DiLeo. She took advantage of the situation by throwing herself in his arms for reporters while flashbulbs popped. The photo made the front pages. Taylor's wife, Barbara Stanwyck, who had a fear of flying, hopped a plane to Rome for a showdown. She returned to Los Angeles and filed for divorce. When he returned to Hollywood, Barbara admitted she had acted on impulse, but Taylor said he wanted his freedom. "I didn't want to be just another divorce statistic in Hollywood," he told Cooper. "And I didn't want to hurt Barbara." Their marriage, like the Coopers', had been considered idyllic.

Pat Neal by accident met the Countess di Frasso while on a publicity tour with several other Warner Brothers' stars in Europe and South America. Elsa Maxwell said, "Dorothy knew about Gary's involvement with her and wished Pat luck. She would need a lot of it, and more."

Cooper, meanwhile, was filming *Dallas* with Ruth Roman, Raymond Massey, and Barbara Payton, with whom he had a "brief encounter." Fortunately, he saw very little of the stunning blond starlet after the picture was finished. A few months later she became engaged at the same time to both Franchot Tone and ex-boxer Tom Neal—she managed to juggle the two men, but when Tom Neal discovered Tone in Barbara's bedroom he beat him up so badly that Tone had to have extensive plastic surgery. Still he gallantly married Miss Payton. They were divorced a year later. Cooper was considering a face-lift—he was relieved that Tom Neal did not force him into having one.

Cooper bounced from one bad film to another. He made a comedy, *You're in the Navy Now,* for Twentieth Century–Fox, with Jane Greer and Eddie Albert, and then went back to Warner Brothers for a cameo appearance in

Starlift. There weren't many good scripts and he was not in demand. His contemporaries were getting all the applause and awards: William Holden in *Sunset Boulevard*, Spencer Tracy in *Father of the Bride*, James Stewart in *Harvey*, Humphrey Bogart in *African Queen*, and Fredric March in *Death of a Salesman*. John Wayne had become a consistent favorite whether he was still fighting World War II in *Flying Leathernecks* or playing cowboys and Indians in *Rio Grande*.

In 1951 M-G-M asked Cooper to do a segment in *It's a Big Country*, a film consisting of several different stories depicting the diversity of the United States. Gary appeared in episode six, "Texas." The picture was such a disaster that M-G-M withdrew it from distribution after a brief engagement.

When Patricia Neal returned from her exhausting publicity tour Gary suggested they visit his good friend, Ernest Hemingway, in Cuba for a while. "We'll do some pigeon shootin'," he said. It's been suggested that Cooper made this trip to consult Hemingway about marrying Pat and that the author, although not overly fond of Rocky Cooper, didn't offer Coop any encouragement. This is curious, considering how similar Hemingway's situation was to Cooper's.

Louella Parsons reported that the Hemingway marriage was in trouble. Hemingway was in love with Adriana Ivancich, a girl who was barely twenty-one. He and she shared love letters. His were filled with such phrases as "I miss your rapier wit and your lovely mind, body, and spirit," and "I want to hold you in my arms." Though Adriana was not physically attracted to Ernest she might have married him for his fame. Papa confided to a friend, "Adriana is as fresh as a young pine tree in the snow of the mountains, strong as a good colt, and lovely as the first ray of the morning sun." He claimed it was possible to be in love with Miss Ivancich and his wife, Mary, at the same time. A few years later he bid farewell to Adriana and sobbed, "Now you can tell everybody that you have seen Ernest Hemingway cry."

Ernest and Gary discussed Pat Neal from sunset to sunrise one night. Mary Hemingway hinted that her husband did not approve of Cooper's flaunting the affair. What Mary didn't say was that she threatened to leave Ernest if he did not stop flaunting his passion for Miss Ivancich.

It is ironic that Adriana and Pat each went on to live such tragic lives. Pat survived, but Adriana hanged herself in 1983 after two divorces, bouts with alcoholism, and nervous breakdowns.

Pat left Cuba for Hollywood with a warm feeling because it was important to Gary that Hemingway liked her, and he did. Cooper flew to New York to appear on a radio show. When he returned to California Pat was doing *Operation Pacific* with John Wayne, who covered for Cooper when he came to visit. During the filming Pat found out she was pregnant. At first she wasn't concerned. After all, if Gary was proud and delighted, so was she.

"But the next morning," she wrote in her autobiography, *As I Am* (Simon and Schuster, 1988), "my joy, my strength, drained out of me as rational terrors whipped my brain. Career. Family. Oh, God—my mother! She would kill herself if I had a baby out of wedlock. And what about Gary? If I pressed him, what would he do?"

There was only one answer. In October 1950, Pat made the decision to have an abortion. Cooper accompanied her to the doctor. "Gary sat rigid in the car," she wrote. "He was also soaked with sweat. We wept together that afternoon. I lay in his arms on the floor and wept."

According to Pat, after Gary told Rocky about the abortion, he packed his bags and moved into the Bel-Air Hotel.

Trying to make a choice between the two women in his life was draining Gary mentally and physically. He was not concentrating on his career. In 1951 Cooper was dropped from the Top Ten box-office stars after being on the list for fifteen consecutive years. Bosley Crowther's review of *Dallas* was intuitive. "There is something about the sadness and the weariness of his walk, something about his manner that is not necessarily in the script."

Yes, Cooper was suffering. His indecisiveness was gnawing away at him. Pat was in pain, too. She yearned for the baby she had aborted. "For thirty years I cried over that baby," she wrote. "If I had only one thing to do over in my life, I would have had that baby."

Rocky was getting along nicely. She had no intention of sitting at home waiting for Gary to return or of giving the impression there was anything wrong. "No one feels sorry for Rocky," Elsa Maxwell said. "She's proud and she's tough. It is Pat who has no friends or had a chance to concentrate on her career. She spends her time alone or with Gary. Pat's a lovely person, but she's the other woman. She has such potential as an actress, too. But when her name is mentioned, Gary Cooper comes to mind."

Hedda Hopper advised Coop to get it over with. "But you'd better be careful," she warned.

"I'm not bein' seen in public," he said.

"I'm referring to a divorce, if it comes to that. Rocky will get everything she can."

"I don't think so."

"She'll make you pay."

"I want Maria to have the best."

"How naive can you be, Gary?"

"Rocky isn't like that."

"I admit she isn't like most women, and that's what worries me. Just tell me one thing. Do you want your freedom?"

"Yes," he said.

"Then do something," Hopper exclaimed.

"Rocky and I are talkin' about a trial separation. What do you think?"

"That's a start, I suppose . . ."

* * *

While Pat had hopes for a future with Gary, she was facing a major career crisis. Warner Brothers declined to pick up her option in 1951, so she moved to Twentieth Century–Fox and took a cut in salary.

Cooper went to Naples, Florida, to make *Distant Drums.* The director, Raoul Walsh, described Gary's foul mood. "We were working in the Everglades, plagued with snakes and mosquitoes. Coop was unhappy and short-tempered in general. He killed a rattler and tore off the skin like a banana peel!"

The reason for Gary's outbursts soon emerged: Rocky's attorneys formally announced the Coopers had separated.

Pat faced the news alone in Hollywood while Gary was peeling snakes in Florida. "I had nothing to do with his marriage problems," she insisted. "No one can break up a happy marriage. Everyone knows that. I hope this talk dies down. I come from an old-fashioned background and this is very upsetting."

Her few friends at Twentieth Century–Fox tried to help Pat deal with the swarms of reporters. Gary might have used his influence or made a statement, but he said nothing. Director Michael Curtiz recalled how Cooper declined to intervene for Pat when she made it clear that she preferred Lauren Bacall's role in *Bright Leaf.* "Cooper could have suggested the reversal of roles. She wanted a chance to talk about it. He did nothing. He didn't want to become involved. I waited, but . . . he did nothing."

Cooper's friends claim Pat could take care of herself—that she had more guts and determination than Gary did. But the fact is she didn't know the right people and never took advantage of her relationship with Gary to further her career. On the contrary, her association with him made her seem all the more "the wanton woman," drawing comparisons with Ingrid Bergman, who had recently left her husband and daughter for another man. Since most moviegoers were women Pat Neal was doomed. Hollywood insiders were divided, but the majority scorned her. Her name was taken off the guest lists at dinner parties and other social gatherings on and off the set. She was left to fend for herself.

There were rumors that Rocky's and Gary's attorneys were negotiating a settlement. The press estimated Cooper's net worth to be around $3 million.

In August 1951, Gary checked into St. John's Hospital in Santa Monica for a hernia operation. A week later he drove to La Jolla Playhouse near San Diego to see Pat appear in T. S. Eliot's *The Cocktail Party,* with Vincent Price. He was cordial to reporters, but chatted only about the play. Because he appeared so pale and tired they did not inquire into his personal life.

After months of silence Pat finally loosened up with reporters. But all she said was "Am I in love with Gary? Maybe." She smiled. "But I'd be foolish to go around advertising it. He is, after all, a married man. I'm very fond of him. We're good friends. He's a wonderful guy."

Meanwhile, Rocky wasn't playing the martyr. She was seen in New York on the arm of millionaire Bob Six, Ethel Merman's former husband. According to close friends, rumors were spread that he was about to propose marriage. Six was serious about Rocky. "I'm cautiously elated," Pat Neal sighed.

High Noon was written by Carl Foreman after he was blacklisted by the House Un-American Activities Committee. Foreman left the United States for England, where he settled down and raised a family. In 1951 producer Stanley Kramer approached John Wayne about playing Marshal Kane, who faces four outlaws alone when the townspeople refuse to support him. Wayne turned down the part. Years later he attacked bitterly: "What about Carl Foreman? I'll tell you about Carl Foreman and his rotten old *High Noon*. Everybody says it was a great picture because Gary Cooper and Grace Kelly were in it. It's the most un-American thing I've ever seen in my whole life! The last thing in the picture is ol' Coop putting the U.S. marshal's badge under his foot and stepping on it. I'll never regret having helped run Foreman out of this country!"

Cooper was not the first, second, or third choice to play the role. After Wayne, Charlton Heston and Marlon Brando were preferred. Gary Cooper was considered over the hill and going down. His marriage was on the rocks and he wasn't in good health. Gary's hip bothered him and he had an ulcer, but Kramer was willing to take a chance. Cooper agreed to do the low-budget Western.

In this, her second film, Grace Kelly portrayed the marshal's Quaker wife. Her soft attractive looks were perfect despite the twenty-eight-year age difference between her and Cooper. Gary wasn't so sure. "They might laugh at me playin' opposite a young girl," he told Kramer, who assured him that Miss Kelly would be insignificant in *High Noon*.

Production began in California's Sonoma Mountains. While Grace was rehearsing her lines and camera positions with the director, Cooper unexpectedly ambled over and offered to read the dialogue with her. The one observer who wasn't surprised was Miss Kelly. She glanced at him fondly.

Gary had invited Bob Slatzer to drop by and discuss a fishing trip. The two men were sitting by themselves on the *High Noon* set. "Coop had just finished a scene with Grace," Slatzer said. "She was getting ready for some close-ups. Coop's eyes were fixed on her although we were a safe distance away."

Gary smiled sheepishly at Bob and asked, "What do you think of that filly?"

"She's all right. Good little actress."

"Yep. She's got a lot goin' for her."

Slatzer said the sparkle in Cooper's eyes revealed more than just admiration of her acting talents. When Grace finished her scene she plopped herself on Gary's lap and kissed him on the cheek. He smiled and looked a little embarrassed, his face flushing red under the makeup. He wiped the lipstick off his cheek with a handkerchief. She teased him about planting one on the other cheek. He said softly, "Not here."

Grace listened intently while the two men talked about their fishing trip. "Going to take *me*?" she teased.

Cooper swallowed hard.

She pressed him for an answer and placed her hand on his knee. He blushed again, looked down at her hand, and tried to be casual. "Well, I don't think you'd enjoy fishin'," he said with a smile.

There was a long pause. Slatzer, sensing Gary's nervousness, asked her, "Have you ever been fishing?"

"Sure I have," she replied. Then she winked and looked at Cooper. "But I was just kidding about going with you fellows."

"I figured," he sighed.

Slatzer recalls that he stayed for lunch, but Grace didn't sit at their table. When she threw a kiss at Gary, he mumbled to Slatzer, "That was for you."

"She was looking your way, Coop."

"Why don't you do something about that? She's available, I hear."

"I can't compete with you," Slatzer said.

"I'm twice her age."

"I wouldn't let that stop me."

"That's all I need." Cooper scowled. "I've had some close calls."

Grace walked over to their table and looked at Gary. "You know that you don't act—you *react!*"

"Ain't that the way it's done?" Cooper asked.

"We have a love scene to do later on. Are you ready?"

Again the silence was broken by Slatzer. "Coop, you're one lucky guy."

"Isn't he?" Grace smiled.

Gary chewed and swallowed hard. "Yep, guess I am."

A few weeks later Slatzer ran into Grace Kelly at the Polo Lounge in the Beverly Hills Hotel. She invited him to a small dinner party.

"Will Coop be there?" he asked.

"He only comes around when I'm alone," she replied.

Gary apparently heard about her comment and casually brought it up while he and Slatzer were on a fishing trip.

"Understand you took Grace out. I guess I'd kinda be out of school if I asked if you went to bed with her."

Slatzer grinned. "You would be."

"I shouldn't ask a thing like that."

Cooper and Kelly made the gossip columns, but like his affair with Ingrid Bergman it was over by the time filming was completed. Their comments about each other for the record? Grace said, "Everything is so clear working with Gary Cooper. When I look into his face, I can see everything he's thinking. But when I look into my own face, I see absolutely nothing." Gary, in turn, thought she was very serious about her work. "She was trying to learn," Cooper commented. "You could see that. You can tell if a person really wants to be an actress. She was one of those people you could get that feeling about."

Gary's closest friends considered Grace one of his cherished lovers. She talked about him all the time and he constantly brought her name up in conversation. They loved each other for the brief spell together, but were not "in love." Gary and Grace were too much alike—each was given to brief, intense affairs.

Cooper went back to Hollywood and Pat Neal.

Grace flew off to a romance with Clark Gable while they were filming *Mogambo* in Africa. She would become intimately involved with Jean-Pierre Aumont, Bing Crosby, William Holden, and Oleg Cassini. Her affair with Ray Milland during Hitchcock's *Dial M for Murder* almost ruined both of them. Twice her age and married, Milland fell head over heels in love with Grace. He left his wife. M-G-M stepped in to prevent the scandal from worsening. Grace said she didn't care. She had been nominated for best supporting actress in *Mogambo* and Hitchcock wanted her for his next film, *Rear Window*. M-G-M reminded her she was under contract. Four public affairs in one year with married men was enough to break her. But Grace had too much confidence in herself to worry. Her parents flew to California to reason with her, but their pleas fell on deaf ears. But when Mrs. Milland filed for divorce, Miss Kelly fled to New York and into Oleg Cassini's arms. The Millands reconciled.

In the early fifties, Clara Bow told Louella Parsons just what she thought about Gary and his flings. "Gary called me about *High Noon* and asked if I'd ever heard of Grace Kelly, but the name didn't ring a bell. He told me she was a vision, very beautiful and very sexy. He was in love again.

"I don't get around much, but I do talk to a lot of old friends in the business. They told me Grace Kelly was not the angel she appeared to be. I should talk, but I did look the part of the girl-about-town. She doesn't.

"I'd heard he was serious about Pat Neal and it's a crazy thing because Gary never mentioned her. I figured he had his reasons so I wasn't going to pry. One of my friends thought it was terrible that he was cheating on that girl . . . Neal. I said, 'What's new?'

"I never regretted what I did for Gary or our times together. I only regret the things I did not do. He had a wandering eye for pretty girls and no woman could stop that—not me, not Lupe and not his wife. If we had put aside our jealousies and coasted, it's possible we might have made a go of it. I missed him. I missed him lots. Yeah, he was great in bed. The best, but he treated me like a lady. His mother thought I was shit. What else is new? She thought Lupe was a floozy and she filled Gary's head full of nonsense about her. Lupe was true blue, you know? She meant well. I am sure Gary's mother lied to him, saying she was cheating and making up all kinds of awful things that weren't true. I read in the gossip columns that she isn't so chummy with Gary's wife, either. If he married the Queen of England, she wouldn't be good enough for him. She poisons his mind. She's the biggest phony of them all. Often I think of how I might have handled her if Gary and I became engaged. We never discuss her, either, but I can tell Gary needs someone to talk to and who else knows him better than me?

"All the damn publicity about my running around, and I did. But Gary didn't do so bad. His appetite for sex was the same as mine, but it's tough to find a man who is not only a terrific lay, but a gentleman, too. He was very hurt when I went to court. Very concerned. Things were so much different then, of course, but I have only myself to blame for what happened. Men can get away with anything, but women are expected to be pure. It's been twenty years since the trial that broke my heart. If it happened today, I'd still be a whore. Grace Kelly, however, will get away with having many lovers. Know why? The damn public will never believe it.

"It's nice to know Gary was the one who helped her get a good start in the movies as I did for him. That's something one never regrets. Love has nothing to do with it."

11

A LOST SOUL

Hedda Hopper knew the end of the Neal-Cooper affair was coming. "Gary was taking Pat out in public. And occasionally to Hollywood parties. It was just a matter of time before they would run into Rocky. It happened at a party that movie producer Charles Feldman gave for Dolly O'Brien, the socialite. When Gary and Pat walked in they went directly to the end of the bar. There they remained until dinner was announced. Rocky, on the other hand, arrived with Peter Lawford, and went immediately to the table assigned her.

"I was sorry Pat didn't look prettier that night. She wore flowers in her hair, like an ingenue. They didn't become her. Rocky, in contrast, being a sophisticated woman of the world and having all the cards in her hand, was very gay, danced every dance, and never took the smile off her face.

"At about midnight—when Pat was dancing—Coop got up and, for a few minutes, visited Rocky's table. Everyone held his breath. I would not be surprised if it was then and there that Pat accepted the fact that things would not work out."

The truth was, Cooper was ill and had not been well for some time. During *High Noon* the pain from his hip and ulcer was evident. The strain of Pat's abortion, his official separation from Rocky, the knowledge that Maria knew about his relations with another woman, and his declining popularity in films all contributed to his deteriorating health.

The day following the party for Dolly O'Brien Cooper flew to New York "on business." The next time he spoke to Pat he was calling from the hospital. He was going to be operated on for a duodenal ulcer. Pat wanted to catch the next plane, but he told her not to come. She was so upset to be shut out of his life that, in desperation, she called Alice Cooper, whom she had met several times. Alice offered her no comfort and even laid responsibility for her son's ulcer on Pat.

Pat dialed the hospital in New York.

"Gary, it's all over," she said and hung up the phone.

Alice had won again.

According to Pat's autobiography, the 1951 Christmas holidays were lonely ones for Pat. Her sadness turned into so many regrets. She loved Gary more than ever. He had given her many expensive gifts during their three years together. This Christmas he did not forget. A card enclosed with the gift read, "I love you, my baby. Gary."

Gary did not reconcile with Rocky. He remained at the Bel-Air Hotel and told friends he wanted to get away and travel, perhaps to Europe. Pat tried to reach him, to apologize, to begin again. When she finally got him on the phone his voice was lifeless. His plans for the future were uncertain; his hesitation forced her to slam down the phone once again. In later years she said, "I was very much in love with him and he was in love with me. But after three years I began to lose weight and I was headed for a nervous breakdown."

Cooper secretly consulted a renowned specialist in New Orleans and checked into a hospital there for another hernia operation. Pat went to stay with her mother in Atlanta, where she, too, was put under a doctor's care. The press knew nothing of this.

In January 1952, Rocky was quoted as saying, "Any time Gary wants a divorce he can have one." Several times a week she was written up in the gossip columns. She was dating Bob Six and the former All-American athlete Howell van Gerbig, and was escorted around town by Rock Hudson, Peter Lawford, and Robert Wagner.

High Noon was nominated in 1952 for Best Picture and for Best Theme Song, and Gary for Best Actor. The studio was elated. From a half-million dollar budget it grossed $8 million. Gary had been sure the members of the Academy of Motion Picture Arts and Sciences would not take a second glance at old Marshal Kane with the haunting eyes and craggy face.

Pat returned to Hollywood with renewed health and a determined outlook despite her assignment to *Something for the Birds,* a dreadful picture with Victor Mature. She went on dates and was slowly getting back into the social scene.

Unfortunately she ran into Gary at one of the parties she went to. This time he approached her. "He looked terrible," she said. "Gary was a mess. He had tears in his eyes and asked me over and over if I was all right. Everyone in the place was watching. Finally he got up and went into another room. I never saw the girl he came with."

Pat Neal made up her mind to put Hollywood behind her and return to the Broadway stage.

One of Cooper's friends recalls, "Coop never asked for a divorce. Rocky knew him better than anyone else and he didn't have the fight in him. He rarely mentioned Pat Neal by name after they parted. It was 'she' or 'her.' I don't think he had the heart to say, 'Pat.' He was shattered when she left him for good. He never got over it, but he admitted he had never given her any hope for the future. Actually, Coop didn't want to give up his place in society. If Rocky hadn't come from a very rich family, Coop would never have given up the Countess di Frasso. He liked people with money. He didn't give that impression, but he thrived on the rich. He had a fabulous wardrobe. Everything was made to order. Coop loved the good life and he was in awe of Rocky because she never knew how to live any other way but rich. Yet he told me how wonderful it was to relax with Pat. There was no pretense with her. No phoniness. She never tried to impress him. 'I can be myself,' he said. I wanted to tell him that every married man says that about his girlfriend."

Very few people actually knew that Gary and Pat had ceased to see each other. Most assumed they were in hiding and covering up by dating others. One day he was seen dining with Rocky and then she was off to ski in Colorado or back in New York dancing with Bob Six.

In 1952, Cooper filmed *Springfield Rifle,* a picture the critics found "satisfactory." Once again he was back in the saddle and number two at the box office. But the cowboy from Montana was a very unhappy man.

Pat Neal found an apartment on Fifth Avenue in New York. "I will not see Gary if I go back to Hollywood," she told Hedda Hopper. "We love each other very much, but when I saw it wouldn't work, I stepped out. I have a lot of living to do and I want to live it with someone who is unattached. Something permanent. Gary is wonderful. But he is a very, very complex person, as you know. We're through. It's over. Wouldn't you know it would be just my luck to fall in love with a married man?"

"How many times have you been in love, Pat?"

"Only once," she sighed. "And I ended up on a psychiatrist's couch. It will take a long, long time for me to get over Gary . . ."

While Patricia Neal was struggling to maintain her sanity and pride, Cooper flew to the South Seas to film *Return to Paradise.* He coated his bleeding ulcer with coconut juice spiked with vodka. Actress Roberta Haynes, his costar, claimed that their relationship was purely platonic. He told her, "Don't be upset if I don't make a pass at you. The medication I'm takin' makes me impotent." But reliable sources insist Miss Haynes was more than his costar. She had had a bit part in *High Noon.* Gary used his influence to get her the lead in *Return to Paradise.*

Working conditions on the Samoan location were deplorable. Because Cooper was a major star, the rest of the cast assumed he would use his influence to make their living quarters, including his own, more bearable. He made some weak threats, but spent his energy fishing and drinking. Miss Haynes said, "When Gary came to the islands, he'd made the decision to go back to Rocky. He was doing it because of his daughter. I don't think it was a happy decision for him. He was not a joyful man. He was beginning to look very careworn."

Cooper returned to Hollywood and spent much of his time hunting and fishing with Clark Gable, recently divorced from Sylvia Ashley; Robert Taylor, who was living with German actress Ursula Theiss, whom he would eventually marry; and John Wayne, who was trying to get a divorce and marry wife number three. Unattached and discontented, the men headed for pheasant country or for the trout streams.

Ralph C., Taylor's buddy, usually tagged along. "For a while in the early fifties, the guys were single or separated, so we got together more often," Ralph said. "Bob was ten years younger than Coop and Clark, but they all had a kind of restlessness. They were running and drinking more than usual. Sometimes we went to a whorehouse. Gable used to say there were no commitments there. I had known them all for a few years, but never envied their fame and wealth. They never flaunted what they had. I remember this particular phase because here were three of the biggest stars in the world and they were confused and depressed. Bob wanted to marry Ursula, but he was afraid of hurting Stanwyck. Gable's marriage to the Ashley woman was a disaster and he still talked about Carole Lombard. He could finish a bottle of brandy at one sitting. Then there was Coop. He liked the upper crust and did not want to take one step backward. That's what bothered him about getting a divorce. He wanted his cake and eat it, too. I found him to be a weak and selfish man and from what I heard, he didn't like the taste of humble pie. Don't take my word for it, though. I thought I knew Taylor, but we had a silly fight over a few bucks and he never spoke to me again."

Gary bounced around and dated no one in particular. He enjoyed the company of beautiful Kay Spreckels, the ex-wife of sugar heir Adolph Spreckels II. (Kay would later marry Clark Gable in 1955 and give birth to his only child four months after his death.) Kay was seen about town with others—always millionaires or handsome actors. How she handled Cooper isn't known, but she did tell Gable "Go shit in your hat!" when he told her to get undressed on their first date.

Gary did not attend many parties while he still carried a torch for Pat; he did not want to link his name with other women for fear of embarrassing Maria. "I was hounded by reporters," he reflected years later. "They asked questions about Rocky and me. If I was seen with a girl twice, the press blew it up into a serious romance. I tried to be pleasant because I was pretty 'hot copy' at that time. There was no place to hide. The only thing to do was get away from Hollywood. I figured I could get myself together in Europe and maybe find some peace." And maybe reduce his 1953 taxes by remaining out of the country for eighteen months, as so many of his peers were doing.

On his way to Europe Gary stopped off in New York and invited Dorothy di Frasso to have dinner with him. Anderson Lawler, who was then producing plays on Broadway, joined them. While Cooper was abroad, the countess died from a heart attack in her train compartment while returning to New York from Las Vegas. She was wearing a diamond necklace and was wrapped in a full-length coat. She had less than $50,000 in her bank account.

* * *

As Joan Crawford once said, "There is nothing like an Oscar to cure one's aches and pains." And it was true. Cooper appeared to regain his good health when he won Best Actor in April 1953 for his portrayal of Marshal Kane in *High Noon.* He had never expected to win against stiff competition from Marlon Brando in *Viva Zapata,* Kirk Douglas in *The Bad and the Beautiful,* Jose Ferrer in *Moulin Rouge* and Alec Guinness in *The Lavender Hill Mob.* But win he did.

Buddy John Wayne accepted the award on behalf of Cooper with a rather amusing speech considering he had turned down *High Noon* and blackballed the author, Carl Foreman.

"Ladies and gentlemen," the Duke said, "I'm glad to see that they're giving this to a man who is not only most deserving, but has conducted himself throughout the years in our business in a manner that we can all be proud of. Coop and I have been friends hunting and fishing for more years than I like to remember. He's one of the nicest fellows I know. I don't know anybody nicer. And our kinship goes further than that friendship because we both fell off horses in pictures together.

"Now that I'm through being such a good sport about all this good sportsmanship, I'm going back and find my business manager and agent, producer, and three name writers and find out why I didn't get *High Noon* instead of Cooper."

No one was more surprised and grateful than Coop. Despite the renewed popularity the Oscar brought him, Gary was happy not to be in Hollywood. European royalty opened their palace doors to him—even Queen Elizabeth of England was no exception. He was seen with many women, but the press did not link him with anyone until he reached the Cannes film festival. There he met actress-model Gisele Pascal. With that familiar twinkle in his eyes, there was no doubt Gary had fallen for her.

The news media were very familiar with Gisele. She had been the mistress of Prince Rainier of Monaco for six years and now had given up hope of ever becoming the Princess of Monaco. Cooper ignored the royal protests and made headlines. When Gary went to Paris, Gisele followed. The paparazzi caught them at dinner, holding hands, dancing. The gossip columns were filled with reports of champagne, moonlight, and romantic kisses. The tabloids announced, "They are in love!" Newsmen asked Gary if he was planning on marrying Gisele.

"I'm afraid I can't talk about that," came his reply. "You see, my wife might not appreciate it, and she's coming over here with our daughter next week."

Gary and Gisele were last seen at a very romantic dinner in Paris. A few days later Gary was driving Rocky and Maria to Italy in his new Mercedes-Benz. They granted private interviews in Rome and posed for pictures as a happy family.

On July 2, 1953, Patricia Neal was married to British writer Roald Dahl after her successful Broadway run in *The Children's Hour.* Thirty-five years later Patricia recalled her wedding night. "Tears rolled down my cheeks. I could feel my heart breaking. I so wanted to be married, but to another man."

At the time the Coopers were in Spain attending the grand opening of the Hilton Hotel in Madrid. When columnist Radie Harris, also a guest, told Gary about Pat's marriage, tears welled in his eyes and he turned pale. Then very quietly he murmured, "I hope he's a helluva guy. She deserves nothing but the best."

Rocky and Maria returned to America, and Gary flew to Mexico to film *Blowing Wild* with Barbara Stanwyck, who played the unscrupulous wife of an oil baron, Anthony Quinn. She falls in love with wildcatter Cooper who will have nothing to do with her, so she "accidentally" pushes her husband into an oil well, where he is killed by a pump. Horrified, Cooper almost strangles her, but is interrupted by a Mexican bandit attack. Barbara is killed, and Gary returns to Ruth Roman, the woman he loves.

In one of the scenes Cooper was badly injured when fragments of a dynamited bridge struck him, resulting in contusions and severe wounds. Bruised and tired, he returned as a "guest" to his Brentwood home. Rocky said her husband needed rest. "Yes, he's home," she told Louella Parsons. "You can put any interpretation on it that you like."

A few weeks later he was back in Mexico to film *Garden of Evil* with Richard Widmark and Cameron Mitchell. On the set he was overheard saying, "I only went home for a little while." He backed up this statement by dating French model Lorraine Chanel. Like the others, that affair ended when the cameras stopped rolling. Tired of being grilled with questions about the women in his life, Gary said, "I'm seeing a few girls. Lorraine isn't the only one!"

Henry Hathaway, director of *Garden of Evil,* saw nothing unusual about Cooper's one-night stands. "The only disappointment was the kind of women he chose," Hathaway commented. "He was still highly charged sexually and needed a variety of girls, but they were floozies. After Pat Neal, he went after anything because Coop didn't want to get involved. In a way it was sad because he was a gentle and sincere guy. Instead of that shy flirtatiousness, he'd make a pass and leave with the girl, park his car in front of her place, and spend the night. We used to wonder when he'd grow out of that boyish approach toward women and when finally he did, it just wasn't our Coop."

Gary had another hernia operation before filming *Vera Cruz* in Mexico with Burt Lancaster. He was again injured when an extra's rifle fired by accident and the wadding from a blank hit Cooper in the left shoulder.

Was the violence worth it? *The New York Times* didn't think so. "Guns are more important in this shambles than Mr. Cooper or Mr. Lancaster. In short, there is nothing to redeem this film." But fans loved *Vera Cruz.* With Cooper and Lancaster on the marquee, it proved to be a box-office success for Warner Brothers.

* * *

Gary returned to Hollywood and moved back home on a permanent basis. Louella Parsons wrote, "If all the women had the good sense of Mrs. Gary Cooper, fewer marriages would end in divorce courts. Rocky was sure Gary would come back to her even when he moved into a hotel and was in Mexico so long, and she waited until he decided that home was the place he wanted to be."

Cooper told the press, "You can't live with a woman seventeen years as I did with Rocky and not know all the good things about her. After that many years together there are moments when everyone feels he'd like a change. Rocky has done a magnificent job with our daughter. I think Maria is the finest young girl I've ever known. She is religious, she is wise beyond her years, she loves to ski, ride horseback, and she participates in all the sports I enjoy."

As a new lease on the marriage the Coopers purchased an elegant modern home in the exclusive Holmby Hills area of Los Angeles. Rocky became more flexible about allowing members of the press into their living room, and Gary began to open up. He said he had learned a lot. "I've led a full life. If I died tomorrow, I'd have no regrets."

Rocky, too, spoke openly. She declared that her husband was free to go wherever he wanted. "I'm never going to object," she said with a smile. "I think we both learned a lesson. It was worth waiting to have him come back."

But a socialite friend of the Coopers revealed that Rocky and Gary occupied separate bedrooms. "That's common in Hollywood," she emphasized, "but this was a marriage of convenience, for Maria's sake. That was the understanding. Gary was a very lonely man . . . a very sick man. I didn't know Patricia Neal well, but well enough to know she was paying her debt to society as was Gary. She told me once at a crowded cocktail party that she didn't know why she married Dahl. I wasn't going to discuss it and I'm sure she had no intention of doing so."

At lunch one day with Bob Slatzer and Richard Arlen, Gary told his friends, "I'm tryin' to get an independent film company together and make some of Hemingway's short stories abroad."

"Abroad?" Arlen smiled. "Like England?"

"They have the best facilities."

"Among other things."

"I don't get ya."

"Coop, don't go around kidding yourself."

"Dunno what you're talkin' about," Cooper said nervously.

"Doesn't Pat spend most of her time in England?"

"Makin' films there is cheaper."

Bob winked at Dick to "knock it off." Soon the conversation got around to *High Noon*.

"The whole damn picture was a success because of the editing," Cooper said, smiling. "When they got that tickin' clock in, it had more lines than I did."

"Seems most of Grace ended up on the cutting room floor," Bob commented.

"Yep," Cooper agreed nonchalantly, "and they dug up every shot of me lookin' half dead . . . shots they weren't gonna use."

"Grace upset?"

"Dunno."

This was the opening Arlen was waiting for. "Say, lover boy, you and that Kelly girl were quite an item."

"Just rumors," Cooper snapped.

"How did she compare to Clara Bow?"

Gary hesitated, swallowed hard, and managed, "Did Clara really take on that football team one night?"

"Did she ever!"

Slatzer said, "There must have been something to it. Duke Wayne told me he was sorry he missed out."

"Duke said that?" Gary perked up.

"The gospel."

"She had hinged heels," Arlen said. "You know that!"

"Sorta, I guess . . ." Cooper scowled.

"Hell, she saw more ceilings than Michelangelo."

Again Bob tried to change the subject. "Grace Kelly is up for an Academy Award in *Country Girl,*" he said. "Nobody wanted her to take such a dowdy part."

"I knew she had somethin'," Gary said, digging into his lunch.

"Quite a picture of her in the paper saying farewell to Gable in London," Arlen said, grinning. "Think they had something going, too?"

"It was the first time she'd ever been away from home alone," Bob commented. "Six months in Africa is no picnic. *Mogambo* was very good, though."

"With John Ford directing?" Gary laughed. "Bet he taught her how to really act. Did Ford refer to her as 'Kelly,' Bob? Someone said so."

"How the hell would I know?"

"Well . . ."

Slatzer looked at Cooper and laughed. "We don't keep in touch, if that's what you're referring to."

"You're the writer."

"You're smart," Arlen teased. "Never put anything down on paper, is that it?"

Cooper shrugged, wiped his mouth, and put his napkin on the table. "As Papa Hemingway used to say, 'Always stand in back of the man who fires a gun and in front of the man who shits. Then you won't get shot at or shit on.' "

"Jesus!" Arlen roared, slapping Gary on the back. "That was great and you didn't even have a script!"

After World War I Brigadier General Billy Mitchell, the assistant Chief of the Army Air Service, tried to show army and navy officials the importance of air power. After many fruitless attempts, he was relieved of his command.

Though Cooper was reluctant to do another biographical film, he thought Otto Preminger's directing of *The Court-Martial of Billy Mitchell* would lend authority to the picture. He was wrong. The movie failed to portray a dedicated man sacrificing himself for the defense of his country. Mitchell was a flamboyant and determined person in and out of uniform, but Cooper had none of his strength and dynamic presence. He was wrong for the part and the weak script failed to tell the real story of Billy Mitchell.

Cooper appeared on "The Ed Sullivan Show" to promote the picture. Because he looked so ill, rumors spread that he was dying. Like every movie star appearing on live television Gary found it a terrifying experience. His fear only intensified the pain of recurring ulcers and the throbbing hip. His health continued to decline.

The Court-Martial of Billy Mitchell was highly publicized. *Time* magazine's description of Cooper was amusing enough to convince the public to see it for themselves: "Gary Cooper plays the flamboyant Billy for a sort of militant old maid, and his historic cry for justice for the air service sometimes seems almost as exciting as an old maid's protest that the neighbor's cat has swallowed her beloved canary."

It was no secret that Cooper had had numerous operations and that his recurring hip ailment made it difficult for him to mount and ride a horse. Yet he traveled abroad with his family whenever possible, mingling with such notables as the Duke and Duchess of Windsor, and Lord Mountbatten.

Why, he was asked, didn't he retire then, or make only an occasional film?

"Because I can't afford to," he replied.

In 1956, Cooper was selected the best-dressed screen actor, an honor he accepted with his characteristic self-effacing humor: "I guess the only time I have my picture taken in public," he said, smiling, "is when I'm all dressed up."

While he was window shopping one sunny day on New York's Fifth Avenue, he ran into Patricia Neal Dahl for the first time in three years. They had a drink together, and found that nothing had changed between them. It was confirmation that what they had shared was rare and everlasting. It was a chance meeting; that was all. They would not see each other again for several years.

Cooper next made *Friendly Persuasion* for United Artists; it told the story of a Quaker family during the Civil War. His costars were Dorothy McGuire and newcomer Anthony Perkins, who had dated Maria Cooper a few times. *Films in Review* wrote, "Gary Cooper as the loving and loved Quaker husband and father has never more aptly utilized his great American face, nor acted more ably."

Both the film and Perkins were nominated for Oscars. The competition was especially stiff that year. Mike Todd ran up the aisle to claim his award for *Around the World in Eighty Days,* but not before dashing back to kiss his bride, Elizabeth Taylor. Anthony Quinn won for Best Supporting Actor in *Lust for Life.* But the most exciting and surprising winner was Ingrid Bergman—who had been banned from the United States for eight years—for Best Actress in *Anastasia.* Her marriage to Roberto Rossellini was coming to an end, and Rossellini refused to accompany Ingrid on her triumphant return.

"I decided to fly to New York for the New York Film Critic's Award," she said, "but I asked Cary Grant to represent me at the Academy Awards. Of course I was frightened about the prospect of returning to America. Ernest [Hemingway] met me in Paris and insisted he go along with me and be my protector. I told him I was afraid, but that I had to be completely alone and unprotected. That's the only way I could go back—all by myself. It was a wonderful homecoming and I'm so glad I did it my way. I went back to Europe and was in the bath listening to the Oscar presentations. Cary Grant accepted my award and began, 'Dear Ingrid, wherever you are . . .' And I was saying, 'I'm in the tub!' "

She had come a long way since *For Whom the Bell Tolls.* Like Patricia Neal, she had continued her work in the theater. Cooper would never again become entangled with women of their stature.

Sonny Tufts, an excellent supporting actor who enjoyed discussing his own sexual exploits as well as those of his buddies, said of Gary's later years, "Coop wasn't going to give up his reputation as a ladies' man. He got smart, though. He went out for the hell of it. The romance bullshit was over. He was going to have fun as long as no one got hurt. Coop said that's all he wanted. He referred to girls as 'fillies' and he said, 'As long as the little fillies want me for a good roll in the hay and not for who I am, that's okay. I'm not for chasin' much these days, though.' Coop always did like a variety and I can't say that I blamed him because I was that way, too. He met a girlfriend of mine at a party, took her home, stayed the night, and went right to the studio in the morning. She told me he was something else for an old man! I thought that was very funny because he was only around fifty-five. She thought it would be a quickie, but he went to work and she stayed in bed for some rest. I knew this girl very, very well and she was capable of handling three men without taking a deep breath. I was a little envious, frankly, because I was ten years younger than Coop and she made me feel like a schoolboy, which I wasn't! I thought Coop would like to hear all about it and he apologized for taking out one of my fillies."

Tufts said he could not have cared less.

"I won't see her again 'cause it was nothing,' " Cooper said.

"Are you nuts?" Sonny howled. "She can't wait to—"

"That's what I *don't* want . . . some who can't wait."

"Coop, I'm sorry I mentioned it, but I thought you'd get a big laugh."

"She never mentioned your name . . ."

"Naturally."

"Not that we did much talkin'," Cooper said thoughtfully.

"Of course." Tufts smirked.

"I don't much like runnin' around in my own backyard. I'd like to do some more films in Europe."

Tufts, who himself deserves a book about his dalliances, also lived life to the hilt. Cooper was amused by his stories. According to Bob Slatzer, "We had nothing much to talk about on fishing trips except women, and Coop loved gossip even though he didn't do much of it himself. But he had a male ego. I realized that when he questioned me about Grace Kelly. Once in a while Coop would talk about how close he came to marrying Lupe and Clara, who snuck away after her marriage to Rex Bell to meet Coop. According to her, the flame never went out—he would always be grateful to her for giving him a break in movies. Clara said, 'I had to push him. He was lazy. I never thought he'd amount to anything. He was clumsy. This embarrassed me. I told him to pick up his feet. He'd stumble over a thimble on a football field. The reason I fought to get him parts was so he could be with me.' "

Slatzer mused that perhaps in his later years Cooper was trying to relive the early days. "He told me on location doing *High Noon* that memories of Lupe were everywhere because they had done *Wolf Song* nearby. Coop never mentioned that Pat Neal came to visit while he was working with Grace Kelly. He apparently carried it off very well. Grace thought it was very funny and that Pat kept an eye on her. She was tempted to make trouble for the fun of it, but decided not to. Knowing Coop he probably told Grace to cool it. It is very difficult to define Coop's standards when it came to women. He was a possessive and jealous guy. He didn't like to share his women regardless of his infidelities.

"He showed me some scars on his arms and body. They were memories of Lupe, but he smiled as if they were important memories of fighting and then making up, something they did beautifully."

Confidential magazine supposedly caught up to Gary Cooper. In their January 1956 issue, headlines on the cover revealed GARY COOPER'S LOST WEEKEND WITH ANITA EKBERG!

He met the actress at a party and took her home. A reporter from *Confidential* gave a minute-by-minute account of their meeting, up to when the lights in Ekberg's apartment went on, and off.

Cooper told a friend, "They must have followed me with a stopwatch!"

12

MAY–DECEMBER

The lead in *Love in the Afternoon,* an international playboy who falls for a young music student in Paris, had been developed with Cary Grant in mind. But Cary had another commitment. Twenty-eight-year-old Audrey Hepburn was cast as the chaste daughter of a detective (Maurice Chevalier) whose police files on adultery and scandal spur her vivid imagination. Gary Cooper accepted the role of the distinguished roué. Some might have thought that playing opposite a girl half his age would have made Gary apprehensive, but he didn't hesitate.

Producer and director Billy Wilder wasn't worried about Cooper's ability to portray the skirt-chasing older man because Gary was acting out the role in real life. It was Gary's aging features that caused some difficulty. Wilder filmed with gauze filters on the camera lens to mask the imperfections. Wilder's other problem was Cooper's two left feet. In the ballroom scene, Wilder called Coop 'Old Hopalong Nijinsky.' The director recalled, "We gave him lessons and he got through it painfully. It came over pretty well on film, though."

As always, Audrey Hepburn was delightful. (She had won an Oscar for *Roman Holiday* with Gregory Peck in 1953.) Happily married then to Mel Ferrer, Audrey was not a likely candidate to be one of Cooper's women. Besides, Gary knew that William Holden was carrying a torch for Audrey. "I was really in love with her, but she wouldn't marry me," Holden said. "So I set out around the world with the idea of screwing a woman in every country I visited, and I succeeded. When I got back to Hollywood I told Audrey about it. All she said was, 'Oh, Bill!' like I was a naughty boy."

Cooper especially enjoyed working on *Love in the Afternoon*—it was shot on location in Paris. His family joined him eventually and he proudly escorted his beautiful twenty-year-old daughter Maria everywhere. When they traveled to Rome on a short break Gary arranged for an audience with Pope Pius XII. Cooper also introduced her to Pablo Picasso. Maria, like her father, was interested in painting. But Gary had no intention of spoiling her. He preferred that she date respectable boys from the East. Her mother was an exceptionally good influence and, though strict, wanted Maria to enjoy life like a normal teenager. She had none of the typical traits of a big movie star's daughter. Maria was a Hollywood rarity.

As a young child she was precociously bright. David Niven recalls, "I was having a Christmas party for my sons. I invited kids from the neighborhood as well as Maria Cooper. Roz Russell's kid, Edgar Bergen's 'Candy,' and so forth. Tyrone Power offered to play Santa Claus and while I was helping him get dressed I mentioned there were about fifty kids at the party. Ty screamed, 'Fifty!? Hand me that bottle!' Well, he kept taking swigs and by the time we got to the party, Santa Claus was feeling no pain. There was a HO! HO! here and he took another swig. HO! HO! there and then another swig. Then Ty finally got to Maria and he blurted out what a very pretty girl she was and to tell her Daddy that old Santa thought he was great in *Unconquered* and could he have Paulette Goddard's phone number. Maria was more sophisticated than the other children and slyly asked where 'Santa' had seen the picture. Ty raised his arm with another slurred HO! HO! and bellowed 'Up there!' motioning to the North Pole. Maria was very sweet about it and played along. I think she was around eleven or twelve years old. Poor Ty was so glad to get out of there. Last I saw he was staggering across the lawn to his house."

When Gary returned home to stay, Maria was nearly eighteen. She loved and idolized her father. In her eyes the three-year "interruption" had not been his fault, but rather that of another woman who had tried to take him away. Maria loved him no less. Now she was comparing her beaus to Gary. Very few came close to the gentle tall man with the glistening blue eyes who looked upon her with such devotion.

Hedda Hopper remarked, "It's a shame that so many children of Hollywood are confused in the shadow of their famous parents. Maria Cooper wasn't one of them."

For many troubled children of Hollywood stars, suicide was the only solution. The sons of such greats as Louis Jourdan, Charles Boyer, Gregory Peck, Dan Dailey, James Arness, Ray Milland, and Paul Newman are among the victims. So were the daughters of Art Linkletter, Jennifer Jones, and her husband David Selznick. According to Christina Crawford her mother tried to kill her, and Cheryl Crane accidentally stabbed gangster Johnny Stompanato when he threatened her mother, Lana Turner. The estrangements are too numerous to mention.

Rocky Cooper set an exceptional example for her daughter by keeping a level head and her house in order. She did, however, tell Maria about Gary's affair with Pat Neal right in front of Gary. Pat tells the story that once, while dining out in New York five years after her breakup with Gary, she looked around the restaurant to find Maria glaring at her with hatred. "It was a terrible feeling," Miss Neal said sadly. "I knew then how much she had been hurt."

Cooper would live the rest of his life trying to make up for his three-year separation from Rocky. One wonders what would have happened had Rocky turned him away. Whatever the new conditions of their relationship, she was in command. If Gary strayed occasionally, Rocky was used to it. She'd been through the worst.

* * *

Love in the Afternoon might have been the one Cooper film his many fans snickered at. *The New York Herald Tribune* wrote, "Love in the Afternoon is the kind of movie that you either like or dislike emphatically." Still, he remained one of the screen's top ten stars. And everyone left the theater humming the theme song, "Fascination." The film's ending seemed to justify the story—a tale of a May–December romance between the gaunt middle-aged man, Cooper, and a wisp of a girl, Hepburn. Cooper leaves Hepburn believing their affair foolish and without a future. At the climax Hepburn chases the departing train, tears in her eyes, her arms outstretched. He reaches out for her and like a feather, she floats into his protective embrace. The reviews were mixed.

The New York Times critic wrote, ". . . what charming performances Audrey Hepburn and Gary Cooper give as the cleverly calculating couple who spar through the amorous afternoons."

Family Circle was more candid: "By keeping Gary Cooper mostly in the shadow, Wilder nearly makes one forget that Coop may be a little mature for the part of an American playboy who woos and wins Audrey Hepburn with the aid of soft lights, champagne and a waltz called 'Fascination.' "

Cooper liked his new image and accepted a similar role in *Ten North Frederick.* One wonders about Cooper's willingness to relive the theme of his own life's sorrow, his affair with Neal. In fact, *Ten North Frederick* has often been referred to by Hollywood insiders as the Gary Cooper Story.

The ailing Spencer Tracy was Twentieth Century–Fox's first choice for the part of the unhappily married man who falls hopelessly in love with a younger woman, and who ultimately returns to his shrewish wife and disillusioned daughter. In the end he dies of a broken heart.

Cooper played himself in *Ten North Frederick*—stoop-shouldered, shy, henpecked, and weary—a man who goes to New York to find his runaway daughter and falls in love with her roommate. Ultimately the difference in their ages forces him to leave her, the only love he has ever known. He returns home to reunite his family before dying. The similarities with Cooper's own life then are astonishing.

Suzy Parker, a beautiful redhead who was America's most highly-paid fashion model, played Cooper's love interest. He behaved as he had with Grace Kelly—rehearsing dialogue together and bolstering her confidence. Everyone who knew Cooper suspected an affair. His name was linked with hers in all the newspapers. The cast and crew on *Ten North Frederick* were divided in their opinions, but alert reporters thought they had all the proof they needed.

One supporting actor in the picture thought Suzy Parker was the most beautiful woman he had ever seen: "She's tall, she has remarkable bone structure in her face and shiny thick long hair. She has poise and patience. Suzy and Gary were a believable couple—a remarkable couple in the film. It was a pleasure to watch them. Any man who could breathe was attracted to her and I doubt that Coop was the exception. He spent a good deal of time with Suzy. There were scenes that reminded me of *The Fountainhead* . . . she sitting on the floor with her head in his lap and he stroking her hair. Coop's been criticized for making love to young girls on the screen like Grace Kelly and Pat Neal and Audrey Hepburn, but he was the master in these roles. There was a helplessness and hopelessness in his face. I recall seeing him at a dinner party with Pat some years ago and he had the same expression in his eyes, the twitching around his mouth and the clenching jawline. He came across as a man who was starved for a little bit of happiness, a moment of intimacy. This was Cooper and I'm not referring to his acting.

"I know that he and Suzy were very fond of one another. A man doesn't change just because he's getting older. You are what you are, and Cooper liked women. If it was only a warm and platonic relationship between him and Suzy, I'd have to say he wasn't feeling well."

Rumors of an affair persisted for quite a while until Paul Shields, Rocky's seventy-year-old stepfather, made headlines in *The New York Daily News* after he was seen cruising down the East River on his yacht with Suzy Parker.

No comment from all concerned.

Ten North Frederick was a fine film. The casting was superb. Geraldine Fitzgerald, as Cooper's bitchy wife, convinced the audience at first glance that she was selfish and domineering. Gary was just right as the middle-aged man reaching out for a moment's happiness. His eyes are pathetic and empty until he meets the warm and sincere Suzy Parker. The dialogue was in good taste, the story was believable, and the characters were convincing. *Ten North Frederick* was a sensitive picture tastefully presented.

To date the critics had generally been kind to Cooper. *Time* magazine, however, pulled no punches—"Gary Cooper is getting a little too old for love scenes."

After two consecutive movies opposite beautiful women half his age, Cooper had his face lifted. He denied it vehemently. "I had a cyst removed from my jaw and they fixed up the other side," he told columnist Earl Wilson. "I don't know why they're makin' such a big thing out of it."

Wilson inquired about his health in general.

"I was up over two hundred pounds, but my ulcers' startin' actin' up and the special diet made me lose about fifteen pounds."

"And your hip, Gary?"

"I should be used to the pain," he replied, "but it's gotten so bad I can't sit a horse for very long. Had to give up skiing and tennis."

"How do you spend your spare time when you're not traveling?"

"I play some bridge and I have my dogs. I miss ridin', though."

Not all the reporters were as sympathetic as Wilson. They pushed and prodded. They wanted to know more about Gary's cosmetic surgery. After all, his face looked different. The consensus was that the lift "didn't take." To this day even Gary's most protective friends admit he had work done on his face, cyst or no cyst.

Robert Taylor, who for the majority of his movie career had been shy and self-effacing about his extraordinary good looks, confessed: "It gets to a point if an actor wants to keep working, he has to have the creases and crow's feet removed from around the eyes. We didn't have much choice. It wasn't a matter of wanting to subtract the years or wanting to play younger men. Let's just say an actor is supposed to grow old gracefully. Squinting under the hot lights and in the bright desert sun took its toll. I might add that the younger actors are having facial surgery done before it's too late, but if I had my life to live over, that would not have been for me."

On January 14, 1957, Humphrey Bogart died.

On April 11, 1957, Patricia Neal Dahl gave birth to her second daughter, Tessa, in Oxford, England.

And very quietly Gary Cooper had another ulcer operation.

Joan Crawford thoroughly enjoyed discussing her fabulous film career and was very candid about the other celebrities with whom she shared the limelight in the thirties and forties. She cursed Spencer Tracy to her dying day because he poked fun at her acting during their brief affair. Of John Wayne she sniffed, "Get him out of the saddle and you've got nothing." Yet she pursued him for years while Duke refused to take her calls. She said "sex is good for the complexion" when she married Franchot Tone. "Now I can do it for love."

"We worked together the year he married Rocky," she said about Cooper. "And he was trying to live down his past indiscretions. He was a homebody then. He told me his wife got up early to make him breakfast and every evening he left the studio in time to have dinner with her. According to him, Rocky read all his scripts and he valued her opinion because she could be objective. He was the one who rushed into marriage. His image needed improving very badly. Any actor who is known as 'Studs' needed a new image.

"I know the press and everybody else expected Gary and me to have a hot affair. The timing was all wrong. We became friends socially during my marriage to Franchot who thought Gary was an empty-headed hick. Franchot was a Phi Beta Kappa and he was a big polished stage actor. Though he liked Gary, he also considered him a big joke. One night he came home during *Bengal Lancer* and said, 'Every time I try to chat with Cooper it's a one-way conversation.' He was annoyed because Gary walked through his scenes in a daze. The truth of the matter is that Gary's great death scene in Ronald Colman's arms in *The Winning of Barbara Worth* was so good because Gary actually fell asleep!

"I think it was Jim Tully who said, 'Cooper's head is like a gorgeous room with no furniture in it.' But, you see, he had the most amazing blue eyes that said so much. And he had a way with his body—the way he walked, that was so special particularly in Westerns. He made Levis popular just as I made shoulder pads the rage. Gary was made for Levis or is it the other way around? He did not look so great in suits. I think he was more comfortable in Western togs. He communed with nature and he loved gardening. Maybe that's why he was a loner."

Life magazine had similar sentiments about the Cooper image: "There's a fellow who doesn't need a Brooks Brothers suit, shoulder pads, a button-down shirt, a hand-painted tie or even a shoeshine. Just give him a pair of tight-fitting pants for his legs to strain against, an old shirt and vest to keep his chest expansion within bounds, a black string tie to hide his Adam's apple, and a dusty pair of boots to die in.

"He'll go riding away tree-tall and grim, looking the way a man should look, a friend to the righteous, a hero to children, and a flytrap to women. Doesn't have to say a word. Doesn't even have to smile. One look at Gary Cooper and the weak take heart, the villains take to cover and the women faint."

When asked what his favorite film was, Cooper answered, *The Virginian.* He spoke about Westerns with great warmth. "To do one is like goin' on a vacation. I get exercise and wear comfortable clothes. *The Virginian* was my first talkie and I knew then that Westerns would improve—they'd have a new life."

Hedda Hopper reminded him about the thousands of letters he'd received since *High Noon.* "That's what the public wants," she sighed. "It doesn't matter what else you do, Gary. They want you in spurs."

He nodded wearily. "I don't know which way to turn these days."

"You told me once that cowboys never complain about their aches and pains. That was Marshal Kane and that's Gary Cooper, right?"

He didn't say anything.

"You can name your own ticket," she reminded him.

"Not if there aren't any tickets left." He smiled weakly.

The advent of television caused a lack of good film scripts, because movies were losing money and script writers were jumping on the TV bandwagon. "But I'm lookin'," Cooper said. "Hell, with a broken hip I went on roundups back on the ranch in Montana. All these years I've been sittin' on a horse with an aching hip. Guess usin' a double once in a while's no sin. Yep, I'd do a Western if I had to."

Cooper gave his fans what they had been waiting for—*Man of the West,* a rousing, shoot-'em-up Western and one of the best Gary Cooper ever made. Julie London, Lee J. Cobb, and Jack Lord were his costars. It was a violence-ridden movie and the first Cooper feature *not* to open on Broadway in over three decades. Its biggest business was in the action-and-grind movie houses where his fans stood in line at the box offices.

The only compliment came from *The New York Times:* "Cooper still rides as if a horse taught him!" If his fans didn't like to see Gary in one of the meanest fist-scrounging duels seen in years on the screen, they were satisfied to see their cowboy in his boots, ten-gallon hat, leather vest, and gunbelt.

Why hadn't he done a Western in five years? "Because most of 'em are just Easterns with men wearing big hats," he replied. "They're cops-and-robbers stories. I turned down ninety-nine out of a hundred offered to me."

The Coopers spent a relaxing vacation in the Bahamas with Mr. and Mrs. Henry Ford II in 1958. Gary took up skin diving, one of the few sports that he found painless. He enjoyed exploring the depths of the clear blue water, but then had to give even this up because of damage to his ear resulting from the dynamite blast in *Blowing Wind*.

But he had more time for vacations now. His fans were satisfied that he was still fast on the draw and still sitting tall in the saddle. After all these years, Jesse Lasky proved he was right when he told the discouraged fellow from Montana, "Your talent is in Westerns." No one will ever know the pain Cooper endured to satisfy his fans and maintain an image.

Gary, however, was concerned about aging. He dyed his hair a sandy brown shortly after the reported face-lift. However, he still looked pretty good for a man in his late fifties and he loosened up somewhat. When Tyrone Power died of a heart attack in 1958 at the age of forty-four, Cooper realized life was short. There was no guarantee tomorrow would come. He had not talked much about his years in Hollywood—the beginning, the hardships, and the movie industry in general. Life would be incomplete somehow if he didn't express his thoughts.

The late fifties were a time of reminiscing. "I've taken acting seriously," Cooper said in an interview. "I'm not very good. You've got to have a fire under you. When you're new, a beginner, you've got to have fire under you all the time. Now when I read stories I think I've read these same lines before. And when I read them I try to keep in mind whether or not it would sell at the box office. Pictures run in cycles. I'd like to do something different, but not startle the world with an artistic floperoo. I just want to do something that isn't running in every other theater."

Gary reflected on his life in Montana, his early years in Hollywood, and some of the women he loved. "I think I was in love with Miss Velez," he said in an interview with several fan magazine reporters, "or as much as one could get with a creature as elusive as quicksilver. You couldn't help being attracted to Lupe Velez. She flashed and stormed and sparkled. On the set she was apt to throw things if she thought it would do any good. She didn't like to be called wild, though. She was a generous girl. Not many people knew that. She took care of her family. She treated her mother like a queen. The whole family kinda took advantage of her, but she did what she could. She was a sensitive and religious girl—that's why she didn't like to be called wild or exotic. She'd say, 'I'm Lupe.'

"The countess took me in hand. I was really down in the dumps when we met. Her villa was where the international set congregated—all kinds of heiresses, celebrities, noblemen, and so forth. They gave me a little confidence. It was hard to tell if the countess gave one party that went on all summer or a lotta weekend parties that lasted all week. People kept coming and going. The countess did everything in a grand manner. She summoned the Italian cavalry to ride with me one day just because I didn't have any company."

Cooper was not available for comment on Lupe's suicide. He suffered alone. When asked about Clara Bow, he said, "That was mostly publicity." His friends thought he might have given her more credit and respect than that. After all these years, he was still afraid of his past linkage to the poor "It Girl." He was also reluctant to discuss Evelyn Brent. It was Joel McCrea who helped her when she was on motion picture relief.

Though he never revealed too many details about their relationship, Gary was delighted to discuss Grace Kelly. He spoke at length with Hedda Hopper about how very special Grace was. "I also feel she filled a much-needed gap in motion pictures," he said. "When she came along we didn't have an actress who looked like she was born on the right side of Park Avenue. She gave the impression she was a cold fish with a man until you got her pants down and then she'd explode."

In an interview with *The Saturday Evening Post,* Cooper gave this weak explanation for his separation from Rocky: "I wasn't satisfied with anything, least of all myself. I talked it over with Rocky. She understood me better than anybody else in the world, and she knew, probably better than I did, that the time had come for me to take another long walk alone. We agreed that the separation should be legal, and I took off. My take-a-walk formula that worked so well in the past was a bust from the very start. I tried Europe, and that was no good."

Director Stuart Heisler, who knew Cooper over the years, remarked, "Coop had a temper that no one likes to discuss. I saw him rip into everyone on the movie set once and he tried it on me. I told him where he could shove it and he apologized. He was a one-liner. I've spent hours with Coop when he said nothing and then popped up with something like, 'I always regretted slapping Lupe.' So, I asked him why he did it. 'She was the one filly I could trust, but I thought she was runnin' around and said so. She threw the first punch, though. Lupe had a violent temper. All I did was try to calm her down.' Another time we were taking a drive in silence when he popped out with, 'Did I ever tell ya that the countess was gonna buy Paramount?' I shook my head and took a stab at asking him when this was. 'When I told her I was leavin' Italy.' Coop half smiled. He gave me the impression that it was a 'cute' gesture on her part—and *that's* how much she wanted to hang on to him.

"As for Clara, she never told him she aborted Harry Richman's baby. That's the only one she ever admitted to. I know Coop believed her story about not being able to have children.

"Then there was Victor Fleming. What a guy he was—one of the best movie directors in the thirties and forties. He was about fifteen years older than Coop, but he had affairs with Lupe and Clara. Ingrid Bergman was in love with him, too. Vic was half American Indian, a real man's man, and women were nuts about him. He and Coop seemed to cross paths when it came to girls, but they were gentlemen about their mutual affairs." Heisler laughed and added, "Clara was crazy about Vic, too, but after he left her house she'd run to Coop for satisfaction."

Jack Oakie was the only one of Gary's friends to acknowledge the role of Anderson Lawler in Gary's life. And all he said was that they were "very close friends for a while." But in Boze Hadleich's *Conversations with My Elders* (St. Martin's, 1986), which consisted of in-depth interviews with famous gays like Cecil Beaton, George Cukor, Sal Mineo, and Rock Hudson, Beaton remarked, ". . . nothing like his [Cooper's] stereotype of the slow-talking cowboy. Erudite, charming, spectacularly constructed man. Eddie [Goulding] once told me he worshipped him—twice a day." (Eddie Goulding directed *Paramount on Parade,* and appeared with Cooper in his one skit.)

Hadleich asked if Beaton was a frequent "worshipper."

"Don't get me back into religious hot waters," was the reply.

"I believe it was Cooper's lover Lupe Velez who said that Cooper had the biggest organ in Hollywood, but no ass to push it with."

"That's probably been said of half the actors in Hollywood."

"And the other half?" Hadleich asked.

"Vice versa," Beaton replied. When Hadleich mentioned Coop's name in his interview with Rock Hudson, Rock just laughed.

Anderson Lawler died in 1959 at the age of fifty-six. In many biographical accounts of Cooper's early days in Hollywood, his involvement with a man is hinted at. Few mention Lawler by name. Yesterday's Hollywood crowd took such rumors in stride.

One old-timer, who was a bit player in films and gave up acting to work as a technician, matter-of-factly said, "No big deal! The public loves that stuff, because it proves that flaws in their idols exist. But they don't know the half of it.

"This generation thinks they invented homosexuals. Hell, we had 'em out here. The others switched because there's a price to pay in Hollywood. Some price, fun! The casting couch is well-known, but who's sharing it? Bisexuals? Common here in Hollywood, but the truth is only surfacing now because gays are standing up for their rights.

"The sad side is that too many actors had no choice. I don't know about the Gable-Haines thing, but . . . it's true Gable was starving to death and needed a job.

"The Cooper rumor was something else. He lived with that rich guy for a few years like Cary Grant did with Randolph Scott. Cooper found out pretty quick that he could do two things well . . . ride a horse and . . . fuck! He used them both to his best advantage. The others had talent, for Christ's sake. He used to hang around the studios but that was a plus, you see, because Gable couldn't get in the gate back around 1925 or 1926. And how did Cooper get inside? He screwed the girls . . . clerks, secretaries, script girls.

"I saw him during *It* with Clara Bow and he was not bad-looking. They put a suit on him and it hung like a burlap bag. She led him around the way she did her dogs. Clara was smart. She wasn't polished, but she had him beat. So did Lupe Velez who came from a distinguished Mexican family. She could speak English better than I could, but the accent made her famous.

"There was a story going around town that Lupe suspected Lawler and unzipped Cooper's fly when she got him alone to find out if there was any sign of Lawler's cologne."

13

". . . SUNSET"

Cooper chose another Western—*The Hanging Tree*—after the great success of *Man of the West*. He costarred with Maria Schell and Karl Malden. Filming took place forty miles from Yakima, Washington. Gary's old friend and double, Slim Talbot, had a small role as a stagecoach driver.

In the film, Gary's unique posture on a horse became exaggerated. He leaned to the left with both hands braced on the horn of the saddle, and rode in considerable pain. Luckily, as a frontier doctor, he wasn't required to do much horseback riding. But he was unable to do several required riding sequences because of the pain.

When the director, Delmar Daves, became ill and had to be hospitalized, Cooper asked Karl Malden to take over. "I wasn't prepared," Malden said, "but Cooper encouraged me. When we went over his scenes I found out he needed to be shown what to do. I'd act it out and then he'd do the scene exactly the same way. He knew the lens of the camera. People mistook his ability to relax on the set for indifference, but he was concentrating."

Despite the constant hip pain during *The Hanging Tree*, audiences saw a healthier Cooper. Undoubtedly it could be attributed to his cosmetic surgery and dyed hair. *Variety* said, "Cooper has one of his best roles. His mystery and tight-lipped refusal to discuss it [his past] perfectly suit his laconic style." *The London Observer* wrote, "Mr. Cooper is still one of the most reliable cowboy heroes on the screen."

That year he also did a TV guest spot in "Alias Jesse James," a Western comedy produced by and starring his friend Bob Hope. Gary played himself, wearing Western attire, a tin star, and six guns. Also in the film were Hugh O'Brien as Wyatt Earp, Ward Bond as Major Seth Adams from "Wagon Train," James Arness as Matt Dillon, Fess Parker as Davy Crockett, Gail Davis as Annie Oakley, James Garner as Bret Maverick, and Jay Silverheels as Tonto. Roy Rogers and Gene Autry also played themselves.

Cooper was next offered *The Sundowners*. He told Hedda Hopper, "I would like to see Australia where it's bein' filmed, but turned it down. I'd like to work with Deborah Kerr, but it's kinda nice having the family with me on location. Rocky said it was okay if I went alone."

Hopper knew the real reason Coop did not want to go on long trips by himself. Everything he did now was planned as a family venture. He was winding down, she thought to herself.

"Is it true you're converting to Catholicism?" she asked.

"Yup, I've been thinkin' about it a long time."

"Are you sure?"

"It was my idea, Hedda. Maybe it started when we had an audience with the Pope. Then I got to thinkin' how our family had tried to do everything together. Rocky was born a Catholic, and Maria is very devout. I felt like an outsider sometimes. We talked about my converting, but I brought it up. There's somethin' peaceful about their outlook on life . . . something I never really had. When things got really tough, Rocky turned to religion and was stronger for it. And I think Maria's religious belief had a lot to do with her serenity . . . I used to say she is wiser than her father. But it's her faith, and I know that now. We're a family and I want it to be complete."

"Something was missing in your life?" Hopper asked.

"Sure. I knew it, but I didn't want to get all wrapped up in religion. I was afraid it would take over—that I'd have to make big adjustments, but that's not the way it was at all. It's very simple because it kinda puts my life in order. I'll never be a saint."

Hedda asked Gary if the rumor was true that Rocky was prepared seven years prior to grant him a divorce. Only Hedda Hopper could have gotten away with such a touchy allusion to Pat Neal.

"Can't say," he mumbled restlessly. "I think she would have given in to make me happy. Rocky suffered through that decision by herself. She was misunderstood then. Anyway, it didn't come to that."

In a separate conversation with Hedda, Rocky commented, "Gary's very, very happy about becoming a Roman Catholic. It took a long time to make up his mind, but he's finally seen the light."

Alice Cooper didn't approve at all. She said that as far as she was concerned her son would always be an Episcopalian at heart.

Gary continued to grant interviews about his new outlook on life, but still denied ever having had a face-lift. He told Hollywood writer Ruth Waterbury: "Until now I spent all my time thinking about what *I* wanted to do, which wasn't always the polite thing. When I was younger all I wanted was to get bigger and better parts and to meet more beautiful and sexier girls. I've had a lot of good things, maybe too many of them. Fame. Success. Money. And of course love. I guess plenty of love. I've had moments of swellheadedness, too . . . moments of horrible conceit. Maybe that's what happens when you make a go of it in this business.

"People brushing my coat and powdering my face and interviewing me and nine million otherwise sensible people wanting to know what my favorite dish is. That's apt to make you think you're a pretty remarkable fellow. One thing my new faith has taught me is that life is as complex as human beings are complex, and you come to judge people and events with less harshness.

Take a little thing like the way I used to talk about people behind their backs. I never meant any harm. Mine was the kind of gossip we all indulge in, particularly in Hollywood. But the next day I'd think, 'Now what the heck did I say that for?' That's sure a small correction to make in my character, but I'm tryin'. I want to be a little better. Maybe I'll succeed."

On April 9, 1959, Gary Cooper finalized his conversion. He became a Roman Catholic at the Church of the Good Shepherd in Beverly Hills.

When Gable was asked why he agreed to make *The Misfits,* his reply was, "For the money. One more film and then I'll retire." He was forced to stay in bed for a week to pass the film's insurance physical.

Hollywood insiders also questioned Cooper's decision to star in *They Came to Cordura.* "I need the dough," he said with a crooked smile.

Stanley Kaufman wrote in *New Republic:* "It is just painful to see a dignified man of almost sixty being dragged a hundred yards on his face by a runaway railroad handcar; socking and being socked. No matter that doubles are employed for the really rough stuff and clever cutting helps the rest. It's the idea that's upsetting. Cooper is not a two-fisted brawler anymore. It hurts. It actually hurts the viewer's joints and back to see him pretend to his earlier admirable activity. In *They Came to Cordura* he had to do such feats. They, the producers, are using this gentleman shamelessly. It ought to stop."

Cooper revealed that the real reason he turned down *The Sundowners* was his doctor's advice. Yet he ignored their protests over *They Came to Cordura,* which was filmed in the blazing Utah sun.

He looked terrible. He looked tired and old. The image of a major in the 1916 Mexican expedition against Pancho Villa hardly befitted him. Despite an excellent cast—with Van Heflin, Richard Conte, and Rita Hayworth—the $5-million film was a disaster.

"Rita and I hit it off fine in *Cordura,*" Gary said. "She does a bang-up job in the picture. I think if I play opposite girls that look over twenty-five I'm all right. It's a funny thing, though. When you play in a Western, nobody is bothered by how old the girl is. Of course when you hit my age you have to have an adult love story."

Fortunately for Gary's health there was no romance between Gary and Rita—only the implication of one.

Tab Hunter, who also appeared in *Cordura,* told writer Hector Arce, in his book, *Gary Cooper,* "I dated Maria Cooper for a while. She was very held back and suppressed . . . a late bloomer. Her mother wanted so much for her, only the best. I don't think she ever allowed Maria her freedom. Maria was always walking on egg shells, afraid to make a mistake. Coop went along with it." About Rocky, he said, "I like ballsy women, but when they get to be too aggressive, it bothers me. I used to find myself saying, 'Yes, you're right.' One day I said to Rocky, 'That's a bunch of shit!' She looked at me and said, 'Well, maybe you're right.' We got along fine after that."

Variety confirmed almost everyone's opinion about *They Came to Cordura*: "Gary Cooper is very good as the central figure, although he is somewhat too old for the role. It is hard to believe that a man of his maturity would only then be finding out the things which Cooper explores as part of his character. Miss Hayworth gives the best performance of her career."

Cooper's last film of 1959 was *The Wreck of the Mary Deare,* in which he plays the role of an aging sea captain. The movie was based on a novel by Hammond Innes, who owned a ten-ton ocean racer that he sailed thousands of miles a year. One night in 1953, off Cherbourg, he came upon a steamer drifting in the mist with only one light visible. Before he could signal, the steamer started its engines, turned on its lights, and moved away.

Cooper plays the captain of the abandoned ship who joins a young skipper, Charlton Heston, in an underwater expedition to solve the mystery of the sunken *Mary Deare*. Heston said the deep-sea diving was difficult. "I had to learn," he explained, "but Cooper knew what he was doing. We worked all day. It was terribly exhausting. He'd come up debilitated. In every scene we had to get wet and dirty and remain under awful physical pressure. He kept himself in fine shape and did all the dives himself."

Heston admitted not making friends easily, but he and Cooper quickly became friends. "We went out for dinner and the theater several times a week. We were leaving a crowded restaurant once and a young kid looked up and said, 'Hey, there goes that cowboy star.' Cooper stopped and glared at the boy and then uttered his famous line from *The Virginian*: "If you wanna call me that, smile!' Nobody said anything for about thirty seconds. Then Cooper nodded and walked out."

Gary was not always so accommodating to his fans. Once at a classical music concert at the Hollywood Bowl, a fan approached Gary from behind for an autograph. Gary pretended not to hear. The man shouted the request. Cooper concentrated on the music without blinking. The eager fan mumbled, 'He must be deaf!' and was about to try yelling a third time when the other symphony lovers told him to leave. The persistent fan appeared again when Cooper and his entourage left the concert. Gary still pretended not to hear the pest who found it hard to believe that his favorite cowboy was going deaf.

Cooper appeared to be more comfortable on European soil. He particularly enjoyed working in England, where he had attended school so many years earlier.

While he was filming *The Wreck of the Mary Deare* at the Elstree Studio near London, Gary had an unexpected visit from Patricia Neal Dahl, who was also filming a movie nearby. Her excuse for visiting the set was to see Charlton Heston, with whom she had attended Northwestern University.

Cooper was rehearsing on the ship's deck when Heston noticed Pat. Heston whispered something in Coop's ear, Gary froze for a few seconds, and then continued on with his dialogue. When he finished rehearsing he went over and sat down beside her. After their brief chat, he thanked her for stopping by, grasped her hand, and kissed her on the cheek.

Pat cannot remember the conversation. They never saw each other again.

Cooper looked emotionally exhausted in *Mary Deare* and, rightly so, a bit mature for underwater combat. *The Beverly Hills Citizen* commented, "Unfortunately, the action calls on Gary to save the obviously younger and stronger Heston's life . . . to engage in a fist fight with him and to worst him in a somewhat preposterous manner. Thus, those in charge of *Mary Deare* have made the same mistake as a number of other filmmakers recently where Cooper is concerned. They insist on presenting him as oh, so noble . . . oh, so virile . . . oh, so pathetic and misunderstood because of his reticence . . . giving him things to do that would be more credible if handled by his younger adversary."

Actually, no one forced Gary into roles more suited to younger men. He had chosen these parts himself, having formed his own production company to give him ultimate say over what parts he took on (he named the company Baroda after the street on which the Coopers lived). The rest of Gary's films, beginning with *The Hanging Tree,* were all of his own choosing, even though they were released and distributed by other companies.

His choice of Westerns proved that he knew what he could do best. Yet *Cordura* and *Mary Deare* did nothing except further damage his health. Those who knew him somehow suspected that he wanted it that way. One friend commented, "When Gary converted to Catholicism, he seemed to rally. It was like a sudden burst of energy, but the real harm had been done. He was a very sick man. I saw him fall down more than once. I was reminded of Clark Gable when he lost Carole Lombard. Gable didn't give a damn. He joined the Air Force with a death wish that lasted until the end. Coop had only one reason to live after Pat left him and that reason was Maria. Oh, Rocky was his strength, too. He needed her. In Hollywood we say a man takes a long time killing himself. Women do it quickly with drugs. Even though Errol Flynn was only fifty when he died in 1959, he had been challenging death for almost twenty years. Flynn didn't want to live. The coroner said he had the corpse of an old, old man."

Following *The Wreck of the Mary Deare* Cooper accepted an invitation from Russian Premier Nikita Khrushchev to visit Moscow as official representative for *Marty,* the first American film to be shown in the Soviet Union in many years. After six grueling days that included a visit to Leningrad, the Coopers returned to their house in Holmby Hills.

Gary was tired. His passion for hunting and fishing slowly diminished. Doctors warned him about his strenuous outdoor activities and his overexertion working in films. Both were blamed for his many hernias.

On April 13, 1960, Gary was admitted to Massachusetts General Hospital for a prostatectomy. Ten days later he was released.

Just one month later he checked into Cedars of Lebanon Hospital, where part of his colon was removed. Doctors found cancer, but they agreed with Rocky that it was best not to tell Gary the truth.

He told the press, "I was living with uremic poison for a couple of years. I knew about it but you just keep putting those things off. Then I made arrangements to make a couple of pictures in Europe. I didn't want to have any trouble while in a strange country, so I had the prostate operation. Then I had an obstruction that was about to strangle my intestines. It's a good thing I got it taken care of."

Around the same time, Coop's friend, Ernest Hemingway, checked into the Mayo Clinic. He was treated for hypertension, liver and kidney disease, high blood urea, and mild diabetes. After his release, Papa lost interest in the outdoors and, tragically, his writing. Unable to concentrate, he told a friend, "I'm losing my marbles." He was readmitted to the Mayo Clinic and given shock treatments to relieve depression. Because of repeated attempts to kill himself Hemingway was placed in a suicide-watch section. When he returned home, he spent his time staring into space and hallucinating. His wife Mary hid the kitchen knives and locked away his guns and rifles.

Ernest confided in Gary, to whom he spoke on the telephone frequently, that he was a "miserable, failed Catholic," but he made no effort to leave the church. "I'll have a Catholic funeral," he said. "I'm sure it will turn out all right. I believe in belief."

While Cooper was recuperating he gave several interviews. He was optimistic about the future—and objective about the past. He told writer Leonard Slater, "Nothing I've done lately, the past eight years or so, has been especially worthwhile. I've been coasting along. Some of the pictures I've made recently I'm genuinely sorry about. Either I did a sloppy job in them, or the story wasn't right. I can't blame anybody else for the stories that didn't come off.

"If I don't get fired up about a story, why should the audiences? I have to take a personal interest in my work to make it believable. And yet I can't force an interest in a character if the story has holes in it that make it illogical or unsound. When I get talked into the project I don't believe in, I'm the one who's wrong, not the fellow who does the talking.

"I intend to take care of myself from now on, so that I can be around a while. As an actor, I want to do something better than I've ever done."

Clark Gable died on November 16, 1960. He had just completed *The Misfits* with Marilyn Monroe, whose tardiness caused countless delays in filming. Restless and bored, Gable insisted on doing his own stunts in the 115-degree Nevada heat. He balanced himself on the hood of a car, rolled across it, and fell to the pavement. In another scene he was dragged by a truck traveling twenty-five miles an hour. He wrestled with a wild stallion, got snarled in a lariat, and was dragged face down until a wrangler stopped the horse.

Two months later Gable had a heart attack. Recuperating nicely in the hospital, the King of Hollywood simply turned a page of the magazine he was reading, put his head back on the pillow, and died.

Cooper was devastated. "Maybe they questioned his acting, but Gable was the greatest star," Gary said. "No one could touch him."

When asked who were the great Hollywood actors he replied, "Spencer Tracy and Fredric March. Also Franchot Tone. I don't know what went wrong with his career in films. Maybe his marriage to Joan Crawford. Who knows? I think Barbara Stanwyck is the finest actress I've worked with. The guys who could play all my roles are Jimmy Stewart and Joel McCrea. Both good friends."

Did he regret not trying the legitimate theater?

"No, but I probably said I wanted to. That was the thing to say, I guess. I've reached the age that I don't particularly care if my words get twisted. Like my acting, for example. I'm supposed to be natural. Well, I found out that's what people wanted. If they didn't, I wouldn't be sittin' here talking about thirty-five years makin' movies."

What about Westerns?

"I'm lookin' for a good one," he said. "A really good Western. By the way, have you ever seen anything so idiotic as some of those TV cowboys? Hell, they grab the saddle with the wrong hand when they mount. And they can't ride, anyway. And look how they carry their guns, down around their knees somewhere so they can make a production job out of drawin'."

What about retirement?

"There's a scarcity of young name stars. That's fine for us old guys, but we hang in there long after we should quit. The urge to act stays with you. Sometimes in the middle of a scene I find myself saying a piece of dialogue from fifteen years ago. Situations tend to repeat themselves and there's a limit to the things you can do with one face and one carcass. For a while I thought about retirin'. Sometimes still do, around five in the morning. But I'd go nuts."

Any plans for the future?

"Yep. I'm goin' to England to make a movie based on a novel by Max Ehrlich, *Last Train to Babylon*. I think they're gonna change the title to *The Naked Edge*. It's a whodunit, I think. Different sort of thing for me. Problem is to play the innocent side and still bring out to the audience the circumstances that seem to make me guilty. Well, there's a bigger problem. I don't know whether people will believe that Gary Cooper would commit a crime! For the picture to work, there has to be some believability that he did kill this other fella. It's gonna be interesting to see how it turns out. Then I might do a Western, *Ride the High Country* . . . maybe the one I've been waitin' for."

When Cooper had recovered sufficiently from his two operations, he took Rocky and Maria along to London for the filming of *The Naked Edge* with

Deborah Kerr. They spent nine weeks at London's Savoy Hotel and were provided with a bulletproof Rolls-Royce.

Eager to chat, Gary didn't mind the presence of the press in his small dressing room. He told one reporter, "Seem to have a cold in my back all the time I'm in this country." He put on a heavy robe and made some hot tea. "I go back to the hotel in the evening. Got a room with a dandy view of the river. I sit there and look at it and the draft hits me." Cooper never liked cold weather, anyway. He knew nothing about the cancer ravaging his body. What bothered him most was getting old.

Cooper talked about working again with Hemingway. "All of a sudden some good stuff's coming along," he told a London reporter. "Papa's not feelin' too good, but he's sendin' someone over here to talk to me about *Across the River and Into the Trees*. We've had some good times, but we're both too pooped to do much huntin' these days. He keeps reminding me to leave him my .22 Hornet with the German telescope sight in my will. Next time he asks, I might give it to him."

Cooper didn't intend to discuss women in this impromptu interview, but he admitted to having dated Mary Pickford after her separation from Douglas Fairbanks, Sr. "No one ever picked up on that one," he said with a smile. It was only natural for the British press to mention Clara Bow and Lupe Velez, but he turned a deaf ear to past love affairs. "It's funny." He smiled. "Nobody thought Rocky and I were right for each other. We were complete opposites, I guess. It took time apart to make me realize how much we really had in common. I didn't talk much back in those days. I clammed up for a long time. I found out if I said things, I would be misquoted and if I didn't say anything, I was misquoted, too."

Cooper would not discuss his prostate and colon operations. "I know some people don't get embarrassed about these things," he said, "but I get embarrassed."

Gary beamed with pride when asked about Maria. "She's studying at the Chouinard Art Institute in Los Angeles. I thought it might be fun if she'd appear in some of my films, but she won't."

The interview ended with the usual question. "Do you have plans of retiring in the near future, Mr. Cooper?"

"I'm not rich!" he snapped. "I don't own oil wells like Bing Crosby and Bob Hope. I couldn't afford to retire and take up painting if I wanted to."

The Coopers returned home in time for the Christmas holidays. A month later, in January 1961, the Friars Club honored Gary with a $200-a-plate charity dinner to honor and "roast" the famous star.

Sam Goldwyn remarked, "Coop doesn't say much, but what he says makes a helluva lot of sense."

Jack Warner laughed. "I've always had a great faith in Gary. What the hell else could you have at $20,000 a week?"

Milton Berle quipped, "Cooper is Randolph Scott with novocaine lips.

He's the Grandpa Moses of the prairie. For thirty years he's lived a clean, respectable life—unfortunately, not his!"

Carl Sandburg thought Cooper was an institution. "He represents something of a clean spirit—the man unafraid in danger—the lack of phony in man."

Cooper had tears in his eyes when he rose to give his thanks. Knees and hands shaking, he said, "The only achievement I'm proud of is the friends I have made in this community . . . and if you asked me if I'm the luckiest guy in the world, all I can say is 'yup.' "

Cooper's next project was narrating an NBC "Project 20" one-hour special called "The Real West." It was aired on March 29, 1961. Though he detested television, Gary wanted to help put the Western in proper perspective.

After it aired Hedda Hopper called to congratulate him. "He didn't return my call for two days," she said. "I found out later he was too ill to talk. When he did he was delighted at the way I felt because he'd dreamed of doing it for many years."

Pete Martin of *The Saturday Evening Post* paid a visit to Cooper and chillingly recalled that the actor's face, with its character seams and lines, somehow had changed.

"When he walked in," Martin said, "a piece of the West always walked in with him. I liked those seams and lines, but they were gone now. Somebody, perhaps a plastic surgeon, had ironed them out, though he denied it. And his hair was a kind of orangy light brown. It wasn't a good dye job. But the voice that came out of that unseamed face was the same voice that had said, 'Nobody wants to read about me.' It gave me a weird feeling."

14

"BET I BEAT YA BACK TO THE BARN"

It was Rocky Cooper who finally told her husband that he had terminal cancer. She had known the truth for two months, but waited for the right time to tell him. He was getting weaker every day and yet continued planning future projects. She did not want him making commitments he couldn't keep.

"Gary didn't bat an eye," she said. "He thanked me for telling him. That's all."

Rocky told writer Richard Gehman in an interview that her husband was running around the house in a bathing suit and she feared he might come down with pneumonia and "go all at once." Cooper's voice was filled with tenderness for her, Gehman wrote, as if he were embarrassed that she had to endure this agony.

Rocky attributed Gary's strength to his conversion to Catholicism two years prior. "Oh, did it stand him in good stead," she said. "Every time he'd receive Communion, he said he felt so much better. He was completely unafraid of the future. He really was. No fear whatsoever."

Rocky wanted finally to set the record straight. She knew that much would be written about her famous husband after he was gone. "You know," she added, "Gary and I had a little trouble about ten years ago. It invariably comes up in articles, and I certainly have no plans to deny it. He left the house . . . but I don't think you could say we were really separated. It was always a temporary arrangement and through it all, we were a family. Gary told me the only thing he regretted was that trouble we had. But at the same time, we both agreed it made a much better marriage, better than it ever had been. He had to find out for himself and I was willing to wait."

Cooper tried to attend an occasional dinner party, but was too ill and weak to pretend any longer. He was confined indoors, spending most of the day in the sun-filled study that overlooked the gardens he had once tended with such pride.

Ernest Hemingway was also deteriorating quickly. He called Gary and pretended they'd both beat the death sentence. "Hell!" he bellowed over the telephone. "We'll be shootin' pheasants this fall. You'll see!"

Coop knew better. "Papa, I bet I beat ya back to the barn."

When Hemingway's friend, writer A. E. Hotchner, paid a visit to Cooper, Gary reached for a crucifix and placed in on his pillow. "Please give Papa a message," he said with tears in his eyes. "It's important and you mustn't forget because I'll not be talkin' to him again. Tell him, that time I wondered if I made the right decision . . . tell him it was the best thing I ever did." And then he put the crucifix against his cheek.

On April 7, 1961, the Academy of Motion Picture Arts and Sciences announced that two honorary Oscars were to be awarded at the ceremony on April 17th—one to Gary Cooper and one to Stan Laurel. Jimmy Stewart, who knew his friend was dying of cancer, received the Oscar on Gary's behalf.

"I am very honored to accept this award tonight for Gary Cooper," Stewart said. "I'm sorry he's not here to accept it, but I know I'll get it to him right away. With it goes all the friendship and affection and admiration and the deep respect of all of us. We're very, very proud of you, Coop. All of us are tremendously proud," he said, his voice trembling. Stewart was shaking, his eyes brimming with tears. "All of us . . . are terribly proud."

Jimmy had hoped to give his speech without breaking down. But his tears told television viewers across America that Gary Cooper was dying. Two days later Rocky confirmed that her husband was suffering from terminal cancer, that he was being treated at home, and that there were no plans to hospitalize him.

President John F. Kennedy phoned, and Coop's close friends Danny Kaye, Sam Goldwyn, Jimmy Stewart, Fred MacMurray, and a few of his hunting buddies, stopped by. They found him ashen and confined to his bed. There were the usual jokes and funny stories. Gary managed a smile.

On May 6, more than five hundred movie personalities gathered at the Cannes Film Festival Palace in France for a special award presentation at which André Malraux, the French cultural affairs minister, made Cooper an officer in the Order of Arts and Letters. Director Fred Zinnemann accepted the award and flew back to Hollywood to present it to Gary.

The Vatican sent this message: "The Holy Father, fondly recalling the visit of Gary Cooper and his family, is grieved to learn of his illness and lovingly imparts a special apostolic blessing, the pledge of abundant comfort, and divine grace and favors."

On May 7, 1961, his sixtieth birthday, Cooper began receiving the sacraments of the Roman Catholic Church every few days.

He was given the last rites on May 12th. Only his mother, Rocky, and Maria remained at Gary's bedside. He was heavily sedated when the end came on May 14, at 12:27 P.M.

Cooper's body was quickly removed through the back door of the Holmby Hills house. Rocky made it clear she did not want her husband's funeral to turn into a typical Hollywood event. Only those who received written invitations would be allowed into the Church of the Good Shepherd.

A solemn high requiem mass was offered before a closed casket. The pallbearers were Jack Benny, Charles Feldman, William Goetz, Henry Hathaway, James Stewart, and Jerry Wald. Honorary pallbearers chosen by Rocky were Fred Zinnemann, Samuel Goldwyn, Danny Kaye, Pat deCicco, Kirk Douglas, William Winans, Irving Lazar, David O. Selznick, William Wyler, Walter Brennan, Dick Powell, Tony Curtis, Peter Lawford, Burt Lancaster, Bing Crosby, Henry Ford II, John Wayne, Dean Johnson, and Ernest Hemingway.

In lieu of flowers, the family asked that any contributions be made in Gary Cooper's name to the Memorial–Sloan Kettering Institute for Cancer Research in New York.

At the funeral, eighty-six-year-old Alice Cooper sat with her surviving son, Arthur. She was unmoved by the Catholic mass. She said, "I'm sure Gary converted to please his wife. He remained an Episcopalian."

Burial was in the Grotto of Our Lady of Lourdes at Holy Cross Cemetery.

Patricia Neal was asked to comment on Cooper's death. Her only words to reporters were, ". . . my love."

Newspapers and friends around the world heaped praise on the man whose fabulous film career spanned film's silent era and golden age, and whose screen career and offscreen life helped define the American image.

Italy's *Corriere della Serra:* "With him there is ended a certain America . . . that of the frontier and of innocence which had or was believed to have an exact sense of dividing line between good and evil."

Germany's *Die Welt:* "He had been a key figure of our days. He was the symbol of trust, confidence, and protection. He is dead now. What a miracle that he existed at all."

Sweden's *Svenska Dagladet:* "He had a soul of a boy, a pure, simple, nice, warm boy's soul . . . he was the incarnation of the honorable American."

A month after Cooper's death, *The Naked Edge* was released. *The New Yorker* described it as "A thriller in which, for a wonder, Cooper himself is suspected of having committed a dastardly murder. It consists of a wholly synthetic piling up of the palest pink herrings. The qualities that made Cooper a great star had little to do with acting, and since he must have been uncomfortable in this absurd and unpleasant role, he leaves the make-believe largely to Deborah Kerr."

Variety commented, "The picture that winds up Gary Cooper's long list of credits is a neatly constructed, thoroughly professional little suspense meller [melodrama] that may seem anticlimactic only because it climaxes a great career.

Time magazine summed up the film this way: "*Naked Edge,* the whodunit that is the late Gary Cooper's last picture, is a waste of a good man."

In one of Cooper's last interviews, he sadly remarked, "People don't recognize me as much as they used to. Only the older people. The kids today have

Frankie Avalon and Elvis Presley. They pretty much leave me alone. It's not like it was in the old days. They've taken all the real glamour out of the picture business by exposing the whole thing to the public—all the inside pictures and stories of how it's done and how that pretty star actually loves to cook a small steak with her own hands and be just like the folks next door."

The New York Times agreed: "A new generation of moviegoers and television viewers may want a different sort of hero—perhaps a man more baffled by life. But it is so sad to see Gary Cooper go . . ."

EPILOGUE

Two months after Gary died Ernest Hemingway got up early on the morning of July 2, 1961, found the keys to the storage room, chose a double-barreled Boss shotgun, walked through the living room to the foyer, slipped two shells in the gun, leaned forward, pressed the twin barrels against his forehead, and tripped both triggers.

Mary Hemingway told the press her husband's death was "accidental." It wasn't until 1966 that she revealed the truth. "He shot himself," she said. "Just like that. For a long time I refused to admit it to myself."

Ingrid Bergman wrote in her memoirs, "It hurts to talk about losing Gary and Papa. It's strange how they went together. I think they planned it."

The bulk of Gary Cooper's $3 million estate was left to Rocky. Trust funds were provided for his mother and daughter; $5,000 each to his brother, Arthur, and his two children; and $10,000 to the Motion Picture Country House and Hospital.

After Gary's death, Alice Cooper moved to Palm Desert to live with her son, Arthur. In 1966 she died at the age of ninety-three in the California Convalescent Hospital.

In June 1964, Veronica Balfe Cooper married Dr. John Converse, the doctor who performed Gary's cosmetic surgery. She was widowed again in 1981 and still resides in Southampton.

Maria Cooper married concert pianist Byron Janis in April 1966. They have no children.

Patricia Neal had a series of paralyzing strokes that left her speechless and crippled in 1965. She praised her husband, Roald Dahl, for nursing her back to health. But in 1983, he left Pat for another woman.

The tragedy of Pat Neal's strokes and valiant struggle to survive prompted a warm letter from Rocky and Maria Cooper. After twenty-five years, the three women Gary cherished most have become close friends. They share fond memories of a man who wanted, above all, to make them happy. The ending is bittersweet, but it is nonetheless a tribute to Gary Cooper.

In May 1974, Gary Cooper's body was removed from the Holy Cross Cemetery and reburied under a three-ton boulder at the Sacred Cross Cemetery in

Southampton, Long Island. There was an outcry from the film colony; they insisted the great star belonged in Hollywood. Rocky explained, "Gary loved Southampton. This is what he would want."

In his novel, *The Virginian,* author Owen Wister wrote, "What has become of the horseman, the cowpuncher, the last romantic figure upon our soil? Well, he will be here among us always, invisible, waiting his chance to live and play as he would like. His wild kind has been among us always, since the beginning: A young man with his temptations, a hero without wings . . ."

CHRONOLOGY OF GARY COOPER'S FILMS

Small Roles

Gary Cooper appeared as an extra in many films in 1925 and 1926. Among the best known are:

Dick Turpin (1925) with Tom Mix
The Thundering Herd (1925) with Noah Beery, Lois Wilson, and Jack Holt
Wild Horse Mesa (1925) with Jack Holt and Billie Dove
The Lucky Horseshoe (1925) with Tom Mix and Billie Dove
The Vanishing American (1925) with Richard Dix, Lois Wilson, and Noah Beery
The Eagle (1925) with Rudolph Valentino and Vilma Banky
The Enchanted Hill (1926) with Jack Holt, Florence Vidor, and Noah Beery
Watch Your Wife (1926) with Virginia Valli and Pat O'Malley

Short Films

TRICKS
(Davis Distributing Co., 1925)

Director: Bruce Mitchell. *Scenarist:* Mary C. Bruning. *Cast:* Marilyn Mills and J. Frank Glendon

THREE PALS
(Davis Distributing Co., 1925)

Director: Bruce Mitchell. *Scenarist:* Mary C. Bruning. *Cast:* Marilyn Mills and J. Frank Glendon

LIGHTIN' WINS
(Independent Pictures, 1926)

Director: Hans Tiesler. *Cast:* Lightin', The Super Dog, and Eileen Sedgwick

Feature Films

THE WINNING OF BARBARA WORTH
(United Artists, 1926)

Director: Henry King. *Producer:* Samuel Goldwyn. *Scenarist:* Frances Marion. *Photographer:* George Barnes. *Editor:* Viola Lawrence. *Cast:* Ronald Colman (Willard

Holmes), Vilma Banky (Barbara Worth), Charles Lane (Jefferson Worth), Paul McAllister (the seer), E. J. Ratcliffe (James Greenfield), Gary Cooper (Abe Lee). Based on a novel by Harold Bell Wright.

IT
(Paramount, 1927)

Director: Clarence Badger. *Producers:* Clarence Badger, Elinor Glyn. *Associate Producer:* B. P. Schulberg. *Photographer:* H. Kinley Martin. *Editor:* E. Lloyd Sheldon. *Cast:* Clara Bow (Betty Lou), Antonio Moreno (Cyrus Waltham), William Austin (Monty), Jacqueline Gadsdon (Adela Van Norman), Julia Swayne Gordon (Mrs. Van Norman), Elinor Glyn (herself), Gary Cooper (reporter). Based on a novel by Elinor Glyn.

CHILDREN OF DIVORCE
(Paramount, 1927)

Director: Frank Lloyd. *Producer:* E. Lloyd Sheldon. *Photographer:* Victor Milner. *Editor:* E. Lloyd Sheldon. *Associate Producer:* B. P. Schulberg. *Cast:* Clara Bow (Kitty Flanders), Esther Ralston (Jean Waddington), Gary Cooper (Ted Larrabee), Einar Hanson (Prince Ludovico de Sfax), Hedda Hopper (Katherine Flanders). Based on a novel by Owen McMahon Johnson.

ARIZONA BOUND
(Paramount, 1927)

Director: John Waters. *Photographer:* C. Edgar Schoenbaum. *Cast:* Gary Cooper (the cowboy), Betty Jewel (the girl), Jack Dougherty (Buck O'Hara), Quinn "Big Boy" Williams. Based on a story by Richard Allen Gates.

WINGS
(Paramount, 1927)

Director: William A. Wellman. *Producer:* Lucien Hubbard. *Photographer:* Harry Perry. *Editor:* Lucien Hubbard. *Associate Producer:* B. P. Schulberg. *Cast:* Clara Bow (Mary Preston), Charles "Buddy" Rogers (Jack Powell), Richard Arlen (David Armstrong), Jobyna Ralston (Sylvia Lewis), Gary Cooper (Cadet White), Hedda Hopper (Mrs. Powell). Based on a story by John Monk Saunders.

NEVADA
(Paramount, 1927)

Director: John Waters. *Photographer:* C. Edgar Schoenbaum. *Cast:* Gary Cooper (Nevada), Thelma Todd (Hettie Ide), William Powell (Clan Dillion), Philip Strange (Ben Ide). Based on a novel by Zane Grey.

THE LAST OUTLAW
(Paramount, 1927)

Director: Arthur Rosson. *Photographer:* James Murray. *Cast:* Gary Cooper (Sheriff Buddy Hale), Betty Jewel (Janet Lane), Jack Luden (Ward Lane), Billy Butts (Chick), and Flash, the Wonder Horse. Based on a story by Richard Allen Gates.

BEAU SABREUR
(Paramount, 1928)

Director: John Waters. *Photographer:* C. Edgar Schoenbaum. *Editor:* Rose Lowenger. *Cast:* Gary Cooper (Major Henri de Beaujolais), Evelyn Brent (Mary Vanbrugh), Noah Beery (Sheikh El Hamel), William Powell (Becque), Roscoe Karns (Buddy). Based on the novel *Beau Geste* by Percival Christopher Wren.

LEGION OF THE CONDEMNED
(Paramount, 1928)

Director and Producer: William A. Wellman. *Photographer:* Henry Gerrard. *Editor:* Alyson Shaffer. *Cast:* Fay Wray (Christine Charteris), Gary Cooper (Gale Price), Barry Norton (Byron Dashwood), Lane Chandler (Charles Holabird), Francis McDonald (Gouzalo Vasques), Charlotte Bird (tart in café). Based on a story by John Monk Saunders.

DOOMSDAY
(Paramount, 1928)

Director and Producer: Rowland V. Lee. *Photographer:* Henry Gerrard. *Editor:* Robert Bassler. *Cast:* Florence Vidor (Mary Viner), Gary Cooper (Arnold Furze), Lawrence Grant (Percival Fream), Charles A. Stevenson (Captain Hesketh Viner). Based on a novel by Warwick Deeping.

HALF A BRIDE
(Paramount, 1928)

Director: Gregory La Cava. *Photographer:* Victor Milner. *Editor:* Verna Willis. *Cast:* Esther Ralston (Patience Winslow), Gary Cooper (Captain Edmunds), William J. Worthington (Mr. Winslow), Freeman Wood (Jed Session), Mary Doran (Betty Brewster). Based on the story "White Hands" by Arthur Stringer.

LILAC TIME
(First National, 1928)

Director and Producer: George Fitzmaurice. *Photographer:* Sid Hickox. *Editor:* Al Hall. *Cast:* Colleen Moore (Jeannine), Gary Cooper (Captain Philip Blythe), Eugenie Besserer (Widow Berthelot), Kathryn McGuire (Lady Iris), Arthur Lake (the unlucky one), Jack Stone (the kid). Based on the play by Jane Cowl and Jane Murfin and the book by Guy Fowler. "Presented by John McCormick."

THE FIRST KISS
(Paramount, 1928)

Director and Producer: Rowland V. Lee. *Photographer:* Alfred Gilks. *Editor:* Lee Helen. *Cast:* Fay Wray (Anna Leė), Gary Cooper (Mulligan Talbot), Lane Chandler (William Talbot), Leslie Fenton (Carol Talbot), Paul Fix (Ezra Talbot), Malcolm Williams ("Pap"). Based on the story "Four Brothers" by Tristram Tupper.

THE SHOPWORN ANGEL
(Paramount, 1928)

Director: Richard Wallace. *Producer:* Louis D. Lighton. *Photographer:* Charles Lang. *Editor:* Robert Bassler. *Cast:* Nancy Carroll (Daisy Heath), Gary Cooper (William Tyler), Paul Lukas (Bailey), Emmett King (the chaplain), Roscoe Karns (an extra). Based on the story by Dana Burnet.

WOLF SONG
(Paramount, 1929)

Director and Producer: Victor Fleming. *Associate Director:* Henry Hathaway. *Photographer:* Allen Siegler. *Editor:* Eda Warren. *Cast:* Gary Cooper (Sam Lash), Lupe Velez (Lola Salazar), Louis Wolheim (Gullion), Constantine Romanoff (Rube Thatcher), Ann Brody (Duenna), Russell ("Russ") Columbo (Ambrosia Guiterrez). Based on a novel by Harvey Fergusson.

BETRAYAL
(Paramount, 1929)

Director: Lewis Milestone. *Associate Producer:* David O. Selznick. *Photographer:* Henry Gerrard. *Editor:* Del Andrews. *Cast:* Emil Jannings (Poldi Moser), Esther Ralston (Vroni), Gary Cooper (André Frey), Jada Welles (Hans), Douglas Haig (Peter). Based on a story by Victor Schertzinger and Nicholas Soussanin.

THE VIRGINIAN
(Paramount, 1929)

Director: Victor Fleming. *Producer:* Louis D. Lighton. *Assistant Director:* Henry Hathaway. *Photographers:* J. Roy Hunt and Edward Cronjager. *Editor:* William Shea. *Cast:* Gary Cooper (The Virginian), Walter Huston (Trampas), Richard Arlen (Steve), Mary Brian (Molly Wood), Chester Conklin (Uncle Hughey), Eugene Pallette (Honey Wiggin), E. H. Calvert (Judge Henry), Helen Ware ("Ma" Taylor). Based on the novel by Owen Wister and play by Kirk La Shelle.

ONLY THE BRAVE
(Paramount, 1930)

Director: Frank Tuttle. *Photographer:* Harry Fischbeck. *Editor:* Doris Drought. *Cast:* Gary Cooper (Captain James Braydon), Mary Brian (Barbara Calhoun), Phillips Holmes (Captain Robert Darrington), James Neill (Vance Calhoun), Morgan Farley (Tom Wendell), Virginia Bruce (Elizabeth). Based on a story by Keene Thompson.

PARAMOUNT ON PARADE
(Paramount, 1930)

Directors: Dorothy Arzner, Otto Brower, Edmund Goulding, Victor Heerman, Edwin H. Knopf, Rowland V. Lee, Ernst Lubitsch, Lothar Mendez, Victor Schertzinger, Edward Sutherland, Frank Tuttle. *Producer:* Albert A. Kaufman. *Photographers:* Harry Fischbeck and Victor Milner. *Editor:* Merrill White. *Cast:* Richard Arlen, Jean Arthur, Mischa Auer, Clara Bow, Evelyn Brent, Maurice Chevalier, Gary Cooper, Leon

Errol, Stuart Erwin, Fredric March, Jack Oakie, William Powell, Charles "Buddy" Rogers, Lillian Roth, Fay Wray.

THE TEXAN
(Paramount, 1930)

Director: John Cromwell. *Photographer:* Victor Milner. *Editor:* Verna Willis. *Cast:* Gary Cooper (Enrique ["Quico"], the Llano Kid), Fay Wray (Consuelo), Emma Dunn (Señora Ibarra), Oscar Apfel (Thacker), James Marcus (John Brown), Donald Reed (Nick Ibarra), Russell ("Russ") Columbo (singing cowboy at campfire). Based on the story "A Double-Dyed Deceiver" by O. Henry.

SEVEN DAYS LEAVE
(Paramount, 1930)

Director: Richard Wallace. *Producer:* Louis D. Lighton. *Photographer:* Charles Lang. *Editor:* George Nicholls, Jr. *Cast:* Gary Cooper (Kenneth Dowey), Beryl Mercer (Sarah Ann Dowey), Daisy Belmore (Emma Mickelham), Nora Cecil (Amelia Twymley), Tempe Piggott (Mrs. Haggerty), Arthur Hoyt (Mr. Willings). Based on the play "The Old Lady Shows Her Medals" by Sir James M. Barrie.

A MAN FROM WYOMING
(Paramount, 1930)

Director: Rowland V. Lee. *Photographer:* Harry Fischbeck. *Editor:* Robert Bassler. *Cast:* Gary Cooper (Jim Baker), June Collyer (Patricia Hunter), Regis Toomey (Jersey), Morgan Farley (Lieutenant Lee), E. H. Calvert (Major-General Hunter), Mary Foy (Inspector). From a story by Joseph Moncure March and Lew Lipton.

THE SPOILERS
(Paramount, 1930)

Director: Edward Carewe. *Photographer:* Harry Fischbeck. *Editor:* William Shea. *Cast:* Gary Cooper (Glenister), Kay Johnson (Helen Chester), Betty Compson (Cherry Malotte), William "Stage" Boyd (McNamara), Harry Green (Herman), Slim Summerville (Slapjack Slims), James Kirkwood (Dextry). Based on the book by Rex Beach.

MOROCCO
(Paramount, 1930)

Director: Josef Von Sternberg. *Photographer:* Lee Garmes. *Editor:* Sam Winston. *Cast:* Gary Cooper (Tom Brown), Marlene Dietrich (Amy Jolly), Adolphe Menjou (Kennington), Ullrich Haupt (Adjutant Caesar), Juliette Compton (Anna Dolores), Francis McDonald (Corporal Tatoche). Based on the novel "Amy Jolly" by Benno Vigny.

FIGHTING CARAVANS
(Paramount, 1931)

Directors: Otto Brower and David Burton. *Photographers:* Lee Garmes and Henry Gerrard. *Editor:* William Shea. *Cast:* Gary Cooper (Clint Belmet), Lily Damita (Felice), Ernest Torrence (Bill Jackson), Fred Kohler (Lee Murdock), Tully Marshall

(Jim Bridges), Eugene Pallette (Seth Higgins), Roy Stewart (Couch), Charles Winninger (Marshal), Jane Darwell (pioneer woman). Based on a novel by Zane Grey.

CITY STREETS
(Paramount, 1931)

Director: Rouben Mamoulian. *Producer:* E. Lloyd Sheldon. *Photographer:* Lee Garmes. *Editor:* William Shea. *Cast:* Gary Cooper (the Kid), Sylvia Sidney (Nan), Paul Lukas (Big Boy Maskal), William "Stage" Boyd (McCoy), Guy Kibbee (Pop Cooley), Stanley Fields (Blackie), Betty Sinclair (Pansy), Terry Carroll (Esther March). Based on an original screenplay by Dashiell Hammett.

I TAKE THIS WOMAN
(Paramount, 1931)

Director: Marion Gering. *Assistant Director:* Slavko Vorkapich. *Photographer:* Victor Milner. *Cast:* Gary Cooper (Tom McNair), Carole Lombard (Kay Dowling), Helen Ware (Aunt Bessie), Lester Vail (Herbert Forrest), Charles Trowbridge (Mr. Dowling), Clara Blandick (Sue Barnes), Gerald Fielding (Bill Wentworth).

HIS WOMAN
(Paramount, 1931)

Director: Edward Sloman. *Photographer:* William Steiner. *Editor:* Arthur Ellis. *Cast:* Gary Cooper (Captain Sam Whalan), Claudette Colbert (Sally Clark), Averill Harris (Mate Gatson), Richard Spiro (Sammy), Douglass Dumbrille (Alisandroe), Raquel Davida (Maria Estella), Harry Davenport (customs inspector), Preston Foster (crewman). Based on the novel "The Sentimentalist" by Dale Collins.

MAKE ME A STAR
(Paramount, 1932)

Director: William Beaudine. *Photographer:* Allen Siegler. *Editor:* Leroy Stone. *Cast:* Stuart Erwin (Merton Gill), Joan Blondell ("Flips" Montague), Zasu Pitts (Mrs. Scudder). *Guest Stars:* Tallulah Bankhead, Maurice Chevalier, Claudette Colbert, Gary Cooper, Fredric March, Jack Oakie, Charles Ruggles, Sylvia Sidney. Based on the book *Merton of the Movies* by Harry Leon Wilson and the subsequent play by George S. Kaufman and Moss Hart.

DEVIL AND THE DEEP
(Paramount, 1932)

Director: Marion Gering. *Photographer:* Charles Lang. *Editor:* Otho Lovering. *Cast:* Tallulah Bankhead (Pauline Sturm), Gary Cooper (Lieutenant Sempter), Charles Laughton (Commander Charles Sturm), Cary Grant (Lieutenant Jaeckel), Paul Porcasi (Hassan), Juliette Compton (Mrs. Planet). Based on a story by Harry Hervey.

IF I HAD A MILLION
(Paramount, 1932)

Directors: Ernst Lubitsch, Norman Taurog, Stephen Roberts, Norman McLeod, James Cruze, William A. Seiter, H. Bruce Humberstone. *Producer:* Louis D. Lighton. *Cast:* Gary Cooper (Gallagher), George Raft (Eddie Jackson), Charles Laughton (the clerk), Jack Oakie (Mulligan), Frances Dee (Mary Wallace), Charles Ruggles (Henry Peabody), W. C. Fields (Rollo), May Robson (Mrs. Walker), Gene Raymond (John Wallace), Mary Boland (Mrs. Peabody), Roscoe Karns (O'Brien). Based on a story by Robert D. Andrews.

A FAREWELL TO ARMS
(Paramount, 1932)

Director: Frank Borzage. *Photographer:* Charles Lang. *Editor:* Otho Lovering. *Cast:* Helen Hayes (Catherine Barkley), Gary Cooper (Lieutenant Fredric Henry), Adolphe Menjou (Major Rinaldi), Mary Philips (Helen Ferguson), Jack La Rue (the priest), Blanche Frederici (head nurse). Based on the novel by Ernest Hemingway.

TODAY WE LIVE
(M-G-M, 1933)

Director and Producer: Howard Hawks. *Photographer:* Oliver T. Marsh. *Editor:* Edward Curtis. *Cast:* Joan Crawford (Diana Boyce-Smith), Gary Cooper (Bogard), Robert Young (Claude), Franchot Tone (Ronnie), Roscoe Karns (McGinnis), Louise Closser Hale (Applegate). From the story "Turnabout" by William Faulkner.

ONE SUNDAY AFTERNOON
(Paramount, 1933)

Director: Stephen Roberts. *Producer:* Louis D. Lighton. *Photographer:* Victor Milner. *Editor:* Ellsworth Hoagland. *Cast:* Gary Cooper (Biff Grimes), Fay Wray (Virginia Brush), Neil Hamilton (Hugo Barnstead), Frances Fuller (Amy Lind), Roscoe Karns (Snappy Downer), Jane Darwell (Mrs. Lind), Clara Blandick (Mrs. Brush). Based on the stage play by James Hagan.

DESIGN FOR LIVING
(Paramount, 1933)

Director and Producer: Ernst Lubitsch. *Photographer:* Victor Milner. *Editor:* Francis Marsh. *Cast:* Fredric March (Tom Chambers), Gary Cooper (George Curtis), Miriam Hopkins (Gilda Farrell), Edward Everett Horton (Max Plunkett), Franklin Pangborn (Mr. Douglas), Isabel Jewell (lisping stenographer), Jane Darwell (housekeeper). Based on the play by Noël Coward.

ALICE IN WONDERLAND
(Paramount, 1933)

Director: Norman McLeod. *Producer:* Louis D. Lighton. *Photographers:* Henry Sharp and Bert Glennon. *Editor:* Ellsworth Hoagland. *Cast:* Charlotte Henry (Alice), Richard Arlen (the Cheshire Cat), Gary Cooper (the White Knight), Leon Errol (Uncle

Gilbert), W. C. Fields (Humpty-Dumpty), Cary Grant (the Mock Turtle), Jack Oakie (Tweedledum), Edna May Oliver (the Red Queen), May Robson (the Queen of Hearts), Charlie Ruggles (the March Hare). From *Alice's Adventures in Wonderland* and *Alice Through the Looking Glass* by Lewis Carroll.

OPERATOR 13
(M-G-M, 1933)

Director: Richard Boleslavsky. *Producer:* Lucien Hubbard. *Photographer:* George Folsey. *Editor:* Frank Sullivan. *Cast:* Marion Davies (Gail Loveless), Gary Cooper (Captain Jack Gailliard), Jean Parker (Eleanor), Katharine Alexander (Pauline), Ted Healy (Doctor Hitchcock), Henry Wadsworth (John Pelham). Based on the story by Robert W. Chambers.

NOW AND FOREVER
(Paramount, 1934)

Director: Henry Hathaway. *Producer:* Louis D. Lighton. *Photographer:* Harry Fischbeck. *Editor:* Ellsworth Hoagland. *Cast:* Gary Cooper (Jerry Day), Carole Lombard (Toni Carstairs), Shirley Temple (Penelope Day), Sir Guy Standing (Felix Evans), Charlotte Granville (Mrs. J. H. P. Crane), Gilbert Emery (James Higginson), Akim Tamiroff (French jeweler). Based on the story "Honor Bright" by Jack Kirkland and Melville Baker.

THE WEDDING NIGHT
(United Artists, 1935)

Director: King Vidor. *Producer:* Samuel Goldwyn. *Photographer:* Gregg Toland. *Editor:* Stuart Heisler. *Cast:* Gary Cooper (Tony Barrett), Anna Sten (Manya), Ralph Bellamy (Fredrik), Helen Vinson (Dora Barrett), Siegfried Rumann (Nowak), Walter Brennan (Jenkins), Esther Dale (Kaise), Leonid Snegoff (Sobieski), George Meeker (Gilly). Based on a story by Edwin Knopf.

THE LIVES OF A BENGAL LANCER
(Paramount, 1935)

Director: Henry Hathaway. *Producer:* Louis D. Lighton. *Photographer:* Charles Lang. *Editor:* Ellsworth Hoagland. *Cast:* Gary Cooper (Lieutenant McGregor), Franchot Tone (Lieutenant Fortesque), Richard Cromwell (Lieutenant Stone), Sir Guy Standing (Colonel Stone), C. Aubrey Smith (Major Hamilton), Monte Blue (Hamzulia Khan), Kathleen Burke (Tania Volkanskaya), Akim Tamiroff (Emir), J. Carroll Naish (Grand Vizier), Mischa Auer (Afridi). Based on the novel by Major Francis Yeats-Brown.

PETER IBBETSON
(Paramount, 1935)

Director: Henry Hathaway. *Producer:* Louis D. Lighton. *Photographer:* Charles Lang. *Editor:* Stuart Heisler. *Cast:* Gary Cooper (Peter Ibbetson), Ann Harding (Mary, Duchess of Towers), John Halliday (Duke of Towers), Ida Lupino (Agnes), Douglass

Dumbrille (Colonel Forsythe), Virginia Weidler (Mimsey), Dickie Moore (Gogo), Donald Meek (Mr. Slade), Doris Lloyd (Mrs. Dorian). Based on a novel by George Du Maurier and subsequent play by John Nathaniel Raphael.

DESIRE
(Paramount, 1936)

Director: Frank Borzage. *Producer:* Ernst Lubitsch. *Photographer:* Charles Lang. *Editor:* William Shea. *Cast:* Marlene Dietrich (Madeleine de Beaupré), Gary Cooper (Tom Bradley), John Halliday (Carlos Margoli), William Frawley (Mr. Gibson), Akim Tamiroff (Police Official), Alan Mowbray (Dr. Edouard Pauquet), Zeffie Tilbury (Aunt Olga), Harry Depp (clerk). From a comedy by Hans Szekely and R. A. Stemmle.

MR. DEEDS GOES TO TOWN
(Columbia, 1936)

Director and Producer: Frank Capra. *Photographer:* Joseph Walker. *Editor:* Gene Havlick. *Cast:* Gary Cooper (Longfellow Deeds), Jean Arthur (Babe Bennett), George Bancroft (MacWade), Lionel Stander (Cornelius Cobb), Douglass Dumbrille (John Cedar), Raymond Walburn (Walter), Margaret Matzenauer (Madame Pomponi), George F. "Gabby" Hayes (farmers' spokesman). Based on the story "Opera Hat" by Clarence Budington Kelland.

HOLLYWOOD BOULEVARD
(Paramount, 1936)

Director: Robert Florey. *Producer:* A. M. Botsford. *Photographer:* George Clemens. *Editor:* Harvey Johnston. *Cast:* John Halliday (John Blakeford), Marsha Hunt (Patricia Blakeford), Robert Cummings (Jay Wallace). Unbilled guest at the bar: Gary Cooper. Based on a story by Faith Thomas.

THE GENERAL DIED AT DAWN
(Paramount, 1936)

Director: Lewis Milestone. *Producer:* William Le Baron. *Photographer:* Victor Milner. *Editor:* Eda Warren. *Cast:* Gary Cooper (O'Hara), Madeleine Carroll (Judy Perrie), Akim Tamiroff (General Yang), Dudley Digges (Mr. Wu), Porter Hall (Peter Perrie), William Frawley (Brighton), J. M. Kerrigan (Leach), Philip Ahn (Oxford). Based on a novel by Charles G. Booth.

THE PLAINSMAN
(Paramount, 1936)

Director and Producer: Cecil B. De Mille. *Photographers:* Victor Milner and George Robinson. *Editor:* Anne Bauchens. *Cast:* Gary Cooper (Wild Bill Hickok), Jean Arthur (Calamity Jane), James Ellison (Buffalo Bill Cody), Charles Bickford (John Latimer), Porter Hall (Jack McCall), Helen Burgess (Louisa Cody), John Miljan (General George Armstrong Custer), George "Gabby" Hayes (Breezy), Fuzzy Knight (Dave). Based on data from the stories "Wild Bill Hickok" by Frank J. Wilstach and "The Prince of Pistoleers" by Courtney Ryley Cooper and Grover Jones.

SOULS AT SEA
(Paramount, 1937)

Director: Henry Hathaway. *Photographer:* Charles Lang, Jr. *Editor:* Ellsworth Hoagland. *Cast:* Gary Cooper ("Nuggin" Taylor), George Raft (Powdah), Frances Dee (Margaret Tarryton), Henry Wilcoxon (Lt. Stanley Tarryton), Harry Carey (Captain of "William Brown"), Robert Cummings (George Martin), Joseph Schildkraut (Gaston de Bastonet), Tully Marshall (Pecora). Based on a story by Ted Lesser.

THE ADVENTURES OF MARCO POLO
(United Artists, 1938)

Director: Archie Mayo. *Producer:* Samuel Goldwyn. *Photographer:* Rudolph Mate. *Editor:* Fred Allen. *Cast:* Gary Cooper (Marco Polo), Sigrid Gurie (Princess Kukachin), Basil Rathbone (Ahmed), Ernest Truex (Binguccio), Alan Hale (Kaidu), Binnie Barnes (Nazama), Lana Turner (Nazama's maid). Based on a story by N. A. Pogson.

BLUEBEARD'S EIGHTH WIFE
(Paramount, 1938)

Director and Producer: Ernst Lubitsch. *Photographer:* Leo Tover. *Editor:* William Shea. *Cast:* Claudette Colbert (Nicole de Loiselle), Gary Cooper (Michael Brandon), Edward Everett Horton (The Marquis de Loiselle), David Niven (Albert de Regnier), Elizabeth Patterson (Aunt Hedwige), Herman Bing (Monsieur Pepinard). Based on a play by Alfred Savoir.

THE COWBOY AND THE LADY
(United Artists, 1938)

Director: H. C. Potter. *Producer:* Samuel Goldwyn. *Photographer:* Gregg Toland. *Editor:* Sherman Todd. *Cast:* Gary Cooper (Stretch), Merle Oberon (Mary Smith), Patsy Kelly (Katie Callahan), Walter Brennan (Sugar), Fuzzy Knight (Buzz), Mabel Todd (Elly). From a story by Leo McCarey and Frank R. Adams.

BEAU GESTE
(Paramount, 1939)

Director and Producer: William A. Wellman. *Photographers:* Theodor Sparkuhl and Archie Stout. *Editor:* Thomas Scott. *Cast:* Gary Cooper (Beau Geste), Ray Milland (John Geste), Robert Preston (Digby Geste), Brian Donlevy (Sergeant Markoff), Susan Hayward (Isobel Rivers), J. Carroll Naish (Rasinoff), Albert Dekker (Schwartz), Broderick Crawford (Hank Miller), Donald O'Connor (Beau at 12). Based on the novel *Beau Geste* by Percival Christopher Wren.

THE REAL GLORY
(United Artists, 1939)

Director: Henry Hathaway. *Producer:* Samuel Goldwyn. *Photographer:* Rudolph Mate. *Editor:* Daniel Mandell. *Cast:* Gary Cooper (Doctor Bill Canavan), Andrea Leeds (Linda Hartley), David Niven (Lieutenant McCool), Reginald Owen (Captain Hartley), Broderick Crawford (Lieutenant Larson), Kay Johnson (Mabel Manning), Charles Waldron (Padre Rafael), Russell Hicks (Captain Manning).

THE WESTERNER
(United Artists, 1940))

Director: William Wyler. *Producer:* Samuel Goldwyn. *Photographer:* Gregg Toland. *Editor:* Daniel Mandell. *Cast:* Gary Cooper (Cole Hardin), Walter Brennan (Judge Roy Bean), Doris Davenport (Jane-Ellen Mathews), Fred Stone (Caliphet Mathews), Paul Hurst (Chickenfoot), Chill Wills (Southeast), Forrest Tucker (Wade Harper), Dana Andrews (Bart Cobble).

NORTHWEST MOUNTED POLICE
(Paramount, 1940)

Director and Producer: Cecil B. De Mille. *Photographers:* Victor Milner and W. Howard Greene. *Editor:* Anne Bauchens. *Cast:* Gary Cooper (Dusty Rivers), Madeleine Carroll (April Logan), Paulette Goddard (Louvette Corbeau), Preston Foster (Sgt. Jim Brett), Robert Preston (Constable Ronnie Logan), George Bancroft (Jacques Corbeau), Akim Tamiroff (Dan Duroc), Lon Chaney, Jr. (Shorty), Richard Denning (Const. Thornton), Robert Ryan (Const. Dumont). Based on *Royal Canadian Mounted Police* by R. C. Fetherston-Haugh.

MEET JOHN DOE
(Warner Bros., 1940)

Director and Producer: Frank Capra. *Photographer:* George Barnes. *Editor:* Daniel Mandell. *Cast:* Gary Cooper (John Doe–Long John Willoughby), Barbara Stanwyck (Ann Mitchell), Edward Arnold (D. B. Norton), Walter Brennan (Colonel), James Gleason (Henry Connell), Spring Byington (Mrs. Mitchell), Gene Lockhart (Mayor Lovett), Rod La Rocque (Ted Sheldon), Irving Bacon (Beany). From a story by Rochard Connell and Robert Presnell.

SERGEANT YORK
(Warner Bros., 1941)

Director: Howard Hawks. *Producers:* Jesse Lasky and Hal B. Wallis. *Photographer:* Sol Polito. *Editor:* William Holmes. *Cast:* Gary Cooper (Alvin York), Walter Brennan (Pastor Rosier Pile), Joan Leslie (Gracie Williams), George Tobias (Michael T. "Pusher" Ross), Stanley Ridges (Major Buxton), Ward Bond (Ike Botkin), Noah Beery, Jr. (Buck Lipscomb), June Lockhart (Rose York), Dickie Moore (George York). Based on the diary of Sergeant York as edited by Tom Skeyhill.

BALL OF FIRE
(RKO-Radio Pictures, 1941)

Director: Howard Hawks. *Producer:* Sam Goldwyn. *Photographer:* Gregg Toland. *Editor:* Daniel Mandell. *Cast:* Gary Cooper (Prof. Bertram Potts), Barbara Stanwyck (Sugarpuss O'Shea), Oscar Homolka (Prof. Gurkakoff), Henry Travers (Prof. Jerome), S. Z. Sakall (Prof. Magenbruch), Tully Marshall (Prof. Robinson), Dana Andrews (Joe

Lilac), Dan Duryea (Duke Pastrami), Gene Krupa and his orchestra. Based on the story "From A to Z" by Thomas Monroe and Billy Wilder.

THE PRIDE OF THE YANKEES
(RKO-Radio Pictures, 1942)

Director: Sam Wood. *Producer:* Samuel Goldwyn. *Photographer:* Rudolph Mate. *Editor:* Daniel Mandell. *Cast:* Gary Cooper (Lou Gehrig), Teresa Wright (Eleanor Gehrig), Walter Brennan (Sam Blake), Dan Duryea (Hank Hanneman), Babe Ruth (himself), Elsa Janssen (Mom Gehrig), Ludwig Stossel (Pop Gehrig), Virginia Gilmore (Myra). From a story by Paul Gallico.

FOR WHOM THE BELL TOLLS
(Paramount, 1943)

Director and Producer: Sam Wood. *Executive Producer:* Buddy De Sylva. *Photographer:* Ray Rennahan. *Editors:* Sherman Todd and John Link. *Cast:* Gary Cooper (Robert Jordan), Ingrid Bergman (Maria), Akim Tamiroff (Pablo), Arturo De Cordova (Agustin), Vladimer Sokoloff (Anselmo), Mikhail Rasumny (Rafael), Fortunio Bonanova (Fernando), Eric Feldary (Andres). From the novel by Ernest Hemingway.

THE STORY OF DR. WASSELL
(Paramount, 1944)

Director and Producer: Cecil B. De Mille. *Photographer:* Victor Milner. *Editor:* Anne Bauchens. *Cast:* Gary Cooper (Dr. Corydon M. Wassell), Laraine Day (Madeleine Day), Signe Hasso (Bettina), Carol Thurston (Tremartini), Dennis O'Keefe (Benjamin "Hoppy" Hopkins), Carl Esmond (Lt. Dirk Van Daal), Paul Kelly (Murdock). Based on the story by Commander Corydon M. Wassell and a story by James Hilton.

CASANOVA BROWN
(RKO-Radio Pictures, 1944)

Director: Sam Wood. *Producer:* Nunnally Johnson. *Photographer:* John Seitz. *Editor:* Thomas Neff. *Cast:* Gary Cooper (Casanova Brown), Teresa Wright (Isabel Drury), Frank Morgan (Mr. Ferris), Anita Louise (Madge Ferris), Patricia Collinge (Mrs. Drury), Jill Esmond (Dr. Zernerke), Emory Parnell (Frank), Isabel Elsom (Mrs. Ferris), Mary Treen (Monica). Based on the play *The Little Accident* by Floyd Dell and Thomas Mitchell.

ALONG CAME JONES
(RKO-Radio Pictures, 1945)

Director: Stuart Heisler. *Producer:* Gary Cooper. *Photographer:* Milton Krasner. *Editor:* Thomas Neff. *Cast:* Gary Cooper (Melody Jones), Loretta Young (Cherry de Longpre), William Demarest (George Fury), Dan Duryea (Monte Jarrad), Frank Sully (Cherry's Brother), Russell Simpson (Pop de Longpre), Arthur Loft (Sheriff). From a story by Alan Le May.

SARATOGA TRUNK
(Warner Bros., 1945)

Director: Sam Wood. *Producer:* Hal B. Wallis. *Photographer:* Ernest Haller. *Editor:* Ralph Dawson. *Cast:* Gary Cooper (Col. Clint Maroon), Ingrid Bergman (Clio Dulaine), Flora Robson (Angelique Buiton), Jerry Austin (Cupidon), John Warburton (Bartholomew Van Steed), Florence Bates (Mrs. Coventry Bellop), Curt Bois (Augustin Haussy), John Abbott (Roscoe Bean), Ethel Griffies (Mme. Clarissa Van Steed). From the novel by Edna Ferber.

CLOAK AND DAGGER
(Warner Bros., 1946)

Director: Fritz Lang. *Producer:* Milton Sperling. *Photographer:* Sol Polito. *Editor:* Christian Nyby. *Cast:* Gary Cooper (Prof. Alvah Jesper), Lilli Palmer (Gina), Robert Alda (Pinkie), Vladimir Sokoloff (Polda), J. Edward Bromberg (Trenk), Marjorie Hoshelle (Ann Dawson), Ludwig Stossel (the German). Story by Boris Ingster and John Larkin.

UNCONQUERED
(Paramount, 1947)

Director and Producer: Cecil B. De Mille. *Photographer:* Ray Rennahan. *Editor:* Anne Bauchens. *Cast:* Gary Cooper (Capt. Christopher Holden), Paulette Goddard (Abigail Martha Hale), Howard Da Silva (Martin Garth), Boris Karloff (Guyasuta, Chief of the Senecas), Cecil Kellaway (Jeremy Love), Ward Bond (John Fraser), Sir C. Aubrey Smith (Lord Chief Justice), Virginia Grey (Diana). Based on a novel by Neil H. Swanson.

VARIETY GIRL
(Paramount, 1947)

Director: George Marshall. *Producer:* Daniel Dare. *Photographers:* Lionel Lindon and Stuart Thompson. *Editor:* Le Roy Stone. *Cast:* Mary Hatcher (Catherine Brown), Olga San Juan (Amber La Vonne), De Forest Kelley (Bob Kirby), William Demarest (Barker). *Guest Stars:* Bing Crosby, Bob Hope, Gary Cooper, Ray Milland, Alan Ladd, Barbara Stanwyck, Paulette Goddard, Dorothy Lamour, William Holden, Burt Lancaster, Robert Preston, Veronica Lake, Billy De Wolfe, and others.

GOOD SAM
(RKO-Radio Pictures, 1948)

Director and Producer: Leo McCarey. *Photographer:* George Barnes. *Editor:* James McKay. *Cast:* Gary Cooper (Sam Clayton), Ann Sheridan (Lu Clayton), Ray Collins (Reverend Daniels), Edmund Lowe (H. C. Borden), Joan Lorring (Shirley Mae), Ruth Roman (Ruthie), William Frawley (Tom). Based on a story by Leo McCarey and John Klorer.

THE FOUNTAINHEAD
(Warner Bros., 1948)

Director: King Vidor. *Producer:* Henry Blanke. *Photographer:* Robert Burks. *Editor:* David Weisbart *Cast:* Gary Cooper (Howard Roark), Patricia Neal (Dominique),

Raymond Massey (Gail Wynand), Kent Smith (Peter Keating), Robert Douglas (Ellsworth Toohey), Henry Hull (Henry Cameron), Ray Collins (Enright). From the novel *The Fountainhead* by Ayn Rand.

IT'S A GREAT FEELING
(Warner Bros., 1949)

Director: David Butler. *Producer:* Alex Gottlieb. *Photographer:* Wilfrid M. Cline. *Editor:* Irene Moore. *Cast:* Dennis Morgan (himself), Doris Day (Judy Adams), Jack Carson (himself). *Guest Stars:* Gary Cooper, Joan Crawford, Danny Kaye, Patricia Neal, Eleanor Parker, Ronald Reagan, Edward G. Robinson, Jane Wyman. From a story by I. A. L. Diamond.

TASK FORCE
(Warner Bros., 1949)

Director: Delmer Daves. *Producer:* Jerry Wald. *Photographers:* Robert Burks and Wilfrid M. Cline. *Editor:* Alan Crosland, Jr. *Cast:* Gary Cooper (Jonathan L. Scott), Jane Wyatt (Mary Morgan), Wayne Morris (McKinney), Walter Brennan (Pete Richard), Julie London (Barbara McKinney), Bruce Bennett (McCluskey), Jack Holt (Reeves), Stanley Ridges (Bentley).

BRIGHT LEAF
(Warner Bros., 1950)

Director: Michael Curtiz. *Producer:* Henry Blanke. *Photographer:* Karl Freund. *Editor:* Owen Marks. *Cast:* Gary Cooper (Brant Royle), Lauren Bacall (Sonia Kovac), Patricia Neal (Margaret Jane), Jack Carson (Chris Malley), Donald Crisp (Major Singleton), Gladys George (Rose), Elizabeth Patterson (Tabitha Jackson), Jeff Corey (John Barton). From the novel by Foster Fitz-Simons.

DALLAS
(Warner Bros., 1950)

Director: Stuart Heisler. *Producer:* Anthony Veiller. *Photographer:* Ernest Haller. *Editor:* Clarence Kolster *Cast:* Gary Cooper (Blayde "Reb" Hollister), Ruth Roman (Tonia Robles), Steve Cochran (Brant Marlow), Ramond Massey (Will Marlow), Barbara Payton (Flo), Leif Erickson (Martin Weatherby), Antonio Moreno (Felipe), Jerome Cowan (Matt Coulter), Reed Hadley (Wild Bill Hickok), Jay "Slim" Talbot (stage driver).

YOU'RE IN THE NAVY NOW
(Twentieth Century–Fox, 1951)

Director: Henry Hathaway. *Producer:* Fred Kohlmar. *Photographer:* Joe Mac Donald. *Editor:* James B. Clark. *Cast:* Gary Cooper (Lt. John Harkness), Jane Greer (Ellie), Millard Mitchell (Larrabee), Eddie Albert (Lt. Bill Barron), John McIntyre (Commander Reynolds), Ray Collins (Admiral Tennant), Harry Von Zell (Capt. Eliot), Jack Webb (Ensign Anthony Barbo), Ed Begley (Commander). From an article in *The New Yorker* by John W. Hazard.

STARLIFT
(Warner Bros., 1951)

Director: Roy Del Ruth. *Producer:* Robert Arthur. *Photographer:* Ted McCord. *Editor:* William Ziegler. *Cast:* Doris Day, Gordon MacRae, Virginia Mayo, Gene Nelson, Ruth Roman. *Guest Stars:* James Cagney, Gary Cooper, Phil Harris, Louella Parsons, Randolph Scott, Jane Wyman. From a story by John Klorer.

IT'S A BIG COUNTRY
(M-G-M, 1951)

Directors: Richard Thorpe, John Sturges, Charles Vidor, Don Weis, Clarence Brown, William A. Wellman, and Don Hartman. *Producer:* Robert Sisk. *Photographers:* John Alton, Ray June, William Mellor, and Joe Ruttenberg. *Editors:* Ben Lewis and Frederick Y. Smith. *Cast:* Ethel Barrymore (Mrs. Brian Patrick Riordan), Keefe Brasselle (Sgt. Maxie Klein), Gary Cooper (Texas), Nancy Davis (Miss Coleman), Van Johnson (Adam Burch), Gene Kelly (Icarus Xenophon), Janet Leigh (Rosa Szabo), Fredric March (Papa Esposito), William Powell (Professor), George Murphy (Mr. Callaghan).

DISTANT DRUMS
(Warner Bros., 1951)

Director: Raoul Walsh. *Producer:* Milton Sperling. *Photographer:* Sid Hickox. *Editor:* Folmer Blangsted. *Cast:* Gary Cooper (Capt. Quincy Wyatt), Mari Aldon (Judy Beckett), Richard Webb (Lt. Richard Tufts), Ray Neal (Private Mohair), Arthur Hunnicutt (Monk), Robert Barrat (General Zachary Taylor), Clancy Cooper (Sgt. Shane). From a story by Niven Busch.

HIGH NOON
(United Artists, 1952)

Director: Fred Zinnemann. *Producer:* Stanley Kramer. *Photographer:* Floyd Crosby. *Editor:* Elmo Williams. *Song:* "Do Not Forsake Me Oh My Darlin" by Dmitri Tiomkin and Ned Washington. *Cast:* Gary Cooper (Will Kane), Thomas Mitchell (Jonas Henderson), Lloyd Bridges (Harvey Pell), Katy Jurado (Helen Ramirez), Grace Kelly (Amy Kane), Otto Kruger (Percy Mettrick), Lon Chaney (Martin Howe), Henry Morgan (William Fuller). Based on the story "The Tin Star" by John W. Cunningham.

SPRINGFIELD RIFLE
(Warner Bros., 1952)

Director: Andre De Toth. *Producer:* Louis F. Edelman. *Photographer:* Edwin Du Par. *Editor:* Robert L. Swanson. *Cast:* Gary Cooper (Major Alex Kearney), Phyllis Thaxter (Erin Kearney), David Brian (Austin McCool), Paul Kelly (Lt. Col. Hudson), Philip Carey (Capt. Tennick), Lon Chaney, Jr. (Elm), James Millican (Matthew Quint), Martin Milner (Olie Larsen), Quinn "Big Boy" Williams (Sgt. Snow). From a story by Sloan Nibley.

RETURN TO PARADISE
(United Artists, 1953)

Director: Mark Robson. *Producers:* Theron Warth, Robert Wise, and Mark Robson. *Photographer:* Winton Hoch. *Editor:* Daniel Mandell. *Cast:* Gary Cooper (Mr. Morgan), Roberta Haynes (Maeva), Barry Jones (Pastor Corbett), Moira MacDonald (Turia), John Hudson (Harry Faber). Based on the book by James A. Michener.

BLOWING WILD
(Warner Bros., 1953)

Director: Hugo Fregonese. *Producer:* Milton Sperling. *Photographer:* Sid Hickox. *Editor:* Alan Crosland, Jr. *Song:* "Blowing Wild—The Ballad of Black Gold" by Dimitri Tiomkin and Paul Francis Webster, sung by Frankie Laine. *Cast:* Gary Cooper (Jeff Dawson), Barbara Stanwyck (Marina Conway), Ruth Roman (Sal), Anthony Quinn (Ward "Paco" Conway), Ward Bond (Dutch).

GARDEN OF EVIL
(Twentieth Century–Fox, 1954)

Director: Henry Hathaway. *Producer:* Charles Brackett. *Photographers:* Milton Krasner and Jorge Stahl, Jr. *Editor:* James B. Clark. *Cast:* Gary Cooper (Hooker), Susan Hayward (Leah Fuller), Richard Widmark (Fiske), Hugh Marlowe (John Fuller), Cameron Mitchell (Luke Daly), Rita Moreno (singer). From a story by Fred Freiberger and William Tunberg.

VERA CRUZ
(United Artists, 1954)

Director: Robert Aldrich. *Producer:* James Hill. *Photographer:* Ernest Laszlo. *Editor:* Alan Crosland, Jr. *Song:* "Vera Cruz" by Hugo Friedhofer and Sammy Cahn. *Cast:* Gary Cooper (Benjamin Trane), Burt Lancaster (Joe Erin), Denise Darcel (Countess Marie Duvarre), Cesar Romero (Marquis de Labordere), Ernest Borgnine (Donnegan), Charles Bronson (Pittsburgh). From a story by Borden Chase.

THE COURT-MARTIAL OF BILLY MITCHELL
(Warner Bros., 1955)

Director: Otto Preminger. *Producer:* Milton Sperling. *Photographer:* Sam Leavitt. *Editor:* Folmar Blangsted. *Cast:* Gary Cooper (Billy Mitchell), Charles Bickford (General Guthrie), Ralph Bellamy (Congressman), Rod Steiger (Allan Guillion), Elizabeth Montgomery (Margaret Lansdowne), Fred Clark (Colonel Moreland), Jack Lord (Zach Lansdowne), Darren McGavin (Russ Peters). From a story by Milton Sperling and Emmet Lavery.

FRIENDLY PERSUASION
(Allied Artists, 1956)

Director and Producer: William Wyler: *Associate Producer:* Robert Wyler. *Photographer:* Ellsworth Fredricks. *Editors:* Edward A. Biery and Robert A. Belcher. *Song:* "Friendly Persuasion (Thee I Love)" by Dimitri Tiomkin and Paul Francis Webster, sung by Pat Boone. *Cast:* Gary Cooper (Jess Birdwell), Dorothy McGuire (Eliza Birdwell), Marjorie Main (Widow Hudspeth), Anthony Perkins (Josh Birdwell), Robert Middleton (Sam Jordan), Mark Richman (Gard Jordan). From the novel *The Friendly Persuasion* by Jessamyn West.

LOVE IN THE AFTERNOON
(Allied Artists, 1957)

Director and Producer: Billy Wilder. *Photographer:* William Mellor. *Editor:* Leonid Azar. *Song:* "Fascination" by F. D. Marchetti and Maurice De Feraudy. *Cast:* Gary Cooper (Frank Flannagan), Audrey Hepburn (Ariane Chavasse), Maurice Chevalier (Claude Chavasse), John McGiver (Monsieur X), Lise Bourdin (Madame X). Based on the novel *Ariane* by Claude Anet.

TEN NORTH FREDERICK
(Twentieth Century–Fox, 1958)

Director: Philip Dunne. *Producer:* Charles Brackett. *Photographer:* Joe MacDonald. *Editor:* David Bretherton. *Cast:* Gary Cooper (Joe Chapin), Diane Varsi (Ann Chapin), Suzy Parker (Kate Drummond), Geraldine Fitzgerald (Edith Chapin), Tom Tully (Slattery), Barbara Nichols (Stella). From the novel by John O'Hara.

MAN OF THE WEST
(United Artists, 1958)

Director: Anthony Mann. *Producer:* Walter M. Mirisch. *Photographer:* Ernest Haller. *Editor:* Richard Heermance *Cast:* Gary Cooper (Link Jones), Julie London (Billie Ellis), Lee J. Cobb (Dock Tobin), Arthur O'Connell (Sam Beasley), Jack Lord (Coaley), John Dehner (Claude), Royal Dano (Trout). Based on a novel by Will C. Brown.

THE HANGING TREE
(A Baroda Production; Warner Bros., 1959)

Director: Delmer Daves. *Producers:* Martin Jurow and Richard Shepherd. *Photographer:* Ted McCord. *Editor:* Owen Marks. *Cast:* Gary Cooper (Doc. Joseph Frail), Maria Schell (Elizabeth Mahler), Karl Malden (Frenchy Plante), Ben Piazza (Rune), George C. Scott (Dr. George Grubb), Slim Talbot (stage driver). From the novelette "The Hanging Tree" by Dorothy M. Johnson.

ALIAS JESSE JAMES
(United Artists, 1959)

Director: Norman McLeod. *Producer:* Jack Hope. *Executive Producer:* Bob Hope. *Cast:* Bob Hope (Milford Farnsworth), Rhonda Fleming (the Duchess). *Guest Stars* (unbilled): Hugh O'Brien (Wyatt Earp), Ward Bond (Major Seth Adams), James Arness (Matt Dillon), Roy Rogers (himself), Fess Parker (Davy Crockett), Gail Davis (Annie Oakley), James Garner (Bret Maverick), Jay Silverheels (Tonto), and Gene Autry, Bing Crosby, and Gary Cooper as themselves. Based on story by Robert St. Aubrey and Bert Lawrence.

THEY CAME TO CORDURA
(A Goetz-Baroda Production)
(Columbia Pictures, 1959)

Director: Robert Rossen. *Producer:* William Goetz. *Photographer:* Burnett Guffey. *Editor:* William A. Lyon. *Cast:* Gary Cooper (Major Thomas Thorn), Rita Hayworth (Adelaide Geary), Van Heflin (Sgt. John Chawk), Tab Hunter (Lt. William Fowler), Richard Conte (Cpl. Milo Trubee), Dick York (Pvt. Renziehausen). From a novel by Glendon Swarthout.

THE WRECK OF THE MARY DEARE
(A Blaustein-Baroda Production)
(M-G-M, 1959)

Director: Michael Anderson. *Producer:* Julian Blaustein. *Photographer:* Joseph Ruttenberg. *Editor:* Eda Warren. *Cast:* Gary Cooper (Gideon Patch), Charlton Heston (John Sands), Michael Redgrave (Mr. Hyland), Emyln Williams (Sir Wildred Falcett), Cecil Parker (the chairman), Alexander Knox (Petrie), Richard Harris (Higgins). Based on a novel by Hammond Innes.

THE NAKED EDGE
(A Pennebaker-Baroda Production)
(Released through United Artists, 1961)

Director: Michael Anderson. *Producers:* Walter Seltzer and George Glass. *Executive Producer:* Marlon Brando, Sr. *Photographer:* Edwin Hillier. *Editor:* Gordon Pilkington. *Cast:* Gary Cooper (George Radcliffe), Deborah Kerr (Martha Radcliffe), Eric Portman (Jeremy Clay), Diane Cilento (Mrs. Heath), Hermione Gingold (Lilly Harris), Peter Cushing (Mr. Wrack), Michael Wilding (Morris Brooke). Based on the novel *First Train to Babylon* by Max Ehrlich.

INDEX